Flight of the Dancing Bird

Flight
of the
Dancing
Bird

Tanjas Darke

JOHN BLAKE

Published by Metro Publishing,
an imprint of John Blake Publishing Ltd,
3 Bramber Court, 2 Bramber Road,
London W14 9PB, UK

www.blake.co.uk

First published in 2001 by HarperCollins Publishers (New Zealand) Ltd
This edition first published in hardback in 2007

ISBN: 978-1-84454-419-6

Disclaimer: Apart from the author's name and that of her father, husband, members of the Police, Crown Prosecution and Defence legal teams and Chief Verembat, all names have been changed.

This book is a work of non-fiction.

British Library Cataloguing-in-Publication Data:
A catalogue record for this book is available from the British Library.

Design by www.envydesign.co.uk

Printed in Great Britain by William Clowes Ltd, Beccles, Suffolk

1 3 5 7 9 10 8 6 4 2

Papers used by John Blake Publishing are natural, recyclable products made from wood grown in sustainable forests. The manufacturing processes conform to the environmental regulations of the country of origin.

Dedication

To the countless women, men, girls and boys living behind drawn curtains, fearing what the day will bring, what the future holds; I wrote this book for you.

I managed to get away despite seemingly hopeless odds and I hope that in some small way this book will help you. Help you to find the strength to escape from the darkness of the 'nightmare' and into the sunshine of freedom.

We share an amazing gift – survival. The fact that we survive is the proof that we can achieve the seemingly impossible.

Rob Hanna, thank you for believing in me, and telling me I should go home and start writing again. Somehow, you persuaded me that I could, and I did.

Bill, my husband, my hero and my best friend, I especially want to thank you, for your unfailing support and understanding, and for sharing the happiest years of my life.

Chapter 1

My name was called and I was led into the courtroom. I stepped into a room filled with faces – so many people, I remember thinking, as I was conducted to the witness box.

I was shaking as I sat down and nervously looked at the prosecution team. I didn't look at the jury. I didn't look at the judge. I knew where my father would be sitting, between two guards behind a screen. I heard him clear his throat.

The clerk of the court placed a Bible in my hands and I took courage from the feel of the worn leather binding against my fingers.

The time had finally come. Unbidden, the words of Lewis Carroll leapt into my mind. 'The time has come,' the walrus said, 'to talk of many things...'

I was born in Wellington, New Zealand, on 4 October 1960. My earliest memory is of a tiny house where I'm standing in a doorway, clinging to it for support. My mother sits sewing nearby. A door slams, frightening me and I take a few stumbling steps towards her before falling over. My very first steps. My first word was 'fall-over'. Apparently, I fell over so many times that 'fall-over' preceded Mama or Dada.

I was the heaviest baby in the ward, but perhaps all proud mothers say that. I don't know if my mother was proud of me – by some accounts the pregnancy was unwanted. Perhaps it was fortunate she was five and a half months gone before she discovered my existence. My father went to bed, pulled the covers over his head and stayed there for several days.

My mother tried the old methods. Her version is that my father made her get into scalding hot water and forced her to drink copious amounts of gin. His version is a little different; whichever, I survived. Eventually they realised I wasn't going to go away.

Early baby photos reveal a plump, contented baby. I remember one in particular – I was sitting on the floor and clutched in my fat little fists was the then banned book, *Lolita*. I used to think it was funny, but in retrospect it was a chilling foretaste of things to come.

My father moved to Australia and eventually my mother and I followed, renting a flat in a rundown house. When I was six, my maternal grandfather, my Opa, died. My mother and I were in the garden when the postman came with the black-edged telegram. She tore the envelope open and had to sit down on the concrete steps when she read the contents. I asked her what happened when someone died and she told me they turned into dust and ashes.

She spent the next two days sitting with her knees under her chin, rocking backwards and forwards. Sometimes she'd talk to herself – saying she wished Ronald was there. That's when I learned my father was called Ronald. But my father wasn't there; he was somewhere in the outback with a woman from the Finnish Embassy in Canberra. Apparently she became pregnant and resigned, returning to Finland, and as far as I'm aware didn't keep up contact with my father.

When I was six my parents separated again. My mother and I moved to a seedy little flat and my father eventually moved to the tropics. My mother worked long hours in a small city boutique and we lived on yoghurt, bread and cheese. During the week I'd go to kindergarten, and she collected me at about six in the evening.

I spent a lot of time by myself. At first I used to explore our rundown apartment block. Once I climbed on top of some old cupboards and found a collection of violins, dusty but beautifully carved, and played with them until the strings broke.

A month before Christmas a wonderful thing happened. One of the mothers gave Mrs Manaham, the kindergarten owner, a box of clothes for me. Inside were the most beautiful summer frocks, some thick woollen jumpers and two pairs of pyjamas printed with little donkeys. I asked where the nice lady lived, and was told she lived over the road. I decided to thank her. I wasn't sure which was the correct house, so next morning I walked down the road knocking on all the doors, asking people if they'd given me the clothes. None of them had, so I never did get to thank her.

Then came the kindergarten Christmas party. For days we cut out stars and angels, painting them silver and gold for Mrs Manaham to string around the room. The party was on a Saturday afternoon. I got all dressed up in one of my new frocks and waited for my mother, excited because we were all going to get a present.

As promised, my mother came home and said we'd be

leaving in a moment. Then David arrived. David was in love with my mother and was always very kind to me. I liked him a lot. He suggested we drive to the kindergarten. When we were almost there, they decided to visit his parents instead. I was terribly disappointed, but I never stayed unhappy for long, and enjoyed the long drive.

On Monday my friends told me about the party and my present, an amazing doll with eyes that opened and shut. My mother came to collect me at six o'clock and explained to Mrs Manaham that we hadn't come on Saturday because I'd been naughty. I couldn't understand why she lied. Mrs Manaham told me naughty girls didn't deserve presents and that was that. I don't know what happened to the doll; perhaps someone else got it.

In the autumn, after a wonderful morning jumping in drifts of fallen leaves, I found my way into a church. I was guided into a room full of children, which is how I secretly started going to Sunday school, and how I got my *Children's Pictorial Bible*. I was enthralled with the lovely stories, especially as the teacher told us they were true. I was very happy to meet God. The woman told us he was with us all the time, and knew everything we were feeling and doing. I found his presence very comforting.

The months passed until one Sunday when my mother hadn't been home the night before. It didn't worry me, I knew she was with David and she didn't always come home. When I saw how late I'd slept, I hurriedly dressed and ran to church. Unfortunately, just as I arrived, my mother and David drove past. They were very cross and I was forbidden to go to Sunday school again. I hid my Bible under my mattress, scared it would be thrown away. I read it every night by torchlight, there were some big words I didn't understand, but mostly I didn't have a problem. I didn't want God to think I'd forgotten him, because I didn't want him to forget me.

Around this time I started school. I hated it; I couldn't stand having to stay indoors, trapped after my life of wandering. I sat near a window and spent most of my time watching the world go by. I was bored; I already knew my alphabet and had been reading since I was four.

I remember being given a maths exercise and I started doing the sums. They were simple, and after the third one I looked out the window and completely forgot what I was meant to be doing. I couldn't understand my teacher's anger when he found I hadn't finished. After all, if he knew the answers what was the point of me doing them?

I was sent to see the headmistress, a hugely overweight woman with horn-rim spectacles. We secretly referred to her as the Dragon and I lived in constant fear of her. As I sat outside her office, a little boy told me all about the cane in great detail. He'd been caned before and was close to tears. Then the Dragon appeared and hauled him off. I could hear the whistle of the cane and his screams filled me with horror of what was to come.

When the door opened, the boy came out sobbing, wiping his face as he ran down the corridor. I began to tremble. She told me to go into her office, but my legs wouldn't respond. Infuriated, she reached over and grabbed me by an arm, lifting me clear off the bench.

As she closed her office door behind me, I stared at the cane lying on her desk. Then I did an unforgivable thing. I wet myself. The warm liquid streamed down my legs and formed a puddle, which slowly spread across the floor. Her face was one of shocked disbelief. I shifted uncomfortably from one foot to the other. We stared at each other for a long moment, then she swept out into the corridor calling for the janitor. While the puddle was being mopped up, she told me what a filthy little girl I was. But the maths wasn't mentioned and better still, she forgot to cane me.

I would love to say I paid more attention in class after this, but I didn't. The days dragged on and merged together in awful uniformity. Anzac Day came closer and I was given a form to take home. The entire school was going to attend religious services to pray for the souls of the Australians and New Zealanders who gave their lives during the First World War. But my mother wouldn't sign the form – apparently we were agnostics, a big word for a little girl. I understood it to mean we didn't speak to God. I wondered if my mother and God had had a fight. I thought it wiser not to mention I spoke to God every night.

On Anzac Day the school ground was empty, save for two little girls. Karina was in my class and her parents hadn't signed the form either, so we were put under the Dragon's supervision.

'Hope you're not going to pee in here again,' was her greeting to me. She stomped off to get a cup of coffee, muttering 'No gratitude, no patriotism, our boys died fighting your war.' Eventually she settled to work at her desk; pausing only to glare at us over her spectacles.

Karina and I sat and whispered together, trying to understand agnostics and what the war had been about. We became firm friends, inseparable during school hours. Word spread that we hadn't attended the Anzac service and we became fair game for the school bullies. After a while they tired of teasing us, with the exception of one girl.

She was several classes ahead of us and really mean.

Overweight, with frizzy blonde hair, she'd follow us round the playground, taunting us and pulling our hair. We did everything we could to avoid her. One day she pulled my hair and started punching me. I took it as I always did, knowing that eventually she'd get bored. Then she turned on Karina, punching and scratching. Karina started to cry and I turned into a wildcat.

I lunged at her, yelling at the top of my voice, punching, kicking and biting until her bottom lip began to tremble and tears rolled down her plump cheeks. But I wasn't finished. I followed her when she tried to take shelter near the teachers, and made her sit down, forcing her to push flowers up her nose. When she hesitated I told her I'd bite her again if she didn't, and crying all the while, she stuffed them up her nose one by one. She never bothered us again. In fact, none of the kids bothered us again.

I still used to explore the neighbourhood after school, sometimes not arriving at the kindergarten until after five to wait for my mother to arrive back from work. Nothing was ever said, until one day when I arrived well after six. My mother was waiting with Mrs Manaham. They were absolutely furious. I was smacked by both of them, which I felt was grossly unfair, and had to endure a long lecture about what happens to little girls who go about on their own, with dire warnings about what they'd do to me if I ever wandered off again. In future I was to walk directly to and from school, no dawdling and no detours.

With my wanderings curtailed I played at housekeeping, and I'd sweep and dust, wash the dishes and make beds. Sometimes I'd go to the corner shop and buy chocolate Freddo Frogs. When I got home I'd grate them carefully and have them ready on the table with buttered bread for my mother. She loved this and would be happy, although her feet were killing her.

One day a packet arrived from the islands, from my father, full of the most wonderful cowry shells with spots and stripes, so smooth and shiny. I played with them for hours. Another packet came with bottles of shampoo for my mother and books for me, in English and French. I loved reading, but I only had two books, *Bambi* and my Bible, hidden under my mattress.

My ninth birthday came with the most wonderful present. It was a doll, nearly as tall as me, with eyes that opened and shut, and when you pulled a little string in her back she'd say, 'Mama, je suis fatiguée.'

This was French, my mother told me. My mother could speak French, English, German and Dutch. I confided this to Karina, as well as the fact that one day I'd go to the New Hebrides (now Vanuatu) to see my father, and when I came back I'd speak French.

I had no idea how prophetic my words were. Two days later, I was on the aeroplane to Port Vila in the New Hebrides. My evening prayers had been answered.

David came the day before we left and bought me a coconut, telling me I'd see coconuts in the New Hebrides. He cracked it open and broke off a piece of the white flesh for me to eat. It was delicious. He said that because I'd never forget my first coconut, I'd never forget him. He was right on both counts. On the way to the airport, David told me I was going to a new life, where I'd have a mummy and a daddy living together again. I'd live in a house, in the tropics, with a garden all around.

Chapter 2

The flight seemed to go on forever. My mother was absorbed in a magazine, so I leaned against the window and looked out. Far below was a cargo ship, a long streak of white trailing behind. Towards the horizon I caught sight of a swirling kaleidoscope of brilliant turquoise blue and emerald green. Tiny atolls and submerged coral reefs stretched as far as the eye could see and waves raced over the underwater shoals. It was breathtaking. I tugged at my mother's sleeve and she leaned across to get a better view. At that moment, there was an announcement in French over the intercom. My mother told me we'd be landing shortly. I bounced in my seat as she attempted to do up my seat belt. Soon I'd be seeing my father.

The sea gave way to jagged coastline and dense jungle and we flew over a plantation of strange looking trees planted in rows. My mother told me they were coconut trees. We were about to land when unexpectedly, the plane banked steeply, and there was another announcement. My mother laughed and said some fool had parked his car on the runway. As we swept round I saw a tiny red car parked on the tarmac, a man stood next to it, looking up. In the distance, I could see tiny figures running towards the car waving their arms frantically. We circled round and the plane descended, this time with a reassuring bump as we landed.

I'll never forget my first day in paradise. As we stepped into the blazing heat I forgot Sydney. Forgot the cold and the poverty, the greyness and the peeling wallpaper of our tiny flat. I even forgot I'd left my Bible under my mattress.

I walked down the rickety steel staircase towards a new life. I stepped onto the tarmac, and into my new country, which would possess my mind, body and soul in a way no land ever had, and no other land ever would. I felt the heat of the tarmac through the soles of my sandals, while overhead a flock of red and green parakeets shrieked as they flashed past.

My mother held my hand and a warm comforting feeling flowed through me. We couldn't know that it was a point of no return in our relationship, both our lives about to change forever. As we held hands I had no idea the ground between us was already crumbling and a huge chasm would soon separate us. And if we had known ... what then? But we didn't. Perhaps that's one of life's kindnesses.

My mother placed her passport on the immigration officer's counter. I didn't have my own passport yet; I was still on hers. 'French or British?' he asked.

'Neither, I'm Dutch.'

'Which set of laws do you wish to follow? This is a condominium, you have to opt for one of them.'

'Oh, I see,' my mother said, not really seeing at all.

'Well then, go for English,' he said kindly, 'after all, we're speaking English.'

So she picked English, our passport was stamped and we made our way out into the sunshine. Almost immediately, I saw my father running towards us and before I fully realised who it was, he swept me into his arms and we were a family again.

'Sorry about the car,' he said, looking at my mother. 'I was washing it for you, but I wasn't expecting the plane so soon – we all got a bit of a shock.'

Hand in hand we walked to the car park. I clambered into the back seat and wound down the window to let out the stifling heat.

Travelling along tiny coral gravel roads lined with thick tropical growth, I could smell the jungle, a rich loamy smell touched with the perfume of exotic blossoms. Everything was so alive. Chickens scratched in the dirt and a pig wandered across the road. As we drove, we threw up a cloud of thick white dust. Every so often, we passed a group of gaily dressed, smiling brown people. They'd stop whatever they were doing and wave and we'd wave back. My father told me they weren't brown people, they were New Hebrideans.

We drove along a bay with sparkling blue water, Port Vila Harbour, and into the township. It consisted of one main road with several tiny streets, lined with flame trees and old colonial buildings. One of the first buildings we passed was the Hôtel Rossi, with a huge frangipani tree in front. My father stopped and got out of the car, reaching up to pick a blossom. He handed it to my mother and the sweet fragrance filled the car. My mother gave the waxy yellow and white flower to me and I twirled it between my fingers, the white sap making my fingers sticky.

We continued through the tiny town with my father giving a running commentary. Further down we turned up the hill and passed a magnificent building set in a garden filled with hibiscus bushes and frangipani trees. Bougainvillaea grew in wild abandon over the large wooden building, covering it with splashes of vibrant pink and purple. My father told us this was the post office, where we had post box 243. No one had a street address, there were no street numbers, let alone street names.

As we made our way up the hill, we passed a large grassy expanse known as the British Paddock. Despite the heat, some men were playing an enthusiastic game of cricket, watched by listless women and children sitting in the sweltering shade of large mango trees.

The road became narrower, a tiny dirt track, winding through elephant grass so tall the stems reached out towards each other over the car. The track straightened and the elephant grass gave way to jungle on our left and three houses on our right. We turned into the driveway of the last house. My new home. I climbed out but barely noticed the house; I'd seen something amazing.

The fence was made of posts with wire strung between them. Nothing unusual about that; what attracted my attention was the thick luxuriant growth of heart-shaped leaves and yellow flowers crowning the top of each one. The fence posts were growing! There was more to come. My father called me over and as I crouched next to him, he showed me a tiny plant with feathered leaves and tiny pink puffball flowers. 'It's called sensitive grass, watch what it does when you touch it.'

He gently stroked the leaves and one by one they closed up and folded back. I remember giggling – a country where grass grows taller than a house, fences grow and plants move all by themselves!

A large ginger tom wandered over and rubbed against my father's legs. 'And this is Monsu, our cat.'

When I rubbed his tummy he purred loudly in appreciation, his eyes half closed. Then abruptly, he walked off into the undergrowth, without so much as a backward look, but I soon learnt cats are like that.

It was a large sunlit bungalow, sparsely furnished, with whitewashed walls. I walked into the spacious living room; a huge teak bookcase covered one wall, lined with books and strange carvings. A light breeze billowed through the room, lifting the edges of the muslin curtains.

I stepped out through the open French windows onto a terracotta-tiled terrace. Running the full length of the terrace was a concrete planter, overflowing with orange marigolds. I looked out over a huge expanse of elephant grass, an ocean of elegantly waving stems. Tiny brightly-coloured finches flitted from stalk to stalk, the delicate stems bending as they alighted. A sudden eddy of wind startled them and they flew up in a cloud of red and green.

My father came up behind me. 'Come and look round the house.'

My mother was already unpacking. First, he showed me my new bedroom. It was a lovely room, looking out across the track to thick jungle and tangled vines. The large window was covered with a fine mesh screen, to protect against the mosquitoes, he explained. Under the window was a fold-up bed, which had been opened out and covered with a soft blue blanket; my small suitcase stood in the middle of the room.

We stepped back out into the hall and into another room. 'And this is the bathroom.'

A large glass shower cabinet took up one corner, there was a blue porcelain washbasin and matching toilet and a funny shaped thing like a toilet with taps. I turned the taps on and off and asked my father what it was for. He told me it was a bidet and women used it to wash their bottoms. I was very impressed but I wasn't sure my father should have said bottom. I'd have had my mouth washed out with soap for saying bottom.

Next, we went into my parents' bedroom. My mother was putting her dresses on hangers in a large cupboard. She looked so happy, and smiled as I came into the room. A huge teak bed with short posts dominated the room. I sat on the edge swinging my legs, as my father described how he'd made the bed himself.

The only other way to get a bed was to order it months in advance and then hope it was put on 'the Polly'. The Polly was the local name for the *Polynesia*, a cargo ship that came roughly every six weeks, depending on the weather. As I ran my fingers along the finely grained wood, feeling the satiny smooth finish, I had no idea how much I'd grow to hate that bed.

The kitchen was up-to-date with a large double sink, new stove and a huge fridge, filled with an astonishing array of food – exotic cheeses, pâtés, ham, strange looking vegetables and tropical fruit, including two pineapples. My mother and I stared, normally there were only one or two yoghurts in our ancient, rust-flecked fridge, sometimes a couple of slices of Spam, but not much else.

My father began to slice French bread while my mother hunted for the plates. We ate in the living room, looking out through the French windows. My mother and I tentatively tried the different fruits, each more delicious than the last.

We heard the front door open and a slender woman came into the living room followed by another woman and two men. 'Hi, I'm Tisha,' she said as she walked over and held out her hand. 'Welcome to the New Hebrides. I'm the one who's been helping get this house tidy for your arrival.'

She introduced her companions. 'This is Grant, a pilot for Air Mélanésie, and this is Mike and his wife Sue. Mike also works for Air Mélanésie.'

Everyone shook hands and they pulled up chairs and joined us at the table. My father went to get some more plates and glasses and another loaf and soon they were deep in conversation.

My mother decided she'd like a cup of coffee so my father went off to make it. I followed and watched as he put the pot of water on the stove to boil and measured out the coffee into a large green enamel coffeepot. I'd forgotten what my father looked like. He was tall with black hair and dark brown eyes and he smiled a lot. His thick black-rimmed glasses were all the rage back then.

'So what do you think of the New Hebrides?' he asked as he tipped sugar into a stainless steel bowl.

'I think it's so pretty, and painted such wonderful colours,' I said earnestly.

He laughed at my choice of words. I carefully carried the sugar bowl to the living room and then went back to fetch the cups.

When Monsu wandered off in the direction of the kitchen and meowed to be let out I opened the door and we both went out into the afternoon heat. We spent an hour or so exploring the overgrown garden, him stalking intriguing rustling noises, me making them in high excitement.

I discovered a cage containing a parakeet, which screeched lustily when it spied me and puffed out its green breast feathers. I went over and said hello. After a few minutes I pushed my fingers through the wire and scratched its head. Monsu went and sat in the shade of a low shrub, panting. I agreed; it was too hot to be outdoors.

That night we went to the Hôtel Rossi, a local institution. The lives of the European population revolved around the Rossi. It was owned and operated by Madam Rossi and with an ample bosom and a larger heart, she mothered all her patrons. Her Corsican cuisine was legendary and the best food I've ever eaten was prepared in her kitchens.

That night mingled in my memories with so many other nights, but I remember eating bürek, a deep-fried cheese roll, and lobster. I attacked the lobster with gusto, quickly coming to terms with the claw crackers. Hot butter dripped off my chin but nobody seemed to mind; they were all preoccupied with their own lobsters. After dessert I was sent to play outside. It was already dark. Night had fallen abruptly at around six; there was no twilight. A breeze swept in off the harbour, carrying a salty tang of sea air, replacing the savage heat of the day. There were several French children playing nearby and I joined them on the swings, watching the harbour lights as I soared up into the sky and swooped back down to earth.

That first night, as I was tucked up in bed, I asked for Monsu to sleep in my room. He was duly brought in and deposited on the bed. My mother kissed me goodnight and switched off the light. Sleepily I lay back in bed under a sheet; it was too hot for the blanket.

For a while, Monsu purred on the pillow next to me, then decided he wanted to go out, so I pulled the mosquito screen down and let him out the window. He obviously had things to do and cats to see. I drifted to sleep listening to the unfamiliar sounds of night birds and other strange creatures.

I slept soundly, not even waking when someone placed a lighted mosquito coil on the floor beside my bed.

The weeks passed and one delightful day followed another. Sun-filled days of happiness and new discoveries, from the relative coolness of the dewy mornings when I ran barefoot in the garden playing with Monsu, to dusk, when the flying foxes came out, silhouetted against the last rays of the orange, red and dusty pink of the setting sun.

Left alone most of the day, I was free to explore the jungle. Sometimes Monsu would come with me. I climbed trees, and looked under rocks for snakes, but never found any. I tore my clothes on thorny undergrowth and never combed my hair if I could help it, and always managed to get muddy. When I was hungry I'd make my way back to the house and look in the fridge. I saw very little of my parents, they were always coming back from somewhere or just about to leave. Late one afternoon I came back as they were just getting into the car, they'd been invited to Mike and Sue's. They called out, 'Come with us, you're invited as well.' I bounded over the road and hastily wiped a smear of mud, hoping no one would notice my grubbiness.

When we arrived, Mike said he had something to show me. We went inside, and my father and I followed him down the corridor to a spare room. He opened the door very carefully and to my amazement, snuffling at the edge of the door was a baby rabbit, a ball of white fluff. Mike placed it in my arms. The rabbit was so soft, I buried my face into his fur and he smelt clean and gentle.

And so I became the proud owner of a white rabbit with pink eyes. All the way home I worried about where I'd keep him, but to my surprise the problem had already been solved. On a grassy strip next to the front door was the perfect rabbit hutch. A soft carpet of grass poked through the wire-mesh bottom, and running along the back was a lovely wooden house for him to sleep in. Through the opening, I could see a thick layer of dried grass, and later that evening when I sneaked outside to check, he was snuggled up in it, fast asleep.

Next morning when I was playing with my rabbit, a little girl appeared at the other side of the fence and stared at me. She was white with dark hair cut into a French bob.

'Hello, I'm Claire. You're new aren't you? Mummy says I should come and play with you. We're English you know, expatriates. I can tell you're new. Mummy says only new people wear socks. She says it's too hot to wear socks, you'll get a rash. These are the tropics.'

I stared back at her, speechlessly clutching my rabbit. She continued unperturbed. 'My brother Stephen wanted you to be a boy, I'm glad you're a girl because there aren't many girls here. I have a rabbit too, and mine is bigger.'

Her rabbit was indeed bigger, so big it was awkward dragging it out of its hutch. It was bigger, and it bit. My rabbit never bit. After a while we put the rabbits back in their respective hutches and sat on the front porch, swinging our legs. Suddenly she leapt off and crouched on the ground. 'Come and look at this plant, it's very clever.'

I got down and watched as she stroked the leaves. 'Ha,' she exclaimed triumphantly, as the plant pulled its leaves back out of her reach. 'Bet you didn't know about that.'

I told her I did, and said my father had showed me on my first day.

'Oh,' she said dejectedly, then cheered up almost immediately as she saw a shrub growing at the far edge of the house. 'Have you eaten any of these yet?'

I stared at the fruit, tiny carrot-like shapes ranging in colour from deep green to bright red and orange. I shook my head. 'No, I haven't. Are they nice?'

'Mmm,' she said, 'specially the red ones, they're really sweet. Here, try one.'

She picked one and offered it to me. It looked delicious and I popped it into my mouth. It was a second or two before fire filled my mouth and flashed up my nose. I spat it out, my eyes streaming. I tried wiping my tongue on the back of my hand, and drank some water at Claire's suggestion.

'At least you don't cry,' she said. 'Robin cried, and I got into lots of trouble. You aren't going to tell are you?'

I became quite indignant. 'I don't tell tales.'

Later as we shared a pineapple in a tall tree in her garden, we giggled over the whole affair. 'You did look funny, wiping your tongue on the back of your hand.'

Then she looked serious. 'You are a silly-billy, it might have been poisonous. Mummy says there are lots of poisonous berries here, and I mustn't eat any of them unless I show her first.'

About a week later, I started school. My father walked with me, holding my hand. I wasn't sure about going to school; I knew my freedom would be curtailed again.

The school was situated at the edge of the British Paddock. It was a simple construction – three classroom blocks laid out in an untidy U shape. Outside each classroom was a mad jumble of flip-flops, which seemed to be the universal footwear. I felt very conscious of my new leather sandals and white ankle socks.

The headmaster was in the staff room; classes weren't due to start for another ten minutes. He shook hands with my father and then gravely shook hands with me. He looked at me for a moment with a slightly distasteful look on his face and then turned to my father.

'So, this is Tanja.'

My father nodded.

'Which grade was she in?'

My father hesitated. 'I was in grade three,' I said, when it became apparent he didn't know.

He completely ignored me. 'Well,' he suggested, 'best thing we can do is go round the classrooms and see where she fits.'

He had a rather novel way of determining my grade level. 'This is the fourth grade,' he explained, as we stepped into one of the classrooms. As soon as everyone had quietened down, he introduced me to the class. 'This is Tanja, she's joining us from Australia.'

He made it sound as though he was talking about another planet. Then he asked them all to stand up and there was a huge scraping of chairs. The pupils stared curiously at me with unfamiliar black and white faces.

'No, no good,' he said to my father, 'they're much taller.'

He told them to sit down and we continued on our way, the class whispering behind us.

As we went into the next classroom, I was pleasantly surprised to see Claire. As before, he introduced me and asked everyone to stand. This time the average height matched my own and I was placed in grade three. A desk was found and once I was settled my father left for work.

Claire grinned broadly at me as I looked around the room, carefully laying out my new pen and rubber. I wondered what my new teacher would be like. I soon discovered my new teacher was the headmaster, and he was called Mr Proctor.

We never saw eye to eye. Very early on I learnt to distrust him, he had a habit of sneaking up behind and if you weren't paying attention, or he suspected you'd been talking, he'd slap you across the side of your face. The first time he did this I'd been talking to a boy sitting next to me. I'd just written my name on the front of my exercise book when he leaned over. 'That's a Dutch name – van der Plaat.'

I nodded, 'Yes, I'm Dutch.'

He was most excited at this, 'Spreek je Nederlands?'

'Natuurlijk!' I exclaimed, surprised to find someone who could speak Dutch.

We continued speaking – my Dutch wasn't as fluent as his, but I could follow him well enough. We were so engrossed in our conversation we didn't notice a deathly silence had fallen as Mr Proctor came up behind us. The next thing I knew was this whack across my face; I wasn't even sure what had hit me. I sat stunned into silence. 'We don't allow talking in this class,' was his only comment.

The day before my father had beaten me for the first time, Claire and I had come across a clearing near the far edge of the jungle, filled with a tangled mass of dwarf tomato plants. There were hundreds of ripening tomatoes, each the size of a marble. It had been getting late; the first flying foxes were already out, so we agreed to come back the next day.

We met early the next morning. This time we had a woven, native basket and I slung it over my shoulder as we set off down the road. We heard the sound of a car behind us and moved out of the way; pressing up against the bushes lining the road. It was my father on his way to work. He stopped the car and leaned out the window. 'Wondered where you were,' he smiled. 'Can you feed the parrot? He hasn't got anything to eat. There's some pawpaw in the fridge.'

I said I would and he drove off with a cheerful wave. We decided to feed the parrot straightaway and turned back to the house. The parrot had a full bowl of birdseed but no water. I washed and refilled his water bowl and we played with him for a few moments, scratching the top of his head before we set off again.

We soon found the tomatoes and set about filling the basket, popping more than a fair share into our mouths. It was fiercely hot and the air was full of the smell of the leaves we crushed as we searched for the tomatoes. Soon the basket was half-full and heavy and we were both perspiring.

We walked further into the jungle searching for a cool place and settled down against the huge root of a tree, fanning our skirts up and down to cool our legs and watching tiny skinks darting about.

We became aware of the tantalising sound of running water. Leaving the basket of tomatoes tucked amongst the tree roots, we left the shade of the jungle and walked over an area strewn with thick vines.

The tinkling of water grew louder. I was walking ahead when suddenly the vines gave way and I plunged through, feet first. I'd walked straight off the edge of a cliff. The vines grew so prolifically it was impossible to tell they no longer grew on the ground, but covered the uppermost branches of several tall hardwood trees below.

The branches saved me from serious injury; one of them caught in the leg of my underpants and broke my fall. I hung suspended in the air, vaguely aware of a smarting pain where a branch scraped across my stomach.

Below I could make out the shimmering of sunlight on the stream we'd been looking for, then I felt a frantic grasping at my hair and there was Claire, reaching over the edge, trying to catch hold of my plaits. She stretched precariously over the edge until she managed to seize my hair, then carefully wriggling back to a more secure position, began to haul me up. I felt as though my hair would come out by the roots. I didn't care, I was too afraid of falling on the rocks below.

In a blind panic, I kicked out with my feet, trying to get a foothold on one of the branches so I could lever myself upwards. Finally, my foot made contact and between us, we managed to get me back to safety.

When I finally caught my breath I became aware of the pain in my stomach. I lifted my skirt and found a piece of branch had broken through the skin, and a large sliver of bark was still lodged there. When I pulled it out it left a neat round hole, about half a centimetre across. I could see it was quite deep and it began to bleed profusely.

We decided to go back to Claire's house because her mother had sticking plasters. When Claire lifted up my skirt and revealed my bleeding stomach, she immediately went off to get the medicine kit. Then, sitting me on a kitchen chair, she gently cleaned the wound with a ball of cotton wool soaked in Dettol. She patted it dry and put a large plaster over it. We didn't tell her how I got it, and she didn't ask. After I was all fixed up she invited me to have lunch with the family. Much later, I remembered the basket of tomatoes still sitting under the tree. We found them where we'd left them, and ate a few more on our way back up the road, talking all the while.

I stopped in mid-sentence, catching sight of my father standing outside the gate. He looked furious, and completely ignored Claire's cheery greeting.

Instead he grabbed me by the back of my neck, his nails cutting into my flesh as he pulled me, stumbling, through the open gate. The basket slipped off my shoulder scattering the tomatoes. Claire stood transfixed by the roadside.

'Come and look at this,' he bellowed and thrust me down in front of the parrot cage, pressing my face painfully into the wire netting. 'Look at what you've done, you little bastard.'

I looked. The parrot hung suspended by his neck in the fork of a branch, gently swinging. A breeze ruffled a few feathers of his lifeless body.

'You've starved him to death.' He shook me as he spoke.

I tried to stand up, 'But, he had seed, lots of seed,' and I pointed to the bowl.

This only angered him further, 'Are you stupid? He was a fruit-eating parrot, he can't eat seed.'

I stood silently for a minute, horrified to think the parrot had starved to death while I'd been feasting on tomatoes. Then I wondered why the birdseed was in the cage if the parrot couldn't eat it.

'Why ... ' I began, but was silenced by a resounding slap across my face. Mortified, I looked over at Claire, but she was running up the road.

He slapped me again, and shoved me forward. I ran into the house, to the sanctity of my bedroom, but he followed me. He said I had to be punished and I saw he had my mother's hairbrush in his hand. He roughly turned me over his knee, pulled my pants down, and proceeded to spank me. As the blows fell, I screamed and cried with the pain and the unfamiliar indignity of having my pants pulled down; but my mother was out. She couldn't help me. Finally he pushed me away. I was forbidden to leave the room and he slammed the door. A moment later I watched him back out of the driveway, his mouth a thin hard line, and turn down the road.

I sat carefully on the bed, still shaking from this unexpected violence, tears rolling down my cheeks, when

Claire's mother appeared at the window. 'Would you like to come shopping?'

I shook my head, 'I can't, I'm not allowed to leave my room.' I told her about the parrot, sobbing all the while.

'That's ridiculous! That's not your fault, at your age you can't be expected to be responsible. Come on, come shopping with us, it'll cheer you up.'

So in spite of my father's words I came out of my room and went outside. She wiped my tears and gave me a hug, then Claire and I hopped in the car. She bought us milkshakes at the coffee shop and we went to the Chinese tailor, where she had a final fitting for a new summer frock. Claire and I looked though the bolts of material, imagining all kinds of wonderful dresses we'd have made from the silks and lace.

We were nearly home when we spied my father's car turning into the drive just ahead. My heart sank. Claire's mother discreetly pulled over at the far end of our garden. I climbed over the fence, hoping to get over the terrace wall and into my bedroom before he came into the house.

I was too late. He was waiting under the terrace. He didn't say a word, he dragged me by my arm round the house and in through the kitchen. Once inside he struck me several times across the side of my head, heavy open-handed slaps that left my ears ringing. His face was suffused with rage as he dragged me into my room and threw me on the bed. He now used his closed fists as I screamed. Then he was gone, slamming my door as he left. I heard the key turn in the lock.

I gingerly got up; making my way painfully to the door, and in disbelief tried the handle. He'd locked me in. I sat on the floor in a patch of sunlight and stared out the window, watching the clouds. Eventually the room began to fill with shadows, and still I sat. I listened to the plaintive calls of night birds as they passed overhead, the sound echoing in my head, reflecting the feeling in my heart.

The shadows deepened into night and when I could no longer see my hands in the blackness, I crawled under the sheets, still dressed. I slept almost immediately.

The next morning I awoke, a feeling of dread rushing through me as I stood before my bedroom door. Tentatively I tried the handle, to my relief it was unlocked. The house was silent. I crept into the kitchen and found an apple in the fridge, and nibbled on it as I made my way out of the house.

It was early; the grass was still wet with dew. I walked quietly past the red car parked in the drive, expecting to be called back at any minute. Then with a feeling of freedom, I passed through the gate and went up the road, to wait for Claire and Stephen.

Claire was all agog, wanting to know what had happened. I told her about the beating and she carefully rolled up the back of my blouse. 'You're covered in bruises,' she exclaimed, sounding horrified.

I was lying on my stomach on the pleasantly cool floor of my bedroom, looking over my live beetle collection. I had more than ten jam jars lined along the wall. One by one, I carefully unscrewed the perforated tops and sprinkled a little water on the burou leaves; I could hear my parents in the living room. They were fighting again.

An iridescent blue beetle about the size of my thumbnail scuttled over the edge of the open container; dropping to the floor before I could stop it. I put the lid back on, careful not to crush any of the others; keeping an eye on the runaway as it headed under the bed.

Claire said they were stinkbugs, but they were too beautiful to be called stinkbugs so I didn't believe her. We'd found them sheltering on the underside of the burou leaves, the growing fence posts. My prize possession was a leaf dotted with tiny orange eggs. I couldn't wait for them to hatch; hopefully they'd do it when I was home from school.

The argument became louder and more intrusive. The peace between them hadn't lasted long, not even three weeks. There was no sign of my six-legged runaway. I finally pulled the bed away from the wall and found him up against the skirting board. I picked him up carefully between my finger and thumb, holding one hand beneath in case I dropped him. His tiny little black legs waved frantically as he tried to escape. 'There you go beastie,' I murmured, as I dropped him back in the jar and screwed the lid back on. I placed the jar back in line with the others and settled down to watch them drinking. My mother was yelling, her voice a rising crescendo of fury. Then there was a terrific crash, the sound of breaking glass, followed by my mother's high heels clicking loudly past my bedroom door and down the tiled corridor. The bedroom door slammed, the sound reverberating through the house, followed by a heavy silence.

After a while I opened my door and peered out. There was no sign of life so I stepped out of my room and made my way to the living room. My father was sitting at the table, calmly making himself a sandwich. On the floor near the French windows lay the shattered remains of a crystal vase. African daisies lay scattered in a pool of water, shards of crystal sprinkled over their colourful petals. It wasn't the first thing my mother had broken in the last couple of months. I wondered if I should get the dustpan and sweep up the glass.

My father looked up as I entered the room. 'Have you eaten?'

I shook my head, and made my way over to the table, careful not to step in any glass. I was hungry and pulled up a chair and sat down. 'What were you and Mummy fighting about?'

He didn't answer, offering me a thin slice of cheese, covered in a thick layer of tiny black seeds. It was delicious. 'Do you want to know where it comes from?' Then he added, 'Very few people know the true story of this rare and wondrous cheese.' He had a twinkle in his eye as he said this.

'Please tell me,' I begged, more than a little curious.

'Well,' he began, 'it comes from a wild mountain tribe in a faraway land, many days' trek from civilisation.'

I listened enthralled as he went on to tell me how this tribe made cheese from goats' milk. Because they didn't have paper they rolled the cheeses in seeds to prevent them sticking to each other on the long dangerous ride through the mountains to where they exchanged them for fine cloth and presents for their families.

I loved it when my father told me stories, I knew they were mixtures of truth and wild imagination, but even so, I could imagine the wild horsemen galloping over the mountaintops with their precious load.

We sat for a moment, each with our own thoughts; I was away riding across the mountains. As for my father, I don't know where he was; perhaps he was thinking about the fight with my mother. Suddenly, he asked if I'd like to go for a drive.

I nodded; I loved going for drives. 'Can Mummy come too?'

He got up from the table, 'Go and ask her.'

However, she had a headache and didn't want to come. My father and I set off in the little red car. He decided we'd go to Lelepa Landing, which both surprised and pleased me because it was several hours away. Once out of the residential area the road became narrow and snaked through the thick jungle, occasionally coming out to run along the coast. He decided we should play a game. The idea was to tell the other person to do something and they had to do it immediately. I got him to touch his nose, put the window wipers on; giggling with childish glee as the coral dust smeared over the window, temporarily blinding us. Then I got him to wind his window up and down, a puerile game, but I was only a child and easily amused.

Then for my pièce de résistance I yelled, 'Stop the car!' There was a screeching of brakes and I slipped forward in my seat as the car slewed to one side and stopped in the middle of the road. Through my open window, I could hear the sea pounding on the reef, and my heart pounded in my chest. I had no idea he'd stop the car, at least not like that.

As the dust settled he turned the key in the ignition and slowly drove on. 'Do you know why it's so important to play this game?' he asked, looking straight ahead, watching the road. I didn't, and told him so.

'Well,' he said quietly, 'imagine if you were just about to jump in a river and I yelled out for you to stop, what would happen if you jumped in anyway?'

I shrugged my shoulders. 'Nothing I guess.'

'What if I'd seen the river was full of crocodiles waiting to eat you?'

This made me think.

'Now it's my turn,' he said, 'because it's very important that you do exactly as I say, without hesitating. One day it could save your life, even if it doesn't make sense at the time. That's why I stopped the car, for all I knew you'd seen someone running across the road. If I hadn't stopped, some-one might be lying dead now.'

I squirmed in my seat. This was beginning to sound like another lecture. He told me to put both my hands on top of my head, I did. Then I struggled to touch my big toe to my nose, but I was laughing too much. We drove many kilometres, taking turns at this new game. We left the main road and turned down the track leading towards Lelepa Landing. The way was so narrow that leaves and branches scraped against the side of the car and pressed against the windows. Unexpectedly, he stopped the car halfway down the track and turned the motor off. I sat silently for a moment, wondering why we'd stopped.

A precious moment, that last moment of childhood. I took a last glimpse of the make-believe world we all grow out of, forgetting to wave, and then my father told me to take my underpants off. I looked sideways at him, shocked. Fathers weren't meant to talk about underpants.

'Haven't you learnt anything?' he exclaimed, looking at me strangely. I picked nervously at a scab on my knee. Was he angry? I didn't know, and I didn't want to find out, I still remembered the hairbrush and his fists.

'I said, take your underpants off, that way I'll know I can trust you to listen to me.' He flipped up the edge of my frock as he spoke, exposing my thighs. I squirmed uncomfortably in my seat, biting my lip. Then slowly I pulled my pants down, lifting my bottom off the seat to free them, then yanking them down over my knees to my ankles. I tried to kick them off. For a moment, they snagged on one of the buckles of my roman sandals and I had to lean forward to disentangle them. Self-consciously, I sat back in my seat, scrunching up my white cotton underpants in my hands, not knowing what to do with them. My father took them, and leaning across, opened the glove box and shoved them inside, away out of sight. I smoothed my skirt back down over my legs.

'You see, everything is for a reason,' he spoke easily, confidentially. 'You're a big girl now. Quite grown up for your age.'

He casually put his hand in my lap as he spoke.

That's true I thought, a little less stricken, I am nearly ten.

'It's time you learnt about sex,' he continued and his hand pushed my skirt back up again, uncovering my legs once more. I stiffened.

'Relax,' he laughed, 'it's all right, I'm just going to show you something.' His hand slid down between my legs. 'You see, girls have a hole down here, it's for boys to put their penises in.' His fingers probed, persistent, and found what they were looking for. 'Here it is.'

Despite my uneasiness, I was momentarily intrigued, I didn't know I had a hole down there. I wasn't sure about letting a boy put his penis in though; a little boy said he'd show me his penis if I showed him mine, I readily agreed and he'd pulled his shorts down. It was so ugly, purple and blue-looking, I screamed in disgust and ran away.

However, I was only momentarily intrigued; what my father was doing began to hurt. 'Ouch,' I exclaimed, and pushed his hand away.

'Didn't that feel nice?' he asked in a soft voice. 'It's supposed to feel nice, perhaps you're too dry.'

Then he did a disgusting thing, he spat on his hand, and spittle clung to his chin as he pressed the wetness between my legs; rubbing his fingers up and down.

'There, doesn't that feel better?'

It didn't, but I didn't know what to say so instead I stared out the window, ignoring what was happening. A solitary leaf had caught the wind and fluttered back and forth. Later I learnt spirits do that when they're around to let you know they're there. I didn't know that then; if I had, perhaps I wouldn't have felt so alone.

After a couple of moments my eyes caught sight of movement further down the track. Two men were crossing the beach, heading towards us. My father spotted them at the same time and whipped his hand from between my legs, hastily pushing my skirt down.

It would have looked strange if we'd reversed up the track, so he drove slowly down to the beach, waving as we passed the villagers. He got out, but I sat in the car feeling slightly sore and horribly embarrassed. I couldn't get out, my pants were still in the glove box.

The drive home was mostly silent, without the laughter we'd shared earlier. When we were only a few kilometres from home, he told me not to tell my mother. I wanted to know why not.

'Because we'll fight again. She doesn't want you to know about sex yet, she thinks you're still a child, she doesn't know you very well, anyone can see you're quite grown up.'

I guess he was right; I had done a lot of growing up that day.

Chapter 3

Tisha was getting married. The evening before, while my mother was at work, my father decided to visit her. I sat in bed reading and was still awake when I heard him come in and head for the bathroom.

It was nearly time for him to drive to Hôtel Le Lagon to fetch my mother. She was working the night shift, sometimes not coming in until 4am because my father had fallen asleep, leaving her to walk home. I got out of bed to ask if I might go with him. I hadn't seen her all day and I missed her. In fact, I hardly saw my mother at all these days.

My father stood in the living room, completely naked. It was the first time I'd seen him undressed, but he was unconcerned. I asked him if he knew where his underpants were and he told me it was perfectly normal to be naked. His penis twitched as I looked at it, and he caught hold of it. He stood looking at me, then told me he'd just had sex with Tisha. 'Got my revenge on that bastard, now he's marrying damaged goods.'

I didn't understand what he meant, so I said nothing.

'She'd taken a sleeping tablet and I carried her to bed. I put it in all the way.'

'But it's too big,' I exclaimed, a little sceptical and a little scared of the idea.

'It'd never fit in you, you're too little, but Tisha isn't.'

There was a momentary silence and I remembered why I'd come into the hall. 'Can I come with you to pick up Mummy?'

'Only if you promise not to tell her what I told you, it's our little secret and she mustn't know.'

I assured him I wouldn't.

Tisha came back from her honeymoon, proudly showing her wedding ring. One lunchtime she came back to the house with my mother, deeply distraught. She'd lost her wedding ring the previous evening while swimming. I suggested we go and look for it. Everyone laughed, the tide had been in and out, and it'd be impossible to find. I persisted, saying that if we asked God, perhaps he'd help. This brought another round of laughter, but in the end we all piled into Tisha's car. Once there, I had to agree. It was an impossible task. The sand was so fine, something as tiny as a wedding ring would simply disappear. I was soon bored, so I pulled off my dress, tugged on my mask and flippers and plunged in. I chased tiny fish along the shoreline, occasionally glimpsing Tisha and the others searching the beach.

A tiny orange and white clown fish darted out and attacked my mask. They are very territorial and this one must have seen its reflection in my facemask. Satisfied it had made its point, it sank down to safety.

I spied a tiny patch of white sand – a good place for cowries. I swam down and something glinted within the rusting remains of a tin can, half-filled with sand. I returned to the surface for air and dived again, pulling myself along the coral. I saw the sparkle again. I pried the tin out and it crumbled in my grasp. As the sand slipped through my fingers I was stunned to see a gold wedding band sitting in my hand.

I was so overjoyed, I tried to call out before I reached the surface and swallowed a mouthful of seawater. Coughing and spluttering, I broke through the surface, shrieking with excitement. Everyone came running as I clambered out of the water. 'What's the matter?' they asked anxiously, thinking I'd been stung by something.

'I found it, I found it!' I shrieked.

Then as I unclenched my fist and revealed my treasure, they shrieked as well. We all jumped up and down and I did a little war dance. I was a hero. My Sunday school teacher was right; God had been listening!

I still can't believe the odds against finding the ring. Perhaps, if I'd known then what I know now, I would have flung it back into the sea, cutting one of the tangled threads that were already weaving a trap around me.

Most afternoons after school Claire and I played with our rabbits, watching them nibble the sweet grass and enjoy their freedom. My rabbit was as fluffy and gloriously white as ever and growing rapidly.

Just before dawn one morning, I was awakened by a bloodcurdling sound – a high-pitched screaming, footsteps running down the hall and the front door slamming. I leapt out of bed to find my mother standing in the hall, white faced. 'The rabbit,' was all she could say.

I tore into the garden. The hutch was empty, one side crushed and the wire netting torn from the wooden frame.

My father stood naked in the road, clutching the lifeless remains of my rabbit, a vivid smear of blood across the white fur, scarlet against white. Further down the road I saw the Elly twins dragging their dog into their garden. My father was crying, 'I couldn't get the dog to let go.'

I stroked my dead rabbit's face, gently smoothing back his ears. His neck was broken. Together we went indoors and laid him on the table. My father had been bitten and my mother hunted for something to cover it.

We buried my rabbit outside the back door, wrapping him carefully in a new towel to keep the dirt off his fur and I covered the tiny mound with marigolds. I said a prayer, but my father told me animals don't have souls and don't go to heaven. But I did anyway; I felt he must be wrong, heaven would be a very sad and lonely place if there were no animals.

As Claire and I walked to school I told her what had happened. She squeezed my hand and promised I could play with her rabbit. But I wanted my own rabbit; I wanted to run my hand down his soft fur and whisper into his long velvety ears.

Morning playtime was a rude surprise. The Elly twins had been whispering behind their hands all morning. Once I saw Jerry passing a note to the Chinese boy sitting behind me. When the bell finally rang, I hurried out into the sunshine, glad for a moment of freedom, but a jeering crowd soon surrounded me.

'You father runs round the street naked,' Jerry yelled.

'We saw his penis,' snickered his twin brother.

'He was trying to rescue my rabbit from your dog,' I yelled back, 'he didn't have time to get dressed, he was still in bed.'

This only made it worse. They continued with their

barrage, saying he was rude for not wearing pyjamas. I dissolved into tears and put my hands over my ears, feeling deeply ashamed. Finally, it was too much and I ran home, their taunts burning in my ears.

These days, I rarely saw my parents. Their fighting continued, day after day, only stopping when one of them had to go to work. I stopped coming home for lunch because I couldn't bear it any more. They never spoke to me and there never seemed to be anything to eat.

I have clear memories of my parents circling the coffee table, looking as though they were about to lunge at each other's throats. They were yelling terrible things and weren't even aware of my presence. Once my father screamed, 'If you didn't fuck around with everybody in sight ... ' I sat forward. Had he really said that? Perhaps he only said muck, so I asked, 'Did you say fuck or muck?'

There was a deathly silence and two pairs of eyes swivelled in my direction. Needless to say, he didn't answer me; they turned away and continued where they'd left off.

The fight that upset me most was the one they had when my father crossed me out of my mother's passport. She stood in the middle of the living room, waving her passport in his face, so incensed it took me a while to understand what she was saying. 'You bastard, you had no right to do this ... ' and on and on. From where I sat, I could make out the thick black lines where my father had deleted my name. I didn't understand the sinister implications until much later, but I understood her next words. I was shocked into stillness. 'She's not my daughter any more, from now on I have no daughter. Are you happy now?' Mad with rage she flung the passport across the room. Without looking at me she turned and walked away, her high heels clicking down the hall.

My father picked up the passport and put it on the table. 'Doesn't Mummy love me any more?' I asked tentatively, looking for reassurance.

He looked at me, an angry expression on his face. 'No, she doesn't, she never loved you.' He started to say something else but I ran away to Claire's place. They weren't home, so I sat and talked to her rabbit. I couldn't believe my mother didn't love me, but it had to be true because my father said so and I'd heard her terrible words. I didn't cry, perhaps I was too numb.

After that I avoided them. I'd hurry back from school and scrounge around in the kitchen for something to eat then climb the huge tree next to the fence. From here I'd watch their coming and goings and know when the coast was clear.

Once or twice I saw them looking for me, but they never thought to look up. Claire's mother found out and several times a week she'd send Claire to call me over for lunch. I'd go to bed before my parents came home, reading by torchlight under the covers, feigning sleep if they looked in my room. But all that changed one day.

I was feasting on apples in my lookout, throwing the cores into the road, waiting for the red car to drive off. Finally, after what seemed an uncommonly long wait, I heard the car door slam and spied its departure. After allowing a reasonable amount of time, I slid to the ground and went inside. Imagine my shock when I saw my parents waiting for me. It had been a trap. I backed up, ready to make a run for it, but my father caught hold of me. The long and the short of it was that I was put under house arrest. I was allowed to walk to and from school with Claire, I wasn't allowed to get into any more fights, I was forbidden to climb trees and on and on. They finished up by telling me they'd decided to hire a housegirl to clean the house and keep an eye on me. The postmaster was bringing her around after work that evening.

Chapter 4

When Lidia came into my life she was only fourteen and beautiful – her skin the colour of the finest burnished teak. When we were together, just the two of us, she laughed frequently, hiding her mouth with long slender fingers, huge mischievous brown eyes sparkling. When the adults were around she kept her eyes shyly downcast, calling my father 'Masta', and my mother 'The Missus'.

I watched as she cleaned the house on her first day. She smelt lovely, of baby powder and eau de toilette. She left at six, leaving a note for my father.

Dear Masta, Please you must buy 1 Vim, 1 brush for scrubbing floor, 1 packet Bonux soap powder for washing clothes. Thank you very much, Yours faithfully, your Lidia, housegirl.

For all her shyness, she was in control – she ran the house efficiently and did whatever she thought needed doing – no one dared tell her what to do. When she'd finished, we'd lie in the shade, reading and eating oomais, a Chinese sweet.

The house was full of friends; it was Sunday and unbearably hot. My mother had bought an electric fan and it sat on the table giving momentary relief before it swung on to cool someone else. We picked at the food, a slice of pâté here, a piece of Camembert there, Monsu sitting with us as usual. My father went off to get some more Evian water. While he was out of the room, Tisha leaned over. 'I have a little present for you,' she said, handing me a tiny red box.

Inside was a tiny gold ring. I slid it on my finger and it was a perfect fit. I beamed up at Tisha. It was beautiful, criss-crossed with a diamond pattern and perfect in every way. I held out my hand, admiring how the gold reflected in the sunlight.

'It's real gold,' said Tisha, 'it's the only way I can think of thanking you for finding my wedding ring'.

I leaned over to kiss her, but suddenly we were all sprayed with a fine mist. Monsu had chosen that moment to spray up against the fan blades. We all shrieked, leaping out of our chairs and Monsu was chased off in disgrace while we mopped ourselves frantically.

The school holidays finally arrived, two months covering the worst of the hot season. My house arrest was forgotten – perhaps my parents thought Lidia was keeping an eye on me, perhaps they were simply too involved with their own lives.

My mother had become a stranger. Occasionally we'd meet in the corridor or at breakfast. Sometimes she'd look at me and ask me when I'd last combed my hair, or didn't I think I should have a shower?

I'd stopped taking showers; I only washed if I was sure no one else was home. My father had taken to watching me showering. At first I hadn't cared. He'd sit on the toilet and talk to me through the shower door. I loved to talk and I'd chatter away about things I'd seen and what I'd been doing. Then one day he pulled the shower door aside, and without any warning stuck his hand between my legs, rather roughly. 'Make sure you wash yourself properly there.'

I backed up against the shower wall.

'With soap,' he added.

I nodded and said I would, but I don't think he believed me because he bent down and picked up the soap. Water spattered on his head and shoulder and splashed out all over the floor. He rubbed the soap between my legs. 'Like that.'

His glasses had fogged up and he handed me the soap and began to wipe them on his shirt-tail. It was slippery and I dropped it, but I didn't pick it up. The soap began to sting and I frantically tried to rinse it off, but it was awkward, especially with him watching.

After that I wasn't so happy about him coming in. I started locking the door, then the key to the bathroom mysteriously disappeared. My mother and I spent ages searching, but no one knew where it was.

Not having a key meant the door could never be locked and it wasn't long before my father started coming in when I was on the toilet. I used to sit at an awkward angle trying to aim my stream of wee against the side of the porcelain bowl so he couldn't hear me. My cheeks flamed when I miscalculated and a sudden stream hit the water, the trickling seeming to echo round the bathroom. I noticed he never came in while my mother was home. I used the toilet in the house as little as possible; more often than not I'd disappear into the elephant grass, preferring the company of the creepy crawlies. Often Monsu would appear, rubbing against my legs. Once he squatted next to me and made me laugh, the two of us crouched in the elephant grass, weeing.

One day, while visiting a friend of Claire's, I was given two ducks. I carried them proudly home, one tucked under each arm and my father agreed to make a duck run for them on the weekend; meanwhile they would stay in the house.

At the weekend my father arrived home with fence posts and a roll of chicken wire. We spent the next couple of hours digging holes for the posts and hammering the chicken wire onto them, modifying the rabbit hutch into a duck shelter. Finally it was ready; we stood back and admired our handiwork. We'd built the run around my tree, to give them shelter in the hot season. My father sent me to get the ducks. I hunted all through the house and in the end had to come out and tell him they'd gone.

'They can't be gone,' he exclaimed irritably, but they were. The gate had been left open, somehow they'd wandered out and must have waddled straight past us.

My father was furious, I had a sinking feeling in my stomach when I saw his face. I knew what was coming. He grabbed me by my hair and shook me, 'How can you be so stupid, leaving the gate open?'

Then I was back to sitting in my locked room, my bottom glowing with the assault of the hairbrush, watching the sun go down.

I awoke the next morning with a plan. I decided an empty duck run would only serve as an reminder of my muddle-headedness. I'd have chickens instead. There were wild chickens everywhere, all I had to do was catch some babies. Unfortunately, my father didn't agree. The subject was dropped.

I talked to Claire about my idea of having chickens and she came up with a brilliant idea. 'Let's get some eggs out of the fridge and hatch them.'

We went back to her house and took two eggs out of the fridge. Back at my house we agreed it would be best if I hatched them, and we put them in a sock I sneaked from my father's cupboard. For the next two weeks I carried them stuffed down my front. At night I put them under my pillow.

Two weeks passed, and I have to admit I was getting fed up with caring for them. One morning, while my parents were eating breakfast, I saw a gecko run up the wall. I clambered up onto a chair to try to get a better look. Somehow in my haste I missed my footing and in my attempts to regain my balance the chair tipped up and I fell.

The eggs broke, soaking through my top; my mother looked at me in horror as the stench filled the room. I was devastated. There was no sign of any chickens, only a thick black stinking mess. My mother went round opening windows as my father dragged me outside to the laundry tub and pulled off my top. Then he went back inside, Lidia following him with a bucket and mop.

Once I'd changed my clothes and the stench had gone, my father said I could have some chickens. He ordered a dozen Rhode Island Reds from overseas and the eggs duly arrived at the agricultural station. I waited on tenterhooks, until my father finally got the call to say they'd hatched. I was so excited. There were thirteen tiny little yellow balls of fluff. I had my chickens.

Each day dawned hot and dusty and rolled into each other as the holidays began to draw to an end. My chickens lost their baby fluff and slowly turned deep brown, there were nine hens and four roosters.

One day it was even more unbearably hot than usual. Lidia and I played in the garden taking turns with the hose, then went and sat on the grass, enjoying the coolness of our wet clothes. There was an eerie stillness in the air; even the birds were silent. The chickens sat in the shade, their beaks open, their wings spread a little. Monsu was nowhere to be seen.

Lidia said, 'I think we're going to have an earthquake, it's always like this when an earthquake is coming. The trees and animals are waiting.'

'How do the trees and the birds know?'

'The spirits tell them; the lizards bring messages from the spirit world.'

I believed her absolutely and suddenly understood her fear of geckos and lizards. She talked for hours as I listened, entranced.

That day she opened a whole new world for me. She told me about the spirits that live in banyan trees, but assured me it was all right if I climbed the trees, providing I asked the spirits first and didn't damage the trees. She told me about the little people who live in the bush with long blonde hair and how a man from her village had tried to catch one, somehow in the ensuing struggle to hold the little person, he suffered a broken arm. It was his own fault, he should have known better. She told me about clevas (witch doctors) and leaf medicine (magic), and the many signs that spirits are around, such as a solitary leaf fluttering in the wind or hearing breathing in the night. Spirits were all around us, good spirits and bad ones, they could be seen, you just had to learn how to look for them.

The day continued, still and waiting. At five o'clock, we sat together in the living room, reading. The first we knew of the earthquake was a far off rumbling, like distant thunder. It seemed to come from the depths of the earth, followed immediately by the rattling of ornaments and crockery. Lidia sprang to her feet, her book falling to the floor as she tugged me up. She pulled me over to the doorway leading to the corridor. 'Safest place to stand,' she breathed anxiously. At first it didn't seem to be much of an earthquake, two or three violent tremors, followed by a momentary swaying of the ground. We were just about to leave the safety of the doorway when the rumbling began again; this time there was one savage lurch, sending the huge teak bookcase crashing through the window.

The noise was terrific as glass cascaded and books and ornaments tipped all over the living room and scattered outside on the lawn. Silence returned and the dust began to settle. So that was an earthquake! We went outside to collect the books and carry them back in. Several ornaments were smashed but the wooden carvings were undamaged. We tried to shift the shelves, but they were far too heavy. We left them for my father to sort out when he came home.

School started again. I was kept in the third grade; I still didn't know my multiplication tables. I didn't care, I was in no hurry to go anywhere; it made no difference to me if I was in fourth grade or third grade. Robin was in my class now and we sat next to each other. I no longer had a window seat. I think Mr Proctor was on to that one.

Our circle of friends gradually widened, and my father met a businessman called Maurice, who was married to Jeanne and had two daughters, Gabrielle a year younger than myself, and Yvonne a year older.

The weekends were filled at this time with trips around the island. Long days on the coast, with swimming and luxurious picnics prepared by Jeanne. Often we'd go to Tukutuk at Devil's Point. Sometimes we'd fish, swimming the huge nets out and then pulling them in, tipping out the tangle of flapping fish onto the sand.

Once, Maurice made a furrow in the sand and lined it with rocks; it gradually filled with water and he placed our catch there. I sat and watched them swimming, knowing this was their last day. The flames were dying down and the embers were nearly ready for cooking, the tin foil already spread out, waiting for their bodies. I couldn't bear it any more and caught up one of the brilliantly coloured parrotfish. I carefully placed it in the sea and watched as it darted away. Then I caught another one. Maurice came and sat next to me. 'Why are you doing that?'

'Because it's too beautiful to die.'

'Why only the beautiful ones? Should only the beautiful ones be rescued?'

I didn't know how to answer this; I stared silently down into the pool, biting my lip looking at the brown triggerfish swimming between the brilliant colours of the others. I didn't want any of them to die.

We didn't say anything for a while then Maurice pulled the rocks aside, and the sea swirled in through the opening. In a flash, the fish were gone. Together we walked back up the beach.

'The fire is ready, where are the fish?' Jeanne was stirring the embers with a stick and little sparks flew in the air. I said nothing.

Maurice spoke for me. 'They escaped, the wall collapsed.'

We looked at each other, sharing our secret; I had a delicious warm feeling as I thought of our fish, free again to live another day. The others were thoroughly put out; they'd been looking forward to freshly grilled fish with baguettes smothered in French butter. Well, they'd just have to have pâté and ham instead, and I didn't think that was such a bad thing.

During the week I was alone in the evenings, Lidia went home at six and I'd wait for my parents. I'd read all the books by this time. Sometimes I would talk to Monsu and my beetles. The eggs had long hatched. I had missed their arrival in the world, but I'd found others and watched them hatching. They were no bigger than a pinhead but grew rapidly.

Not long after this, I stayed overnight at Claire's house. It was a wonderful evening, and after our baths we dressed in our pyjamas and got into bed. Mrs Mason came into our room and read us a story.

The next evening as I showered, my father came in to the bathroom. He asked me about the previous evening and I chatted away telling him everything that had happened, describing the roast chicken, chips and pudding. Then I told him Claire and I had bathed together, innocently adding that normally Claire had a bath with her brother. Last night Stephen hopped into our bath after we'd finished.

This set my father off down a familiar track. He told me he was sure Claire and her brother had sex. He went on to say most brothers and sisters did, it was perfectly normal. This upset me and I didn't believe him. I couldn't understand why he would say such things. To me Claire's home was a place of goodness and decency and I couldn't accept that was happening. He wanted me to ask Claire. I never did, but somehow the closeness I'd felt with Claire fell apart. I can't really put my finger on what went wrong, I guess my feelings just changed. I saw less and less of her and when her father's job supervising the construction of the new wharf came to an end, she disappeared out of my life, returning to England.

I came home one day from school to find all my beetle jars empty, drying upside down on the sink. The living room was full of boxes. Years later, I learned we'd been kicked out; my father had received numerous warnings about the garden. The owner didn't like elephant grass and wanted a lawn but my father refused to cut it.

It was very difficult to find a house so we moved onto Maurice's cabin cruiser, moored off the jetty near his house. We walked back at night to feed my chickens. I'd since caught about fifteen bush fowl chickens. It must have looked funny, me running up the road, my skirt filled with babies, and a mad hen, wings outstretched, chasing after me. In the end, I gave her back three, which calmed her down. I guess she couldn't count.

I also had two guinea fowl. I had been sitting up my tree when a pair of guinea fowl, surrounded by about twenty or thirty half-grown chicks wandered into our garden. In my excitement, I practically fell out of the tree. I called out for Lidia and my father, and the three of us ran round the garden, trying to catch them, but they were too quick and most flew up into my tree.

Lidia suggested we hose them, as they can't fly when they're wet. Eventually two landed in the chicken coop, sopping wet. In the morning the others had all gone, but these two decided to stay. I'm not sure why, they could have flown out of the coop any time they wanted. They guarded the garden ferociously, making a terrible racket whenever strangers came past.

It was a special time, living on Maurice's boat. I loved sitting on deck watching the sun come up. The water was so flat and still, patches of diesel would float on the surface, pink, purple and green rainbows shimmering, the fin of a karong, or tuna, occasionally breaking the surface. Shoals of glistening, silver sardines would leap out as they tried to evade bigger fish. Tiny little blue and yellow fish hung around the huge twists of rope hanging over the side of the boat, and spiny sea urchins covered the sea bottom.

At lunchtime I'd walk to Maurice's office and eat lunch with Mirabelle, who worked there. I'd also come down to wait at the office after school, until my father collected me. Sometimes he'd stay and share a bottle of wine with Mirabelle, while I played outside with the Vietnamese children next door.

When we walked back to the house to feed the chickens, dusk would be falling and in the dim light I'd rinse out the bowls, give them clean water, and top up their food. Monsu was rarely around. I pleaded with my father to bring Monsu with us, I missed him terribly and I was certain he missed me. My father wouldn't hear of it, I assumed he was waiting for us to find another house.

One night I walked back barefoot, having lost my shoes yet again. We'd been back about an hour; I was sitting on deck when Monsu appeared out of the bushes, meowing. He must have tracked me because I'd been walking barefoot. I called to him and he stood at the edge of the water, plaintively mewing. He wouldn't walk up the gangplank so in the end I went and fetched him. He purred in my arms, rubbing his head against my cheek, all the time mewing as though he had lots to tell me. I cried and cried. I had Monsu back. After a time we went below deck and I fell asleep contented, with Monsu on my pillow, washing himself, occasionally pausing to lick my face. He never stopped purring once.

In the morning Monsu was gone. I never saw him again. My father thought he might have fallen overboard and been eaten by sharks. Such a terrible thought, a terrible end for my friend.

My mother was in love with Maurice. My father had no idea; the first I knew was when Jeanne invited us round for afternoon tea while my father was at work. Somewhere between the second and third cup of coffee Jeanne adeptly changed the subject. 'Do you think you might be good enough to leave my husband alone?'

My mother carefully put her cake fork down and stared at Jeanne. There ensued quite a lengthy discussion, quite heated at times, in rapid-fire French. At the end of it, Jeanne made another pot of coffee and the conversation went back to normal, as though nothing out of the ordinary had happened. It was all very civilised.

Our friends slowly drifted off, everyone knew about my mother and Maurice, but no one was going to say anything to my father. The weekend crowd gradually dwindled until it was only my father and mother, Maurice and Mirabelle, and me.

Chapter 5

We moved again, this time to a flat at Tebakor Corner, upstairs from a Chinese store. It was a nice place. My bedroom was small, overlooking the corrugated-iron roof of the shop storeroom. From here there was good view of the garden, and no mosquito nets covering the louvres. I fell in love with it immediately. Next to this was a bathroom, with a bath but no shower. I noticed with relief there was a key in the door. The toilet also had a key.

The area in front of the shop was always crowded, and without exception everyone would wave or call hello to Lidia and I, and we would call hello back.

Often I'd lean over the balcony and talk to the housegirl from downstairs as she swept the compound, stirring up clouds of dust. She fascinated me because her right foot was swollen to enormous proportions. From a distance, it looked as though she wore an outsized gumboot on one foot. She cheerfully told me that it was elephantiasis. I asked her if it hurt, but she told me she had no feeling in it at all.

My parents took the larger of the two bedrooms overlooking the road. My father used the third bedroom as a sort of storeroom for his clothes; my mother had taken up the entire wardrobe in their room.

The garden was a huge tangle of weeds and wild eggplant trees growing over long-abandoned concrete foundations. The owners gave us permission to keep our chickens there.

Mirabelle made curtains to hang in the living room, orange with bright red flowers and black leaves. My mother was busy as well; she had her sewing machine on the kitchen table and pins and needles scattered all over the place. It had been a long time since she'd used it. She used to be a dress designer and often made our clothes. I took it as a sign that life would finally go back to normal. She was busy for days unpicking the hems of all her dresses and skirts. My father had received a letter, 'On her Majesty's Service', informing him that the length of my mother's skirts were causing offence. She carefully lowered all her skirts by a centimetre – the Resident Commissioner hadn't said how much she had to lower them.

Rachel was much older than the other children in my class, but she was behind because her parents travelled so much. We all hung around her during recess because she had a funny way of talking, was always chewing gum, wore make-up and painted her toenails bright red. The other remarkable thing about her was that she didn't wear underpants. At first, this was just a vicious rumour, then one day a breeze caught the hem of her frock and I discovered the rumour was true.

She always told the most outrageous stories, places she'd been to and people she'd met. Perhaps they were true. Who knows? One day she came to school bursting with importance. She'd seen her parents do 'it'.

'Yeah, right,' sneered one of the Elly twins.

'My dad asked if I wanted to watch and I did.'

I was shocked. That night I told my father, expecting him to tell me it was a pack of lies. Instead, he assured me most parents did that. It was a way to teach children about sex.

I still wasn't convinced, but I was certain I didn't want to see my father and mother having sex. A couple of nights later I was shaken awake from a deep sleep. He wanted me to get up. I peered around, it was very late; the moon was a tight ball of white high in the sky. 'What's happening?' I asked, still not completely awake.

'Come and look,' was all he said.

I followed him across the hall to my parents' bedroom. I came to an abrupt halt, shocked. My mother lay naked on the bed; her legs spread apart. She lolled her head and groaned.

My father went round to the far side of the bed and climbed on top of her. His penis was huge and as he slid it into her, he held her leg up so I could see everything. I didn't want to be there. I didn't want to see my mother naked. As he entered her, she moaned, 'No, don't.' Her speech was slurred.

I wondered why she didn't push him off; she just lay there, looking away. My father kept thrusting it in and out, whispering that it was sexy.

'I want to go back to my room,' I pleaded, afraid to go without his permission. My father got off the bed and came over to me; I was up against the wall near the door. He pulled my pyjamas down and put his hand between my legs, holding his penis with the other hand. Then he bent his knees and thrust his penis between my legs, rubbing it back and forth against my inner thighs. My legs were shaking.

My mother groaned again, I pulled away from him and tugged up my pyjama bottoms as I fled for the safety of my bedroom and locked the door.

I could hear him breathing outside, then there was silence, and I heard the creaking of the bed in my parents' room as he continued with my mother. After a while, I pulled the louvres off their metal tracks and climbed out. I spent the rest of the night with my chickens and didn't go back into the house until breakfast time. Nobody said a word about what had happened the night before.

I was determined to have a proper birthday party with guests and a birthday cake for my tenth birthday. My parents agreed, so I invited my whole class, proudly issuing handwritten invitations. I organised party games and worked out a menu, giving my father the shopping list. My mother said she'd organise the cake.

My party was to begin at four o'clock, the streamers were up, my father was home, everything was going as planned. By five o'clock I started to panic, my mother still hadn't arrived with the cake. We'd played all the organised games, then had a mad romp in the garden playing tag and finally settled down to a game of Monopoly.

At twenty past five my father and I had a hushed council of war and shortly after this he discreetly left. He was going to find my mother and the birthday cake or get another one. He'd been gone about five minutes when my mother arrived with the cake. I was so relieved.

To this day I still don't know exactly what happened. Suddenly my mother was shrieking hysterically, my friends scattering as she sent the Monopoly game flying over the couch. It was absolute chaos, children screaming as Monopoly houses, hotels and money showered down.

I stood clutching the candles I'd been about to place on the cake, hardly able to believe what I was seeing. My mother stepped towards the coffee table and snatched up the cake, throwing it with such force it went right across the room and hit the wall. It slowly slid down, leaving a thick smudge of chocolate cream and walnuts.

Then she had me by my hair and was shaking me like a mad dog, still screeching. I had a glimpse of her wild eyes as I tore free and raced for my bedroom, my classmates Laura and Anita beside me. I slammed the door shut and locked it. I could hear my friends shrieking in panic in the living room and the front door slamming but I was too intent on pulling the louvres out so we could escape to pay much attention.

Later, much later, my father came home. Together we went indoors. My mother had long since departed. The coffee table had been upturned, plates smashed, drinks spilled and some of the streamers torn down. Together, my father and I picked up the Monopoly money, the green houses and the red hotels. Then he scraped the cake off the wall and threw it away, along with the broken plates. I put the unused candles away. He didn't say anything, or ask how it happened and I was still too shocked to explain.

I became a loner again – the daughter of that woman. At first I was terribly upset but there was nothing to be done. I spent time with my chickens and played my one and only record 'Sadie the Cleaning Lady' over and over until my father broke it in two over his knee.

I returned from school one day to find my mother sitting on the couch, completely unresponsive to my questions. There was no reaction when I smoothed her hair off her forehead or when I waved my hands in front of her face. Her eyes remained unfocused and she sat, shoulders hunched, rocking back and forth in silence, lost somewhere in a world of her own. She ended up in the psychiatric ward of the French Hospital for three months, sitting silently in her room. Sometimes we went to visit her; more often than not, the doctors would send us away.

After my mother had been home for a few weeks, things slowly got back to normal. Occasionally, she'd cook a meal and we'd sit down to dinner like a family. One night she cooked lamb chops and put candles on the table. It was a wonderful dinner. Afterwards, as we drank coffee, my mother said she'd go downstairs to buy some biscuits to go with the coffee. We waited for her. Five minutes went by, then ten. When half an hour had gone by, my father got up from the table. 'I'll go down and see what's happened.'

He came back a few moments later to fetch the car keys. 'She caught a taxi into town, I'm going to look for her.'

We found her almost immediately, outside the Hôtel Vate. At first we didn't see her, because of the crowd. As we pushed our way through, we discovered she was one of the reasons for the gathering. Maurice, Jeanne and my mother stood there yelling at each other. Well, Jeanne and my mother were yelling and Maurice was doing his utmost to stop them.

Whatever they were fighting about, it was too much for my father. He pushed me back through the crowd and without a word dropped me at home before driving off again. He came home alone a few hours later and went straight to bed.

I lay in my room, waiting for dawn to break. The sheets had been kicked to the end of the bed, damp with sweat. I slept fitfully, waking in starts, to slap at mosquitoes whining in the darkness, listening for sounds that would tell me my mother had returned. Sounds that never came.

I kept myself busy that morning; feeding my chickens and taking three dozen eggs down to the shop to sell. I spent the rest of the time hovering on the balcony, hoping for a glimpse of my mother. She returned at lunchtime. Maurice waited downstairs, parked in front of the Chinese shop, in his new red sports car. She didn't say anything to me and walked over to where my father was frying eggs.

'I'm leaving you. I've just come for my dresses.' She spoke very calmly, though I suspect she was a jangle of nerves.

I will remember to my dying day the savagery of that lunchtime. My father grabbed her and shook her violently, screaming all the while. 'You whore, you slut, that's all you're good for, screwing around.'

My mother struggled free and began to walk away, unprepared for what happened next. With the speed of a snake, my father grabbed her by the hair, knocking out the comb she always wore. My mother cried out in shock and pain as his fingers twisted and pulled. He yanked her back, lifting her clean off the floor as she struggled frantically.

My mother didn't have a chance; she was no match for his anger. He dragged her past me, still struggling, her hair tangled across her face, the whole time he was yelling 'whore' and 'slut'. As she kicked out, she lost one of her shoes. The white high heel went sliding, turning round and round until it stopped on its side, halfway down the corridor.

I hurried after them, reaching the bedroom door just as he flung her across their bed, face down. Her mini skirt had rucked up her back, and I caught a glimpse of her lacy white panties as my father, still gripping her by her hair, forced her face into the mattress. She still wore one shoe. With his free hand he undid his belt buckle and slid the belt from his trousers.

All the while my mother tried to free herself. He was screaming now, his face twisted with fury, spittle flying as the torrent of abuse flowed from his mouth. I hovered nervously in the doorway, terrified as the belt curled up and whipped savagely through the air, all my father's fury behind it. My mother screamed as it struck her back.

I fled down the hall as it went on and on, my mother screaming and my father grunting with exertion and all the while that awful sound of the belt striking her.

'Help me, Tanja,' she screamed, 'help me, oh God, Tanja please help me!'

But I couldn't move. I was shocked and horrified beyond belief, my heart pounding frantically, tears streaming down my face. Still she called out to me, 'Tanja, help, help me!' her voice pure agony. I was frozen, wanting to move, wanting to do something but my brain seemed to seize up. I put my hands over my ears to try to block out the terrible sound of the belt, willing my father to stop.

I don't know how long he beat her, but finally he stopped. He stomped past me down the hall; sweat streamed down his face and soaked though his singlet.

Still I couldn't move. After a moment or two, I heard my mother get off the mattress. She came into the hall, carefully pulling down her skirt. Moving painfully and awkwardly, still wearing one high heel, she made her way to the mirror where she attempted to tidy her hair, a tiny spot of blood soaking through her dress. I moved back into the shadow of the corridor. When she'd done the best she could with her hair, she retrieved her other shoe. I could see she was in pain. She came to where I stood still trembling, and stopped to look at me. Her face was blotched with tears. 'You little bastard,' she hissed, her face distorted by anger, frustration and humiliation, 'didn't you hear me calling for help?'

I nodded, ashamed of myself. But I couldn't speak. I opened my mouth, but no sound came.

'You can rot in hell for all I care, I hate you.'

She walked into the living room and out the front door. I heard her high heels clicking all the way down the concrete steps. With growing dismay and disbelief, I realised she wouldn't be coming back. She'd gone to Maurice and left me behind. She wasn't going to forgive me. How could she? After all these years, I still can't believe I did nothing.

She left me behind and abandoned me to my fate. Of course, she could have had no idea of the years of misery and despair she was condemning me to. If she had, I'm sure she would have come back up those stairs and snatched me away from my father's clutches, because a mother's love goes beyond hate. At least I hope that's what she would have done.

Chapter 6

I couldn't get the beating out of my mind. The words went round and round in my head, ending with my mother telling me to rot in hell. I climbed into my chicken run, hidden by the thick tangle of weeds.

It was peaceful there – my chickens scratched in the dirt and made contented prawk prawk noises. The roosters strutted back and forth, ruffling their neck feathers.

My father came home just after five. He didn't say anything about lunchtime, behaving as though nothing out of the ordinary had happened. He sat next to me on the couch. 'It's just you and me now your mother's gone off with that pig. We're on our own.'

It suddenly hit home that my mother wasn't coming back and I began to cry. He slipped his arm around my shoulders. 'There, there, everything will be OK, you'll see.'

'It won't, I haven't got a mother any more.'

'No, you don't, but you still have me.'

He pulled me onto his lap and hugged me tight,

murmuring everything would be all right. I lay against his chest, his shirt rubbing against my cheek. I could hear his heart beating and somehow it soothed me, that and his gentle words. Slowly the room filled with darkness and stars began to appear. I was glad he was no longer angry. I wanted to ask if he was sorry about what he'd done to Mummy but I was too afraid of provoking him. After a while he asked me if I felt better. I didn't, but knew instinctively he'd had enough of my tears. I nodded.

'That's a good girl,' he said. Turning a light on, he went to the kitchen and made a cup of tea, opening a packet of chocolate biscuits and giving me a couple. I was famished and ate them quickly – I hadn't eaten since breakfast. Then he put a record on and returned to the couch. As the music filled the room I went and sat next to him, not knowing what else to do. He picked up a book off the coffee table and began to read. 'What would you like to do?' he asked suddenly.

I jumped – I'd been watching the stars through the window, regretting that I'd forgotten to wish when the first one appeared. I could have wished for my mother to come back. 'Nothing,' I said and shrugged my skinny shoulders. An unbidden tear escaped and I felt it run down my cheek.

He leaned over and pulled me to him, and began to tickle me. I struggled and pushed his hands away, giggling. Then I began to tickle him back, but he wasn't ticklish. 'That's not fair, you're not ticklish!' I jumped off the couch and tugged at his shoes and socks. 'Bet you're ticklish under your feet!'

I flung the shoes and socks to one side and began to tickle his soles, squealing with laughter as he twisted and turned to avoid my fingers. 'Stop moving your feet,' I demanded playfully. 'Or I'll have to tie you up,' I said with all the seriousness of a ten-year-old.

'Yes, you will,' he agreed. 'Tell you what, I'll tie you up first and then you can tie me up, how does that sound?'

It sounded a good idea, so I agreed. After all, if he went first he'd have to be careful not to tickle me too much, otherwise I'd tickle him lots when it was his turn.

My father went off to get some rope. When he came back, he began to tie my hands up. Then he seemed to change his mind. Without saying anything he picked me up, carried me into his bedroom and lay me on the bed. I wasn't so sure I wanted to play this game.

He tied my hands to the bedposts, pulling them up above my head, then he took hold of one of my feet, carefully looping the rope round my ankle. I started to protest but he told me I was a silly girl and it was only a game. 'What a sook you are.'

I fell silent as he pulled my other leg down, remembering his savagery with my mother. When he'd finished fastening the rope to the bedpost I was unable to move, my arms and legs stretched tightly to the four corners of the bed. The ropes bit painfully and I asked him to loosen them.

He moved up to the head of the bed and checked the knots. 'They're not too tight, any looser and you could wriggle free.'

I felt his fingers through the thin cotton of my dress as he gently stroked his hands up along my rib cage. I wriggled and giggled, and he laughed, but then it became too much and the tickling became unbearable torture.

Whenever I squirmed, avoiding his fingers, pain would shoot along my legs and shoulders; my hands began to get pins and needles. 'Please untie me, it hurts.'

The expression on his face had changed, and I sensed his mood had changed as well. He didn't untie me; instead, he slid his hand slowly down my belly. He started to breathe heavily. I knew, with dreadful certainty, what was coming.

'Don't,' I said, as he pulled my frock up and began to tug at my cotton pants. I began to twist around, struggling to get loose. The ropes bit deeper and deeper into my wrists, and now one of my feet began to get pins and needles as well. 'Untie me, now, please untie me.' I heard distant laughter from downstairs, producing an overwhelming sense of isolation and loneliness. 'Untie me!'

He ignored me. He'd only pulled my pants down a few inches; he couldn't pull them any further because of my spread legs. The elastic cut into my thighs, where they'd stretched to their limit.

I lay there, waiting, unable to do anything as my father climbed onto the end of the bed, leaning on the ropes. Stabs of pain streaked up my limbs. Crouched there, over me, he put his fingers between my legs, prodding, poking ...

'Stop it, stop it,' I pleaded.

'Doesn't this feel nice?'

'No,' I hissed, 'let me go.' I felt a wave of anger race through me.

Suddenly he got off the bed and I thought he was going to untie me. He undid the buckle of his belt, the belt he had thrashed my mother with at lunchtime, and slid his trousers down. Then he took his white jockeys off. His penis leapt free, larger than I'd ever seen it, a shiny purple at the end. Frightened, I pleaded to be let loose.

'Don't be silly,' he murmured, 'I'm not going to put it in you, just rub it against you.'

'It' twitched as he spoke. I began crying; hot tears streaming down my cheeks and running into my ears.

He put his hand over my mouth, his fingers hard, grinding

my top lip against my teeth. 'Shut up before someone from the shop hears you, stop being such a sookie.' I fell silent and he took his hand away. 'That's better.'

'Please untie me,' I asked quietly, trying another tactic. 'I can't feel my fingers.'

'Not until I've finished,' he said and leaned over and kissed my mouth, a warm disgusting feeling as he tried to press his tongue between my lips. His breath smelt of fish and I pulled my head away. Why didn't he understand I didn't want to be there?

I don't know why I did what I did next; perhaps it was some sort of primal survival instinct. I spat in my father's face, like a wildcat, catching him completely unawares. He stood stock still, in disbelief, my saliva dripping off his nose and chin. 'Why you little bitch,' he began, 'you filthy, filthy little bitch.'

I didn't see the blows coming, and even if I had, I couldn't have done anything to protect myself. His fist slammed into the side of my face and into my chest.

Then he walked round the bed, furiously muttering, pulling the ropes off the bedposts. I lay frozen in terror. I knew I'd done something unforgivable and made him very angry. The tension was unbearable, I was afraid of what was going to happen next. When I was finally loose from the bed he snatched me up violently and carried me towards my bedroom.

'I'll teach you to behave like that!' he screamed, shaking me in his rage. He kicked open my door and threw me into the room. I fell badly, landing on one hip, catching my ankle on the iron bed leg.

I lay there, too scared to move, expecting him to continue punching me but he slammed the door and I heard the key in the lock. I sat in the darkness, not moving, too shocked even to cry. I heard him moving around the house and tensed as he passed my door, muttering angrily. Then I heard the front door slam.

After a long time, I loosened the ropes from my wrists and ankles, using my teeth because the knots were too tight for my fingers. I didn't know what to do with them, so I rolled them up neatly. In the blackness, I could feel the dents the ropes had left in my skin and my left wrist burned. I climbed on top of the wardrobe, curled up in the corner against the wall and fell asleep. When I awoke, it was still dark. I was very thirsty and I urgently had to go to the toilet. As quietly as I could I slid to the ground and tentatively tried the door handle; it was still locked. I didn't dare knock or call to be let out, if he was back he was probably still in a rage. Turning the light on, I went over to the louvres. I bent the metal back cautiously, terrified to make a sound. After a few moments I'd pulled four free and leaned them against the wall. Climbing out, I tiptoed down the corrugated-iron roof. It was a two-metre drop to the ground. I jumped and scrambled across the damp ground to the undergrowth where I hastily relieved myself.

I walked around the back of the shop to the hose and drank thirstily. Then I had the problem of getting back up onto the roof, until I remembered the big iron rainwater drum under the eaves. It was tricky but I managed to get back into my room. That was Friday night.

I stayed in my room for the weekend, the door remaining firmly locked. Sometimes I could hear my father moving round the house. I read and spent most of one afternoon talking to a large green stick insect on top of my wardrobe. The louvres were back in place, but I left the metal bent back, in case I needed to get out again, which I did each night.

On Saturday night I discovered the window of the shop storeroom was open. I looked hungrily at the cartons of biscuits, but there was no way of opening them, and I knew that would be stealing. I discovered a hole in a plastic bag of chocolates. I pulled out a couple, feeling guilty but telling myself a couple wouldn't be that much of a crime. I ate about ten, but I was still hungry. I had a drink from the hose and climbed back into my room.

On Monday my door was unlocked and the ropes had gone. Everything was back to normal. My father greeted me cheerfully and made me breakfast. It was as though nothing had happened but from this point, nothing would ever be the same. A world of dark shadows had opened and I retreated into another dimension. I no longer questioned anything that happened to me. In retrospect, that was when I stopped thinking. I stopped fighting. I stopped feeling.

Sometimes I saw my mother as she drove past with Maurice in his red sports car. She never looked up at the house. Perhaps she didn't want to see me. I heard Jeanne and the girls had been banished to France.

One night my Opa came to visit me for the first time. I woke up because someone was pinching my ankle. Moonlight streamed across my pillow and I looked around me, rubbing my ankle. A dark shadow slipped like a mist into the room and settled next to me. 'Who are you?' I asked, not at all afraid.

'Your Opa, I've come to watch over you.' His deep voice seemed be inside my head, and was strangely reassuring, even though I knew he'd died when I was six. We talked for a long time. Then as the dark time before dawn arrived he told me to snuggle down under the sheet, I felt his hands stroking my hair gently and I fell asleep.

It was a Saturday. My father and I drove to Cook's Corner to buy chicken pellets and fresh bread. On the way home a New Hebridean tripped drunkenly into the street. His companions roared with laughter and I laughed as well. It was very funny. My father didn't think so. 'What's so funny about that?' he asked, his tone warning me to be careful how I answered.

I shrugged my shoulders. 'It just looked funny.'

'That's because you don't know what it feels like to be drunk. You need to learn that it isn't funny.'

He remained silent the rest of the way home and it wasn't until we'd unloaded the bag of pellets and gone upstairs that he spoke. 'Sit down,' he pointed to the kitchen table. 'I'm going to teach you a lesson.' I wondered if I was going to get another beating, watching silently as he searched the cupboards.

My heart was beating fast and there was a mad tangle of ice-cold flutters in my stomach. He opened a bottle of Dutch beer, filling a glass with the frothy liquid. 'Drink it, drink it all down, without stopping.'

I hesitated; his eyes watched me, dark, narrow, unreadable. I picked up the glass and started to drink, gagging halfway through. He became impatient and took the glass, tipping the beer into my mouth; I gulped the bitterness down, shuddering when it was finally all gone. Then he topped up the glass with the rest of the bottle. I drank that too. He stood looking at me and then was gone, coming back with another glass. 'This is gin, there isn't any more beer.'

'No, I'm going to be sick,' I protested.

He pried my lips open with his fingers, pressing the glass

against my teeth. I drank the burning contents, spluttering at the taste. He refilled the glass, this time I refused to open my mouth, and he held my nose, until gasping for air, I opened my mouth and he tipped it in. Fire streaked up my nose and my eyes streamed. I thought I would choke, but somehow managed to swallow. My stomach heaved, I clenched my teeth together. It was an incredible effort to keep the gin down, but I was afraid of what would happen if I threw up.

He seemed to get very far away and the ceiling floated up into the distance, high above and the floor tilted. Then I was lying on my father's bed. Or was I dreaming I was naked and so was he?

'Let me die,' I told this figment of my imagination. I dreamt of his hands between my legs, of his fingers, roughly pressing inside me. I dreamt of him lying heavily on top of me, unable to breathe properly because of his weight. I dreamt of unbelievable pain between my legs, tearing fire inside me, his rasping breath above my head. I dreamt of being alone, rolling off the bed because it wouldn't keep still.

I dreamt I was in the bathroom, propped over the edge of the bath, the yellow light swinging wildly, far above me. My father's face came into focus. I dreamt he forced his middle finger down my throat. 'You have to be sick, you've drunk too much!' He seemed afraid.

I stared into his eyes and bit down hard on the finger raking at the back of my throat. I dreamt he slapped me savagely, but it was only a dream and I felt nothing. Then I fell asleep.

I woke with the sun high in the sky, annoying me. I hurt; there was dried blood on my inner thighs. I didn't think about the blood, washing it off after I went to the toilet. It burned when I peed. I got dressed and brushed my hair. My father was already up. I sat at the kitchen table and he poured me a cup of tea. I stared at his hand as he passed it to me. There was a tooth mark, still bloody, on his middle finger. It wasn't a dream that I bit him. So if I really bit him ... then ... I stopped thinking.

The marigolds on the table were very beautiful, such an intense orange. I remember thinking I'd never really looked at them closely before. They had hundreds of petals, funny I'd never noticed that before.

Chapter 7

I threw the marigolds out. It's a pity flowers have to die. So beautiful and then they turn an ugly brown and the water in the vase stinks. Lidia made soup and together we sat at the table, listening to Radio New Hebrides. Someone called Louis Armstrong had died and they played a song he'd written. He had the most amazing voice; it sent warmth up my spine. I listened, moved beyond words as he sang 'What a Wonderful World,' then went outside and sang it to my chickens.

Later my mother came round with Maurice and a box of cakes. She said I looked pale and my father made coffee. I went to my room to read and when I came out, my mother and Maurice had gone. There was still one chocolate éclair left in the box. I ate it and wandered around the house looking for my father. He was in his locked storeroom, his private place for his secrets. Shortly before my mother left us to live with Maurice, she found the door unlocked and called me in; there was something she wanted to show me, a photo of a little boy. 'Read what's written on the back.'

I turned the photo over and read aloud, 'Reminds me of someone, don't you think?' I looked up at her for an explanation.

'She means he reminds her of your father. That's your half-brother Richard.'

I looked at the photo again; more than a little intrigued, I had a brother!

'Don't tell Ron I showed you, he thinks I don't know.' I promised, and left the room with a brother called Richard. Life went on, I thought about Richard sometimes, but it was difficult to picture him, I didn't even know what country he lived in.

I wished the terrible pain in my side would go away. I first noticed it when I was reaching up to get the eggs out of the nesting boxes, it was a burning the size of a fist. After the second day, it hurt so much I curled up on the bed and tried to sleep. When my father came back from work he came into my room and seeing me hunched up asked what was wrong. I told him about the pain, expecting him to tell me I was a sookie. He came over, full of concern, and prodded my stomach, wondering aloud if I had appendicitis. The doctor said I didn't have appendicitis, he thought I was probably riddled with worms and sent me to hospital overnight for tests.

At the hospital, blood was taken, forms filled out and a bed found. My father left as visiting hours were over and then I was on my own. Bored, I wandered around the hospital talking to patients lying on the mattresses lining the corridors. A man shared some lap-lap with me, making room for me on his mattress as we ate.

I was enjoying myself, until I was found by an irate nurse. I shook hands with my new friend and followed her back towards my ward.

The next morning I woke up feeling really ill. I threw up my breakfast and the room became freezing cold. Ice seeped into my bones, then the shakes began and I was too hot. A nurse arrived, her brown eyes peering closely at me, then a doctor. 'She has malaria.'

I slept and woke to a nurse tapping a thermometer against her wrist. I still felt terrible, but I obediently opened my mouth, and made a real effort not to bite the thermometer while she checked her watch, 41 °C, then she took my pulse, 120. She came back with two tiny white pills and a glass of water, telling me to swallow them straight down; she didn't tell me they would taste disgustingly bitter. I nearly choked on the first one; the second one disappeared under my tongue, leaving a streak of bitterness in my mouth before I finally managed to swallow it. Urgh!

At five-thirty, my father came to visit.

'Is Mummy coming?' I asked.

'No, she says she doesn't have time.'

He brought me some books and grapes but I was too sick to eat them and gave them to the night nurse after my father left. The books were wonderful, in English and French, with beautiful drawings. I was touched, I knew he was really busy and the only bookshop was on the other side of town. He didn't stay long.

A nurse woke me up, and I wished she hadn't. I felt horribly nauseous and sticky; the sheets were damp. To make matters worse I had to take more pills. Then dinner arrived. Liver! I stared in horror as the nurse began cutting it up and I caught a whiff. That was too much, I threw up, all over my damp hospital gown and the sheets.

I remember thinking it was an awful lot of vomit, considering I hadn't eaten all day. More nurses arrived and

I was bundled off to the outside loo, stripped down and sponged clean. Dressed in a crisp, clean hospital gown, I was taken back to bed and tucked into dry, blue sheets, freshly ironed. The liver had gone. They brought me more pills.

Later, much later, after most of the lights had been switched off and I was surrounded by sleeping patients, I lay wide-awake, listening to the fan. Its repetitive creaking made me even more nauseous, like being on a swing too long. The sheets were damp again. I was burning hot and the shakes, those uncontrollable agonising, bone-wrenching shakes, had returned.

It became difficult to breathe, it felt as though my lungs were on fire and I realised with sudden clarity that this is how dragons breathe flames, and all the time I wanted to throw up, but I didn't want to go through all that trouble of cleaning up again. But the fan didn't stop squeaking, squeak, squeak, squeak ... I was going to be sick. I sat up, fighting the shakes. Everything went black – I put my head between my legs and fought back the nausea. After the wave subsided, I slid my legs over the edge and stood up. I'd only taken one step when everything went black and I collapsed.

I was dreaming. I was a bright green light bulb, and someone had rolled me off the top of a flight of stairs. I bounced all the way down to the bottom, making a sound like a fan each time I hit a step. I prayed I'd shatter at the bottom and stop bouncing. But each time I was suddenly at the top, bouncing down again. On and on and on.

I woke up back in bed with a nurse sponging my face. Seeing me awake, she gave me two more pills. I clenched my teeth together, refusing to take them, but she told me she'd get into trouble if I refused. I swallowed them, hating mosquitoes, vowing to squash the next one I saw.

By the fourth day, I was better. They told me I didn't have to take any more pills and I could go home.

My mother came to the house to visit. This time I was too thin, and my hair was knotty. We sat in the living room, my father still at work.

'Did you like the books I bought you?'

I stared at her; 'Daddy bought those books.'

'No, Ron wouldn't let me come and visit you, so I bought you books.'

I stared at her, angry, why did she have to lie to me? Only later while I was cuddling one of my hens did it occur to me that perhaps she'd been telling the truth. But why would my father lie to me? Why would my mother? The only thing I knew for certain was that one of them was lying.

It was nearly Christmas. My father was working for a couple of weeks in Santo and had flown up a few days earlier. I was excited because I was going to join him for Christmas. Mirabelle, my mother, and a couple of people I didn't know were also coming. We were going to travel on the *Kananda*, the boat that went back and forth between the islands.

I could barely contain my excitement. It was going to be wonderful – we'd travel past tropical beaches, with low-hanging coconut trees, and crystal-clear waters. There would be dolphins and maybe even a whale!

The great day finally arrived, my mother was coming to pick me up at ten. I was up long before Lidia arrived to clean the flat and spent hours agonising over what to pack. In the end, I packed two pairs of cut-off jeans and several T-shirts, a dress, in case we went to a restaurant, and my swimsuit. Then I remembered toiletries. I added my hairbrush, and a bar of soap, wrapped in a flannel with toothpaste and my toothbrush.

Lidia had finished her chores and we waited together on the steps. Lidia would catch the bus as soon as I was picked up. My mother was late, but that wasn't unusual, so I didn't start to worry until after eleven. I knew the Kananda was leaving at twelve. I heard a car pull into the driveway and looked over the parapet – Maurice's red sports car. My mother came round the corner and started walking up the stairs; she seemed surprised to see me. 'What are you doing?'

'Waiting for you.' What did she mean by that, I wondered?

'Why?' She reached the top step and we moved aside for her to pass.

'I'm already packed,' I said, thinking she was going inside to pack for me.

She looked at me strangely. 'Why are you packed, where are you going?'

'Daddy said we were going to Santo for Christmas.' I couldn't understand why she was looking at me that way. I'd been there when they arranged it.

'Oh, no, you're not coming. I've given your ticket to Maurice.'

Lidia squeezed my hand tightly. I wasn't going to cry in front of my mother. I couldn't speak, anguished disappointment flooded over me and I needed to sit down. She went into the flat and Lidia came and put her arm over my shoulder, hugging me close. A few moments later my mother came back, silently we shifted sideways to let her down the stairs. We continued sitting there long after the sound of the red sports car faded away. I burst into tears.

Lidia carried my bag back into the living room. I sat on the floor next to it. 'You'll have to come to my village, I'm sure my mother won't mind.' She began wiping the already spotless kitchen table, talking all the while, worrying about what they'd feed me, where I'd sleep and what would happen if I got sick from eating native food. I didn't say anything.

We both heard a car pull into the drive. My heart leapt; my mother had changed her mind. We heard footsteps on the steps and my heart sank. They weren't high heels.

The front door opened. It was Mike. I was too upset to be surprised. I hadn't seen him since we'd moved to the flat. He seemed angry and took one look at my tear-streaked face. 'I thought as much,' he said. 'I saw your mother, she said she's going to Santo. I know Ron's in Santo, so who's looking after you?'

I didn't say anything.

He turned to glare at Lidia, who moved back nervously, as though it were all her fault. 'I am sorry Masta, but I think I am taking Tanja to my village, she can't stay here alone.'

'My oath she can't.' He strode over to the fridge and yanked it open. It was empty apart from half a dozen tins of coke and a packet of butter.

'And just what the hell was she supposed to eat?'

I tucked myself closer to the wall. Why was he so angry? Were we going to get a beating? It wasn't Lidia's fault there was nothing in the fridge.

I found my voice, 'Lidia hasn't done anything wrong, she didn't know either.'

His face softened, 'I know, you can't help having a bloody mother like that, you can come to my house for Christmas.' He gave me a little push, 'Go and get a change of clothes.'

Lidia said, 'She is already packed, Masta.'

'Already packed?'

'The Missus took that Frenchman instead of Tanja, Masta.'

Mike said a very rude word and seemed to struggle with his thoughts for a moment. Then he said, 'OK, let's go, I'll take Lidia home and don't worry, I'll take good care of you, Tanja. Sue's mother is staying with us, and Nanna will be delighted to meet you.'

Many years have gone by, but I can still remember every glorious moment. Walking into Mike's home, the wonderful smells of baking wafting through the air, Sue's arms around me, Nanna's delicious chicken pie for lunch. Sue took me into the spare bedroom, where she made up the bed and unpacked my bag. Nanna found a brush, sat me down in a chair and battled the knots.

'You've forgotten to pack your pyjamas.'

'I don't have any pyjamas.'

I didn't tell her my father had forbidden me to wear pyjamas. I had to sleep naked now, like grown-up people. I'd found my flannel pyjamas, the ones with the little donkeys, in the rubbish bin. It was hard seeing them there. I had taken a last look at them, before tipping the lunch scraps on top.

She looked over my head at Nanna. What did that look mean, I wondered? Then Nanna said. 'Well never mind, I'll find you one of my nighties.'

My clothes all tidily folded in the wardrobe, Sue turned back the bed covers. 'Now it's ready for your nap.'

'My nap?' I was astonished. Why on earth would I want to sleep in the middle of the day?

'Don't you have a nap after lunch?'

I shook my head.

'Well, we all have a siesta, you don't have to sleep. I'll find you some magazines to look at.'

The magazines found, they retired to their siestas and I lay on the bed waiting, anxiously turning the pages, but not really looking at the pictures. Was Mike going to come into my room? Was that why they were so nice to me? Was that why they slept during the day?

In the middle of the afternoon, Sue told me she was taking me shopping while Nanna finished the Christmas baking. 'Us girls together!'

I thought we were going grocery shopping. We weren't. We were shopping for presents for me! First we went to the toy section, and I was allowed to choose anything I liked. I agonised and finally settled on a doctor's set. You had to carefully 'operate' on the patient and if you touched the sides with the scalpel, dozens of red lights started blinking and beeping.

We moved over to the clothing section, where Sue bought me a packet of white cotton underwear and a pair of pink floral shortie pyjamas. I spotted a frock with a lace collar, then felt guilty about drawing attention to it, because she held it against me and it went into the shopping basket. However, Sue wasn't finished – she insisted on buying me a pair of shoes. Such beautiful shoes, shiny black with a low heel and a snap-over strap. I was in seventh heaven. I couldn't wait to get back to try them all on again.

As if the afternoon hadn't been wonderful enough, I came home to a wonderland. The house was decorated with tinsel, and gold and silver stars hung from the ceiling. There was a wondrous smell of crushed pine leaves, and I tried to work out where it came from. Then I spied the Christmas tree. It reached nearly all the way to the ceiling and was topped with a white and gold angel. Coloured tinsel draped across the branches, criss-crossing up and around the tree. Red, green and gold balls fought for space with delicately carved reindeer. I'd seen Christmas trees before, in Sydney, in the shopping mall, but I didn't really believe people had their own Christmas tree. That was only in books.

After supper Sue ran me a bath and left me with lavender bubble bath and a fluffy pink towel. I splashed around for ages, playing with the bubbles, and spilling water all over the floor. Sue didn't seem to mind; she came back in, after knocking first, and put my new pyjamas on the vanity. I stepped out into the hall, squeaky clean, my hair dripping water on the tiles and very satisfied with my new pyjamas.

They all crowded into my room and took turns telling me Christmas stories. All about Santa Claus and his reindeer, and how Santa gave presents to all the good children. I looked at them in astonishment. They didn't really believe that stuff did they?

I woke up at daybreak and tiptoed out into the hall. Everyone was still asleep. I crept over to the tree, where there was a huge pile of presents, all beautifully wrapped. I realised with a twinge of guilt that I didn't have any presents for them. I went out into the garden where I picked flowers and made posies for Sue and Nanna and found a beautiful smooth black pebble for Mike. I couldn't wrap them, so I set them under the tree as they were. Then I curled up on the couch, stared at the tree, and waited for them to get up.

Finally they were all gathered round in their dressing gowns and I presented them each with the gifts I'd gathered. They didn't say very much, and seemed to hug me far too long. Mike carefully put his pebble on the bookshelf and Nanna kept on hugging me and repeating, 'You dear, dear girl.'

The next hour was spent in the bliss of unwrapping and playing with my new gifts. Apart from the presents from the day before, there was a wonderful glass dome with a Santa

Claus and Christmas trees, which snowed when it was shaken. This was from Nanna. Mike gave me a china poodle with a fluffy pink collar and Sue added to the pile with a selection of hair clips.

For Christmas lunch I dressed in my new clothes and new shoes. Nanna brushed my hair and pinned it back. I felt really proud as I sat down at the table. I'd never seen so much food, the house was scattered with bowls laden with iced cinnamon cookies, crystallised ginger, nuts and chocolates.

Sue and Nanna had fussed in the kitchen all morning. There was the biggest chicken I'd ever seen, (they told me it was a turkey) filled with stuffing made from bread, nuts and apricots. There were peas, roast onions, carrots and baked potatoes with thick gravy. The table had been decorated with colourful napkins, candles and Christmas crackers. Mike showed me how to pull them and I giggled at the loud bang they made. Then we got down to the serious business of eating. I don't think I'd ever eaten so much. The adults drank wine and I had cranberry juice in a wineglass so I wouldn't feel left out. The plates were finally cleared and I felt I could never eat again. But there was more to come.

The lights were turned down and the curtains drawn, as Nanna made a dramatic entrance with the Christmas pudding, covered with burning brandy. It was breathtaking. When the brandy had burnt out we each had a slice smothered in custard. I found a sixpence in mine and they told me I could make a wish.

I closed my eyes tightly, 'I wish for a cat,' I said in a loud whisper.

'I thought you had a cat,' said Mike.

I told them about how Monsu had gone to heaven. 'A cat would be good,' I added, 'because then I wouldn't be alone at

83

night. Chickens don't like sleeping in a bed, they need each other too much.'

I stayed with them another week and then one morning my father was standing at the door; he'd come to take me home. Mike had very little to say to him. I didn't want to go back and cried in the car. It had been such a lovely Christmas.

Chapter 8

It was Saturday morning, my father was at work and I was sitting in the henhouse, nestled amongst the straw listening to the soothing prawk prawk of the chickens. It was pleasantly cool out of the burning glare of the sun, and the air was filled with the fragrance of freshly laid straw, chicken feathers and manure. Cradled in my lap were the eggs I'd just gathered. I was wondering whether I could be bothered going back upstairs to get a book, when I suddenly became aware of my mother peering through the wire mesh. I froze, not wanting to be found, but one of the hens betrayed me, cackling loudly.

'I can see you in there, Tanja.' Her voice seemed friendly enough.

I came out, stooping through the low opening, careful not to break the eggs, and stood behind the wire netting.

'What do you want?' I hadn't seen her for a while, and she always seemed to have an ulterior motive for visiting.

She appeared not to notice. 'You need a bath.'

'No I don't, I had a shower this morning.'

'Let me give you a bath,' she continued, as though I hadn't spoken. 'You've been sitting in that filthy henhouse.' Her voice was sweet as honey. 'I've bought special shampoo for your hair.'

In the end I followed her upstairs and placed the eggs in a bowl on the sink. After all, I decided, what harm could there be in a bath? We went into the bathroom and I was surprised to find the bath had already been filled. I started to undress and my mother impatiently tugged off my T-shirt, catching my hair as she slid it over my head.

I dropped my underpants onto the bathroom floor and climbed into the bath. The temperature was just right. She began scrubbing my back and told me to soak my hair. I lay back in the water, watching her; she was smiling at me.

Nothing to be nervous about I decided as I sat up again. She poured shampoo onto her hands and began lathering it into my hair. Soap bubbles streamed down the back of my neck and forehead, I wiped them away before they ran into my eyes and blew a bubble through my thumb and forefinger, it bounced away, all the colours of the rainbow. I was waiting for it to land on the water and burst when suddenly her hands were pulling me backwards into the water. I grabbed at the taps but missed them and slipped down, the water closing over my face.

My eyes still open, I saw her screaming at me. I was desperate, flailing and grabbing at her hands, trying to loosen her grip, grabbing at the side of the bath, anything that came within reach. My scalp was on fire, my lungs were on fire, and I kicked out, the lower half of my body coming up out of the water. I made contact, feeling the softness of her body, and she momentarily loosened her grip. I struggled to the surface, gasping for air as soon as I broke through, water everywhere.

'You have the devil in your eyes,' she was screaming, 'you bastard child.'

Terrified, I struggled to get out of the bath. Then her hands were back tearing at my hair and she shoved me under the water so hard my skull made contact with the bottom of the bath. I kicked out again, but I didn't have the strength any more and everything seemed to fade away and grow dark. Quite peaceful really.

I was on the bathroom floor, lying on my face in a pool of water. Mirabelle crouched over me, screaming at my mother to get out of the bathroom, as she banged my back. I coughed up water and luxuriated in the feel of the tiles against my cheek and the air I was drawing into my lungs.

Then my father was there and everybody was screaming at once. I fled to my bedroom, not listening, not caring, just wanting to be alone. I pulled on my jeans and climbed on top of the cupboard. After a time the voices died down and my father came into the room. He made me get down. 'It's too dangerous up there, you could fall off and break something.'

I came down with the ease of a cat, landing lightly on my feet.

'What happened?' he asked. Was he angry with me? I wasn't sure.

At first, I couldn't talk. I just stared at my father, not knowing how to put any of it into words. 'My mother gave me a bath,' I began. Then fell silent as I noticed my mother standing in the shadows of the hall, listening. 'I didn't need a bath,' I added, as there was a silence that needed filling.

They both stared at me. No one said anything at all for a long time and finally I couldn't bear it any more. I was trembling with rage. 'Why?' I yelled at my mother, 'Why did you push me under the water?'

She flew at me, claws at the ready, screaming all the while, 'You lying little bastard!'

My father grabbed her, restraining her hands, yelling at her to shut up as she continued hurling abuse at me. I stood frozen, not understanding why she was lying, hating the screaming and yelling. Then she started to cry, bemoaning the fact she had such an evil daughter. 'She destroyed my life, our marriage. If it hadn't been for her, everything would still be all right.'

I escaped past them, as my father took my mother into his arms, rocking her gently against himself, comforting her.

I couldn't find Mirabelle anywhere; she must have left. I went out into the sunshine, wondering what to do. I didn't want to go back indoors. Instead, I crossed the road and walked into the jungle. I stayed there until dusk.

Sometimes the loneliness, without a mother, would be unbearable and I would cry and he'd take me in his arms and comfort me, and tell me it was OK, I had him. I didn't need anyone else in the world, and I would be happy for a time. I rarely smiled. I was too sad inside.

School holidays were over. I'd finally been moved up to grade four. I knew my times tables, my father had coached me over and over, getting me drunk again, as he said it would help me. Whatever, I now knew my times tables through to 12 x 12. A new teacher had come from New Zealand, Mr Devonshire. He was kind; he never hit anyone. Every day he read to us for an hour. He said reading was the most important thing one could ever learn to do. We would all sit cross-legged on the floor and listen as he brought the words alive.

He was definitely my favourite person, but I'm not sure if he thought very much of me.

He'd tell me off sometimes, like the time he caught me sucking my thumb when I was meant to be creating a poem. I'd forgotten I was in class. He came over to my desk silently, or perhaps I was too far away in my thoughts. 'Aren't you too old to be sucking your thumb?' he asked, a little louder than I would have liked.

The Elly twins, sitting behind me, sniggered. I snatched the cause of my embarrassment from my mouth, and hid its dampness beneath my desk.

'If I catch you sucking your thumb again I'll bring you a dummy.'

The rest of the class tittered. I hated them all.

I could feel myself going red and realised I was staring defiantly up at him. I dropped my eyes, before he saw the devil in them. However, I think he already knew I had the devil in my eyes; on other occasions I'd glanced up and seen him looking at me strangely. He always looked away, pretending he'd been looking elsewhere.

The first weekend after school started I did something terrible. Something so terrible, only an evil person could have done it. I betrayed a trust, with the most horrific consequences.

It all started when I went into the henhouse to collect the eggs. The largest of the Rhode Island Reds was in a cocky mood, puffing out his feathers and challenging the other cockerels. I pushed him gently to move him out of the way and bent down to enter the nesting area. I saw him coming for me out of the corner of my eye, an angry bundle of red-brown feathers.

The next thing I was aware of was agonising pain in my lower back. I howled and tried to shake him off; he was stuck, his spur imbedded in me, squawking all the while. Then he was gone, scampering off behind the henhouse.

I could feel blood trickling down my back, and wondered if he'd hit a vein. I knew that was dangerous. I forgot about the eggs and ran upstairs to my father and Mirabelle. She made a big fuss about the blood and my father rushed me into the bathroom to see how deep the hole was. He was horrified when he wiped the blood away. I didn't need to tell him what'd happened. It wasn't the first time I'd been attacked; though he'd never drawn blood before. 'That bloody rooster,' he cursed angrily. 'He has to go.'

Once the bleeding had been staunched and a thick wad of toilet paper stuck down over it with plaster, my father insisted we go into the garden, to show him the culprit.

As we reached the wire enclosure, Mirabelle started talking about chicken soup and how back in France she often killed chickens for the pot. I stared at her, horrified, surely she didn't mean what I thought she meant. I looked over at my father. 'You're not going to kill him are you?' I said, desperation creeping into my voice. 'You're not, are you?' I asked again, near to tears. This was murder; they were talking about murdering one of my babies, one of the fluffy yellow bundles I'd raised, nurtured and loved. As we spoke, I watched him, preening himself in the afternoon sunlight, the light catching a thousand burnished browns. This couldn't be happening.

'Of course I am,' my father spoke firmly, convinced by Mirabelle. How I hated her at that moment. 'We're wasting time, which rooster attacked you?'

I stared at the culprit; I couldn't bring myself to betray him, and pointed to one of the bush roosters. I don't know why I did that. I thought my father wouldn't kill the wrong rooster. I thought he'd know I was lying. He didn't and the lie hung heavily over me as he went into the cage. He caught him easily. He didn't squawk, he wasn't afraid. Why should he be? I suddenly remembered running up the road, his mother tearing after me, wings out, determined to rescue her tiny chicks gathered in my skirt.

I was sent upstairs to get the bush knife. I wish I could have refused. I came back downstairs, very slowly. Somehow, the day seemed unnaturally bright. My father put the rooster down on the ground. He stood there for a moment, and then begun pecking at the ground at my father's feet, unconcerned.

Now that my father had the knife in his hand and the full enormity of what he was about to do flooded through me, I began pleading and crying, then sobbing and screaming for him not to kill him.

'Stop it right now,' he yelled, really angry with me. 'Mirabelle is right. It's perfectly normal to kill a chicken.'

'But not my baby,' I wailed, overcome with guilt and horror.

In the end, they let me blindfold him. I took as long as I dared finding a blindfold, hoping for a miracle. As I blindfolded my friend, I was suddenly aware of how the world looked at that moment, the sunlight filtering through the trees, a gentle breeze ruffling the soft pink petals of the hibiscus flowers. I knew he was looking at the world for the last time.

I turned my head when my father swung the bush knife, coward that I was. I was sent to wash it afterwards. I crouched for a long time in front of the hose, staring at the crimson glistening on the metal. Finally, I turned the tap on. When I went upstairs, Mirabelle stood at the sink, surrounded by feathers. Afternoon sunlight caught the kaleidoscope of colour that had been my rooster – gold, blue, scarlet, black and white speckled breast feathers. I went and locked myself in my room. I hated both of them. I hated myself. I knew my mother was right, I did have the devil in my eyes.

Several hours later I was forced out of my room to sit at the table. Mirabelle proudly served up the soup, her face flushed with the steam rising from the pot. Amongst the liquid and noodles were pieces of chicken.

I stared at them both, as they spooned the soup into their mouths. I scraped back my chair and stood up. 'I'm not going to eat this,' I said firmly.

'I'm getting tired of all your complaining,' exclaimed my father, 'you're going to sit down, shut up and eat.'

I remained standing. 'I'm not going to eat your bloody soup!' I screamed, then I picked up the bowl and smashed it onto the floor, hot liquid splattering up my bare legs. They sat there, stunned and I ran to my room and locked the door again, refusing to come out.

Chapter 9

Mike came to visit one night after work. 'I've brought you a present,' he said as I opened the door to find him with a large cardboard box in his arms. As soon as I saw the box I knew what was in it.

My father was in his locked room. I knocked on the door and told him Mike had come, then went back into the living room, where I closed all possible escape routes and sat in front of the box. I folded back the cardboard flaps, barely able to contain my excitement.

Scarcely was the box opened than a ginger and white bundle streaked out and took cover under the couch. That turned out to be the male. The female sat looking at me, a tangle of stripes, black, ginger, white and grey, waiting until I picked her up and cuddled her. They were about three months old, just losing their kittenish look. It took quite some time before I managed to coax the male out into the open. In the end I resorted to bribery and waved a piece of raw meat, just out of reach. After that he was fine.

Mike stayed for a cup of coffee. He told my father his contract had come to an end and he and Sue were leaving Port Vila. They talked while I played with my new friends. I hunted in the kitchen for a bowl for water and a flat plate for their dinner. Mike was leaving as I came back from the shop downstairs, where I'd bought some cat food. He ruffled my hair affectionately. 'Now, you take good care of those two,' he said, smiling down at me. Then he said goodbye, and I never saw him again. He disappeared somewhere into the vastness of this world.

That night, cuddled up in bed with the kittens purring loudly, I thought about names, deciding on Panther for the male and Garbageguts for the female. She'd spent most of the evening turning up the rubbish bin in the kitchen, scavenging for scraps; ignoring her food bowl.

They quickly became the centre of my universe. They'd be waiting for me when I returned from school; Garbageguts would climb up my clothes and perch on my shoulder as I organised their dinner, while Panther would yowl loudly at my feet.

I was in trouble again at school. It was the old story of untidy handwriting.

'Like chicken scratchings,' Mr Devonshire said. 'How can I mark your work, if I can't even read what you've written?' He had a point; even I couldn't decipher some of it. A note was sent to my father, which I thought most unfair. What did it have to do with him? He sat me down at the kitchen table with a note pad and a blue ballpoint pen. 'Let's have a look at your writing.'

He dictated a couple of sentences and I wrote as tidily as I could, trying to keep up. I could see he wasn't impressed by the way he was looking at my attempt. 'What's your favourite book?' he asked.

Surprised by this sudden change of conversations, I naively told him, '*The Happy Prince and other Short Stories*, by Oscar Wilde.'

'Go and get it.'

I brought back the book and laid it on the table.

'You're going to copy this out, the whole book, not missing any sentences or words. If you do, I'll make you start again.'

I look at him horrified. 'But it's such a thick book, it'll take me forever.'

'Then you'd better get started, because there'll be no more reading until you finish.'

It took more than a month. I'd come home from school, feed the cats and the chickens then sit down at the table faithfully copying. Painstakingly checking all the commas, full stops and quotation marks were in place. Carefully rounding my letters, adding tails where required as neatly as I could. Terrified all the while, that if I left something out I'd have to start again. When one exercise book was full, I'd go and buy another one. When the pen ran dry, I bought another one. I wrote until my hand ached, until I began to hate that book. Words, which had evoked so much feeling in me before, now were just clusters of letters to be written down. Even the little swallow dying in the snow meant nothing to me.

I was glad when I could finally crawl into bed, exhausted and secretly read under the covers, the cats pouncing on me as I turned the pages. When I finally fell asleep, I dreamt I was writing. I'd dream I'd forgotten whole chapters and frantically tried to avoid being found out. All my waking hours revolved round copying out that book. I knew that once he decided I had to do something, he'd never relent. I was right. He checked my work against the original every night, and I'd sit, my heart in my mouth in case I'd missed something, in case my writing wasn't neat enough. I developed a callus on my middle finger, which I have to this day, because of the way I held my pen. Finally, it was finished. I carefully wrote out the last sentence and added the final full stop. I felt as though I'd achieved the impossible. He checked my work for the last time. 'Your writing hasn't improved much,' was his only comment as he shut the last exercise book.

I sat frozen as he stood up, surely he wasn't going to make me copy out another book? He didn't say anything and walked out of the room. I heard him open the door to his bedroom, then close it behind him.

The next morning all the exercise books had gone. I found them later in the rubbish bin. I was glad to see the last of them. As for Oscar Wilde, I put the book back in my room, and I've never read it again.

Chapter 10

The next couple of months my father spent a lot of time with Mirabelle, often not coming home till late, if at all. I hadn't seen my mother for a long time. Someone said she'd moved to the Banks Islands with Maurice. I was quite happy, I was old enough to take care of myself. If there was nothing to eat I went downstairs and bought some food and put it on the account. I still sold my eggs to the Chinese woman. These days, she was as round as an egg herself, another baby on the way.

One night, a little while later, I lay listening to her giving birth downstairs. The next morning I was told she had a girl. Her arrival meant we had to move, as they needed the flat.

We began packing our possessions into carton boxes. The cats didn't like it one bit. They stalked round the house, sniffing the boxes suspiciously, mewling in disgust. Panther didn't come home for two days, while Garbageguts frantically searched in all the cupboards, in the boxes, everywhere, meowing pitifully. On the third day Lidia came up and told me Panther had gone to heaven. She'd found his fur hanging to dry over the neighbour's fence. We didn't need to say aloud what that meant. We both knew he'd been eaten.

Our new house was situated at one end of Seaside Village – a collection of huts made of scraps of corrugated iron, fibreboard and scavenged planks, held together with traditional weaving and thatching. Years later I'd see it for the impoverished slum it was, but as a child I only saw the beauty of the flowers surrounding the houses and the smiles of the people who lived there. Ours was the only concrete structure. It wasn't really finished, it hadn't been painted and it lacked power, as did the rest of the village. It did have a toilet and running water, though. The village also had a toilet. One toilet, and a couple of taps, but no one seemed to complain. They had to live somewhere I guess.

I fell in love with the area immediately. Across the road bordering the village was a wide expanse of half-wild bush, interspersed with dozens of enormous banyan trees. Colardo's plantation stretched further beyond, almost out of sight – a wonderland to a wild creature like me.

I settled in quickly, loving the freedom of being able to walk to and from school. There were times when I didn't go to school. I'd leave home after breakfast and walk down the dirt track with the full intention of going to class. However, when I reached the place where the most ancient of the banyan trees spread a huge canopy over the road, the spirits of the trees would gather round me and whisper in my ear. 'Walk with us for a while, just a little way,' they'd say, and it seemed to me their voices were like the rustling of wind through long grass.

I didn't need much encouragement, and in no time at all I'd be climbing over the barbed-wire fence. I'd follow the wind through the half-wild scrub, up over the hill to the darker, deeper parts of the jungle, on the forgotten side of Colardo's plantation, where I'd feast on wild almonds and tiny bush raspberries. Sometimes I'd find a coconut and I became proficient at opening them with my bare hands. The trick is to loosen a tiny part of the husk with something sharp, then tear a strip off with your teeth. When the nut is completely bare, bang it with a sharp rock, turning it all the while until it cracks open. I loved the taste of the creamy pith; it didn't matter that it took a long time to open. Then, with my belly full, I'd curl up in a patch of sunlight and fall asleep.

The new house had its downside. The bedrooms had no glass in the window frames. There were wooden shutters to keep out the wind and the rain, but they didn't keep out the cockroaches. Brown and stinking, they came in by their hundreds in the hot season, drowning in half-full cups and glasses, scuttling and scurrying underfoot at night, unafraid in the half gloom of the hurricane lanterns.

They feasted on the butter, got stuck in the Vegemite and honey and pooped in the sugar. They greeted you first thing in the morning, lying on their backs in the sink, wriggling their revolting legs. Worst of all they laid black scaly eggs everywhere, in the bedding, on the furniture, on the bread. Everywhere! It didn't matter how many Lidia squashed flat with a swift blow of her flip flop; or how many Garbageguts ate, more marched in, and babies hatched every day; as disgusting and smelly as their parents. In desperation, Lidia bought insect spray up at the Chinese shop near the village.

My father became enraged when he found what she'd done. We heard him screaming from the kitchen and went running to see what was the matter.

'Who the hell bought this?' he demanded, holding up the

insect spray, as we entered the kitchen. Poor Lidia looked terrified. 'I did Masta, to kill the cockroaches dead, too many cockroaches, not good Masta.'

'That's the last fucking time, do you hear?' he yelled. 'This is poison, are you trying to kill us?'

Lidia looked at the ground at her feet, dark crimson under her brown skin. 'Yes, Masta, I don't buy it again, Masta. I am sorry.'

'Sorry isn't bloody good enough.' He was so angry he flung the offending canister against the wall and stalked out the back door, slamming it so hard I thought it'd come off its hinges. I hastily put the dented tin into the rubbish bin, covering it with scraps so he wouldn't inadvertently see it later, and become enraged all over again. Lidia and I went back to squashing as many as we could and sweeping their carcasses out the back door every morning.

My bedroom also lacked a wardrobe, which I sorely missed. There were times after my father had called me to his room when I needed a sanctuary where I could climb up out of reach. A place where I could curl up and suck my thumb, and not think. It also meant I had nowhere to put my clothes and other belongings. At first, I just kept them piled up in a corner, then my father gave me an old seaman's chest he'd found years before on Stewart Island, back in New Zealand. I pulled this next to my bed and it also served as a bedside table.

I didn't have any curtains, so for the first few weeks I slept with the shutters closed. I'd lie in bed, eyes wide open, desperately trying to see something in the absolute blackness that filled the room like a mist of evil spirits. I'd stare so hard into the darkness I'd see circles and swirls of scarlet and red before my eyes. Then I'd panic and wonder if I'd suddenly gone blind. Was this what blind people saw? What if I never saw light and colour again, only darkness? What if I never knew he was nearby, until I felt his hands on my body? How could I tell what he wanted until he took it, or until I smelled the baby oil?

I hated the smell of that baby oil. When he tried to enter me I was too tight, and complained too much, it hurt and I said so. It went in a little easier with hand cream, but the hand cream stung where I was torn, and I complained about that too.

'You're always moaning about something,' he said afterwards while I was showering. I hung my head with shame, there was nothing I could say, because it was true. A few days later, while we were shopping, he tried out several different creams on his hand, but none of them were quite right, and then he tried the oil. 'Feel this, it's really slippery.'

I reached over and rubbed my finger on the glistening patch, not really wanting to. I didn't care which cream he used. I didn't want him to use any. I didn't want sex. It was painful and when it was all over you had to have another shower to get rid of the sticky feeling and the smell of sweat.

'So, what do you think?'

'It's OK.' I looked down at the black and white tiled floor between the aisles.

He closed the lid. 'Slippery when wet,' he laughed and added it to the shopping trolley. It became one of the staples of my life, never changing, always there, on the floor next to the bed. Waiting till next time.

I had enough of the darkness. One night I felt my way to the shutters and pushed them open. Cool night air and moonlight flooded into my room, the silvery light chasing away my fears. As for the cockroaches, they had a thousand ways to get in anyway, I couldn't see how one more entrance would make a difference.

Sometimes I'd sit on the windowsill, listening to the night and watching the surrounding village. Families gathered around outside their huts, laughing and talking as they ate. The air filled with the perfume of night flowers and smoke from their cooking fires.

Often they'd call me over and I'd share their food and drink smoky tea. Afterwards, I'd gaze into the depths of the fire feeling totally at home, safe and comforted. Pigs and scrawny dogs would always be nearby, waiting for scraps. Other times I'd sit, tucked into the shadows, unseen, too lonely to join them.

Eventually the village would be still as everyone slept. I'd lie in bed, unable to sleep, and stare up at the stars. Fat geckos pattered across the walls chasing cockroaches and in the stillness of the night I'd hear them crunching their bodies as they ate them. Sometimes my father called to me to come to his bed. Sometimes he didn't. Finally my eyes would stay open no longer and I would drop off to sleep.

'Wake up, wake up, you'll be late for school.'

I opened my eyes, squinting in the early morning sunlight. Lidia was shaking me. My father was away in Santo for two weeks on a business trip and Lidia took her duties very seriously. 'Go and wash yourself, while I make breakfast.'

I stretched and went sleepily outdoors to the rainwater barrel. Lidia preferred me to use the water barrel; she didn't like the shower much. It was too dark and dank in there, in spite of her scrubbing brush. I stripped off the oversized T-shirt Lidia insisted I wear to bed and tipped water over my naked body with the tin mug, gasping at the cold and then began soaping myself.

After breakfast, I walked to school. I took a shortcut through an unkempt paddock, then wished I hadn't, it was filled with knee-high sensitive grass. I scratched my legs badly and the next morning every single scratch had become inflamed. By evening the inflammation was red and angry looking and small painful blisters of pus were forming. Lidia scolded me for being so foolish as she wiped my legs with Dettol. 'What did you think you were doing, are you some kind of bush woman?'

I couldn't sleep for the insistent throbbing in my legs. I woke Lidia before it grew light, the blisters had become ulcers and red streaks were plainly visible, a danger sign of impending blood poisoning. I could hardly walk for the pain.

At seven o'clock we walked to the dispensary in town, sitting outside on the dusty pavement with the other patients until it opened. They gave me a really painful injection. It wasn't the needle that hurt, it was the stuff they injected into my bottom, somewhere between a wall of fire and the feeling of having been kicked, which lasted about twenty minutes.

The nurse gave Lidia a tube of white cream and instructions to clean the wounds every day and I had to come back every day for five days for more injections. The next morning there were more than twenty sores I could stick the tip of my finger in. Every morning Lidia took the crusty tops off with a needle, ignoring my shrieks of agony, releasing the pressure as the stinking yellow pus spurted out, wiping the holes clean and smearing cream into them. Then I'd hobble into town for another injection. On the fourth day Lidia went to her village to see the cleva. She came back with a bottle of thick dark liquid. 'That white medicine no good, we use this one.'

I sat on the kitchen table while she washed the white cream off and patted my legs dry with a towel. She smeared the dark syrupy mixture into every ulcer, and wrapped my legs with bandages. It was really soothing, not like the white cream which stung. A few hours later, my legs only hurt when I moved or accidentally banged an ulcer. When that happened, the pain was so bad I felt like throwing up. But that's the way it is with tropical ulcers, you learn not to bang them.

The next morning, when Lidia unwrapped my legs, there was no pus and no smell. The ulcers were open and pink looking, the pink of healing skin. They still left scars though, little round indentations, to remind me where they'd been.

One morning as I sat with my father at breakfast I recalled the dream of the night before. He was always interested in my dreams. Sometimes he'd tell me what I was going to dream, and in the morning I'd tell him he'd been right, because I knew it pleased him. 'I dreamt I was in a native village, high in the mountains. An old man stood holding a huge wooden bow.'

My father had begun collecting tribal art. 'Describe the bow.'

'It was longer than the man and made from very dark wood. It was slightly curved, and as thick as your two thumbs in the middle, tapering at both ends to a fine point. It was covered in weaving and there were tiny painted clay faces.'

My father laughed, 'You wouldn't be able to use a bow like that.'

A month later my father flew to Malekula and went into the bush, walking with porters to the Small Nambas, a mountain tribe living as they must have in the Stone Age. He went to take photos and buy traditional tribal artefacts, known as 'custom'. He came back in high excitement, with odd-shaped parcels wrapped in jungle leaves. 'You'll never guess what I bought – the bow you dreamt about.'

We peeled off the leaves and uncovered the bow from my dreams. I was flabbergasted. It was exactly as I'd seen it. 'But what's it used for?'

'The old man who sold it told me that when the owner dies they cover his bow like this so it can't be used again.'

I helped my father unwrap the other artefacts he'd bought and put them outside his locked room. When we'd finished dinner my father pushed his plate to one side. 'Why don't you go up to the shop and buy some ice cream?'

It had been such a hot day, ice cream sounded a real treat. I ran up the winding track to the store and bought chocolate ice creams, then hurried back with them wrapped in newspaper. It was very dark, with no moon, and I wished I'd brought the torch. As I rounded a bend in the track I heard snarling and growling. Wild dogs! Then they were all around me, hackles up, shoulders hunched, heads down, yellow eyes watching as they circled.

These weren't indigenous wild dogs, most of these had belonged to Europeans who abandoned them when they returned home. This didn't make them any less of a threat, in fact it made them more dangerous, they were unafraid of people. I was terrified, I knew I was too far away from the house to be heard. One of them made a mock charge; I dropped the ice creams and screamed, turning my back, thinking if I did that they'd think I wasn't afraid. I know now that's the worst thing I could have done.

They attacked, knocking me to the ground. I punched out at their open jaws, their hot breath on my neck and face and one yelped as my fist made contact. I screamed again, a long high-pitched scream and out of the darkness I saw a bobbing hurricane lamp, someone running.

'Woo, woo,' a man's voice yelled as he charged, waving a thick stick, and like magic the dogs slunk off into the long grass and disappeared.

'You all right missy?' he asked as he helped me to my unsteady feet and then held the lamp near my face to see who he'd rescued.

'Yes, I am, thank you.' I looked round for my parcel of ice cream in the pool of light and found it surprisingly undamaged. He walked me back to the house, before going off again into the night.

The dogs began to terrorise our village. Often at night, you could hear them snarling below the windows as they hunted for food. One night they attacked and savaged a child. The boy survived and was rushed to hospital to be stitched back together. During the day they remained hidden in the jungle, only coming out under cover of darkness. One night my father shook me awake, screaming, 'Where's the torch, give me the fucking torch!'

I was still asleep, still half-dreaming. 'It's in the seaman's chest,' I murmured, turning over under the covers. It wasn't, it was under my pillow, but in my half-waking state I didn't know what I was saying.

'What the fucking hell is it doing there?' he roared as he scrabbled in the darkness trying to open the box.

It began to register that he was looking for the torch and I slid my hand under my pillow and I drew it out. 'Sorry, it's not in the chest, it's here.'

He snatched it from my hands. 'Then why the fuck did you say it was in the chest?' I started to reply, but he was so angry he punched me in the side of my face. Without another word he was gone, slamming my bedroom door.

I sat up shaking, my hands wrapped round my knees, terrified he was going to come back. In the end I decided to see why he needed the torch so badly. I pulled on a T-shirt and my jeans and walked through the living room. Garbageguts was in her basket by the front door, with her week-old kittens. My father was standing on the porch with the torch switched off. 'Shh, the dogs will hear you,' he said as I stepped down behind him. 'They're all around the chicken run. Get me the bow and arrow, not the one with the weaving, the other one.'

I ran inside, leaving the front door open and snatched the native hunting bow from the wall and several arrows. I hurried back to the porch and came to an abrupt halt when I saw the pack had gathered around the steps, growling threateningly at my father.

'Get back inside,' he whispered, 'it's too dangerous.'

I stepped back into the living room, and my father began to follow when all of a sudden Garbageguts came flying out the door, fur standing on end, claws at the ready. My father tried to catch her as she hurtled past, yowling and hissing, lunging straight at the leader of the pack.

Sometimes I really couldn't understand that cat. I knew she was a little crazy and protective since she'd had her kittens, but this was insane. For a split second she clung to the dog's head, spitting and snarling, then he was shaking her back and forth in his mouth. Garbageguts screeched horribly and I screamed at my father to do something. In a split second he knocked the arrow in place and sent it flying. Garbageguts was still screeching as the arrow struck the dog side on.

The dog howled, dropping Garbageguts to the ground,

meanwhile the arrow continued clean through him and struck the ground several metres away. The pack turned and fled, the wounded dog following, howling into the distance. Garbageguts lay writhing on the ground, unable to stand. I ran down the steps and carefully picked her up, her eyes pleading with me to help her. I carefully put her down on the floor in the living room. 'There's no blood,' I said, 'what's wrong with her?'

My father cautiously felt her all over. 'I think she has internal injuries.'

I gently stroked her ears, trying to calm her, but she scrabbled with her front paws, meowing pitifully. Her back legs didn't work. I realised she was trying to reach her babies so I carefully moved her over to the basket. Despite the agony she must have been in, she began purring. I carried the basket to my bed and eventually fell asleep with my hand gently stroking her.

She was still alive in the morning, remaining paralysed for several months, yet still managing to raise her babies. She couldn't wee on her own, so several times a day I carried her into the garden and put pressure on her bladder, like the vet taught me, and helped her relieve herself. Gradually she regained the use of her back legs, and one day she walked stiffly down the stairs and proudly squatted on her own.

Chapter 11

My father was sick of me biting my nails. He dragged me into the kitchen and took out a jar with a missing lid, half full of semi-crystalised honey and dead cockroaches. He shoved it under my nose and as the stench filled my nostrils, I struggled not to throw up. When he grabbed my hand and forced my fingertips into the jar I could have died as my fingers squished against the decaying insects. 'Now let's see if you bite your nails.' His grip on my hand was hurting me as he shoved my fingers up to my face. I fought then, turning my head and tugging free. 'You don't like that do you?' he jeered. 'Then you'd better stop, because I'm going to keep sticking your fingers into the jar until you do.'

Afterwards I ran into the bathroom and washed my hands over and over, trying to eradicate the revulsion. He didn't do it again. Lidia found the jar and threw it into the rubbish bin in disgust.

One day, while I was exploring further than I had ever been before, I came to the far side of Colardo's plantation and reached a barbed-wire fence. Over the fence, I could see several houses, surrounded by a neat wire fence, with three girls playing in one of the yards. I climbed over to get a better look and was surprised to see Shona, a girl from my class. She caught sight of me and waved. 'Hi, come and play.'

I opened the gate and began a new friendship. I had so much fun that day with Shona and her two sisters. Her mother invited me to lunch. She was a dressmaker; their living room filled with swaths of cloth and dressmaking paraphernalia. Shona and I became inseparable, walking to school and playing together all our free daylight hours.

I showed her the wonders of my plantation, and taught her how to open a coconut. Together we made bows and arrows and climbed the banyan trees. In exchange she let me play with her toys and dolls. One day, Shona's mother asked to meet my father, and in due course he came round to her house. She invited him in and chased us girls out. We sat outside under the open window and eavesdropped.

'I wanted to talk to you about Tanja, she runs wild. I don't mind her coming here, it's just that I worry my daughters will have an accident. I want my girls to grow into young ladies, don't you want that for your daughter?'

My father launched into a long explanation about the difficulty of raising a daughter on his own, and then asked her what she thought he should do.

'Well to start with she needs new clothes, she can't keep running round half-naked. Perhaps if she had some nice frocks she would be less inclined to play the savage all day. And she is far too thin, all skin and bones. Thinner than a string bean. It's not good for a young girl, it will stunt her growth.'

The next day my father made oxtail soup, buying a new

pot especially. The soup was delicious, thick with chunks of meat, potatoes, onions and carrots. He made so much it took us three days to eat it. He told me I was too thin and needed to eat more. It didn't matter how much I ate; I stayed thin. Lidia thought it was because I had worms and bought some disgusting medicine and forced me to drink it.

That would explain the pain in my side, I decided, and ignored it. It would soon go away, when all the worms had died. I could imagine them writhing by the thousands in my intestines, eating all my food.

The next morning I got out of bed and stood weakly, my underpants in my hand, trying to gather the strength to put them on, when suddenly my door flew open. My father was angry about something, he was screaming at me, but I couldn't work out what he was yelling about. I just wished the room would keep still. 'Are you listening?' he roared.

I stared at him and he grabbed me by the shoulders. Without warning I threw up, it was too much for my full bladder and urine spurted out all over the floor, running into the pool of vomit. I crouched down, trying to stop the flow, but it was impossible. 'You filthy savage, you filthy, filthy bitch.'

I stared up at him, tears in my eyes, 'I'm sorry, I couldn't help it.' I was still clutching my underpants.

'Couldn't help it,' he shrieked, 'you know where the bloody toilet is! Or are you some kind of fucking animal? I'll teach you to piss on the bloody floor.' He grabbed me by the back of my neck and forced me down, banging my head on the floor, through the vomit and the urine. I was lying in it and the foul smell and the slimy feeling made me throw up again. He stood up, incensed with rage and before I could move he swung his leg back and savagely kicked me, crippling pain knifed down my leg as the toe of his shoe smashed into my hip. I instinctively curled up, waiting for the next blow. 'Clean this up, you hear?' he ranted.

I struggled to sit up, fighting through a fog of pain, but I was too slow for him and he grabbed a handful of hair and hauled me to my knees. 'Clean it up, now!' he commanded.

In blind panic I looked around for something to clean the floor with and then remembered my underpants. I started to wipe the vomit up, but there was too much, and I began gagging again. Suddenly my father snatched the sodden pants from me and rubbed them over my face, vomit went up my nose and into my mouth as I screamed for him to stop. He became aware of Lidia standing in the doorway, watching, her face expressionless. 'Oh,' he smiled, anger falling from his face, 'you're early this morning, Tanja is sick. After she's dressed I'll take her to the doctor.'

'Yes, Masta,' she said, as he walked past, her eyes downcast. How much had she seen? I wondered, embarrassed about what I'd done. I ended up in hospital for a week this time, malaria again. The doctor asked about the huge bruise on my hip and my father told him I'd fallen out of a tree.

One day after school my father drove me to Shona's house. He'd decided I needed some new clothes and had bought some fabric in town. Shona's mother tut-tutted over the material. 'This is not the sort of material for a child. It's too slinky, more for an evening dress, and the colours, far too dark. I was thinking more of a simple cotton print.'

'Yes, but I was thinking of something a little more sophisticated,' he said.

I hated the finished clothes the first time I saw them. Trouser suits, very grown up, with long puffed-sleeves tight at the wrist with elastic cuffs. Not at all suitable for tree climbing, you only had to look at the fabric and you'd pull a thread. My father thought they were wonderful, and often told me to wear them, especially if we were going somewhere or people came round to buy artefacts. He also insisted on brushing my hair and pulling it into two tight plaits, which I really hated.

The rainy season had begun, and the air smelt of damp and decaying leaves. My father started carving, copying from his book of Oceanic art. He'd disappear into his locked room after dinner and work till it got too dark to carve. Then he'd bring the gas lantern into his bedroom and read. Often I'd sit on his bed and read as well. I still loved to read. It was better to be in his room, than waiting in mine. In a way, it was better to get sex over with, rather than wait. Because then, after the shower, it wouldn't happen again for a couple of days.

Sometimes he'd bring a carving out for me to admire. When the carving was nearly finished he went over it with a special tool, carefully scraping away all the file marks. He was very good. One time he carved a statue out of a log, about 45 centimetres high, a copy of a Marquesan figure. I thought it was beautiful, but he told me it wasn't ready yet; it didn't look ancient enough. He buried it in the henhouse and waited for nature to age it.

Shona came round to stay the night. We went to bed early after dinner and I put a candle on a saucer so she wouldn't be too disorientated. She had a lovely pink nightie with ruffles. I wasn't going to sleep naked, not when she had a nightie, so I kept my jeans on.

We talked late into the night, giggling about all sorts of things. 'Are you going to see the fireworks next week?' I asked.

She sat up in bed. 'Yes, Daddy's taking us to the

waterfront for dinner and then we'll watch the fireworks. What about you?'

'Yes, Lidia's coming to stay overnight. We'll walk down.'

I was really looking forward to it; afterwards there was always a small fête, with coconut shies and roulette tables. Eventually we fell asleep. I woke up to Shona screaming, 'A mouse, a mouse!'

'That's nothing to scream about,' I soothed, trying to quieten her; I didn't want to wake my father.

'It's inside my nightie,' she wailed, leaping around the bed, clutching at the front.

The poor mouse, no doubt terrified out of its wits, scuttled up until it reached her ruffled collar, pausing under her chin before leaping for freedom. I snatched it before it had time to dart under the bed. Garbageguts sat proudly on the windowsill. It wasn't the first time she'd brought me a live mouse. Perhaps she felt she needed to look after me.

'It's so cute,' I whispered, 'come and look.' It sat trembling in the shadows of my curled fingers. 'It has the sweetest face, and look at his adorable little ears.'

'It's not cute,' she wailed, 'it's probably a rat. Get rid of it.'

In the end I put it in an old empty aquarium, with scrunched up toilet paper for it to sleep in and carefully closed the netting lid. I couldn't understand how she could be afraid of a tiny mouse.

I was glad I hadn't shown her the giant wolf spider that lived under the bed. She'd probably have died of fright – he was bigger than my outstretched hand. He'd come into my life several months earlier, when Lidia put him under my covers as a practical joke, tucking them in so he couldn't escape. When I pushed my feet under the sheets, the huge spider ran up my legs, across my stomach and up over my face, then sat on my head. I hastily brushed him out of my hair, feeling his nails brush my scalp as he flew off. He landed with a soft plop on the floor and scuttled noisily under the bed, where he took up residence. Lidia nearly wet herself when I told her what happened. Strangely, the spider never came into my bed again, perhaps he was too afraid of me.

Shona never stayed overnight again. She said it had been the worst night of her life.

Chapter 12

Bastille Day, 14 July 1972, a night I'll never forget. Lidia cooked dinner and afterwards we sat together in an armchair, reading *The World of Susie Wong*. We came to the part where Susie eats roasted pumpkin seeds. We agreed they sounded delicious and decided that next morning she'd walk to the market and buy a pumpkin.

'We have to go,' my father interrupted, 'or we'll be late for the fireworks.'

Lidia went into the kitchen to fetch her basket, then we all went out to the car.

'I've forgotten the keys. Lidia, can you fetch them? They're next to my bed.'

'Yes, Masta.' She walked back up the stairs. Almost immediately, my father followed. I waited, they seemed to be taking a long time. Eventually I went inside. My father's bedroom door was shut and I could hear voices behind the door. Was my father angry because Lidia hadn't found the keys quickly enough?

Then the door opened, and my father came out.

'We're going to miss the fireworks,' I exclaimed, 'we have to hurry.'

'Don't worry, we'll see the fireworks, but first we're going to play a game. I want you to follow me, you're not to say anything, do exactly what I say.'

I nodded, confused, and followed him into his bedroom. He'd turned the gas lamp down, so it barely gave any light and I looked around for Lidia, thinking she was hiding behind the door, waiting to leap out and give me a fright. Then I saw her – naked, bound hand and foot, spread-eagled on the bed, a black cloth bound tightly over her eyes. She lay motionless. I took a step backwards, horrified, panicking. No, not this, I thought, please no! But I remained silent. I didn't want to anger my father.

He grabbed me by the wrist and dragged me over to the bed. He pushed me onto my knees, so I was leaning into the mattress, my arm touching her leg. I averted my eyes so as not to look between her legs, but he grabbed my hair and forced my chin up, making me look.

I was too scared to close my eyes; I didn't want Lidia to be beaten. He indicated he wanted me to touch her between her legs. I was afraid of him, but I couldn't make my hand reach out and touch her, not there. I was shaking and close to tears. Lidia remained silent, her head tilted, trying to hear what was happening. He grabbed my wrist and forced my hand towards her, holding my fingers tightly between his and moved them up and down.

Lidia moaned, 'Ah wei, ah wei, plis, Masta, mi gud woman.' In her fear, she had reverted to Bislama, a pidgin dialect. My father ignored her. Finding the opening with his fingers he pushed my hand into her; I curled my fingers up, trying to avoid contact. Frustrated, he yanked my hand back and straightened my fingers, squeezing them painfully, fury in his eyes. I surrendered. He grasped my wrist and pushed the tips of my fingers into her vagina. Lidia pleaded for him to stop, because she was a virgin. All the while I remained silent. My father pushed harder, the resistance that had met my fingertips suddenly gave way, and my hand plunged inside her.

'Ah wei,' she cried out over and over again and I tried to shut out the sound of her voice. My hand was all the way inside, up to the wrist. Finally my father released his grip and I pulled my hand free. But it wasn't over yet; he forced me again and again to push my hand inside her. Lidia fell silent, not moving, trembling violently, I could feel it through the mattress where it pressed into my chest. Finally, he released his grip on my hand and I was able to run out of the bedroom. My hand was sticky, not sticky from sperm, or sticky from oil, a different kind of sticky. All I wanted to do was wash my hand, wash away what had just happened.

In the darkness I washed my hands over and over and over. When I walked back into the living room, his bedroom door was shut. I listened, but couldn't hear anything. In the distance I heard the fireworks. I didn't go to the window to see if I could catch a glimpse, I just sat there, a dreadful heaviness in my heart. After half an hour my father came out. He was very cheerful. 'Oh well, we missed the fireworks, never mind, we can see them next year.'

I didn't say anything, then Lidia came into the room, she didn't say anything either, but spent a long time in the bathroom. Afterwards it was as though nothing had happened. Lidia never said a word to me about that night. It was a secret too big to say out loud.

My twelfth birthday came and went, an uneventful day my mother forgot. I cried myself to sleep and woke in the darkest part of the night when Opa came to visit. We talked about Holland, I said I wished I was there, but he said I wouldn't like it, I needed the warmth of the tropics. 'It's in your blood now,' he explained.

A few days later someone shot our hens with an air rifle. When I went to feed them I found Molly lying stiff and dead, riddled with pellets. I found Lola behind the nesting boxes. She was all bunched up, her beak resting on the ground; feathers in disarray. She'd been shot in the leg. I ran inside to find my father. He carefully pried the pellet out, and we put Lola in a box with dry grass and spread a towel over, so she'd be in darkness while she recovered. Lola attended to, we buried Molly, sending her to heaven to join the others. My father was late for work, and I was late for school. Mr Devonshire cornered me and ordered me into the staff room. Once there he motioned me to take a chair and sat on the edge of the desk.

'I was looking through your file this morning, and you've skipped school more than fifty days! I'll have to talk to your father.'

That was the last thing I wanted him to do. 'Please don't,' I asked, in a small voice.

He looked at me for a long time, then his expression softened. 'All right, I'll make a deal, come to school every day, and I won't talk to your father. But if you continue taking time off, I'll have you expelled.'

Put like that I had no choice. It was terrible. I hated being organised, all those wasted hours trapped indoors.

Shona and her sisters came round to play. I showed her my new skipping rope and we decided to go outdoors. It was still muddy from rain the night before and in the end we went onto the small porch. We took turns, seeing who could jump rope the longest. Shona's youngest sister was well ahead, going for a world record, when all of a sudden the rope caught in my father's prize bonsai tree and pulled the planter over. It smashed as it hit the concrete, scattering dirt, fortunately not damaging the tree. I was horrified. It was five o'clock, which meant my father would be home shortly. 'It'd be better if you went before my father gets home,' I insisted, practically pushing them down the stairs.

Oh no, what was I going to do? I found a tube of paper glue and stuck the pot back together, stuffing the soil and the plant back inside. Hurry, hurry, I kept saying to myself, pressing the moss back into place. The crack was obvious on one side, so I turned it against the wall, hoping he wouldn't notice.

It was ten past five; he'd be home any second. I had to sweep the floor; otherwise he'd notice the dirt. I knelt down and began brushing the concrete with my bare hands, pushing the dirt under the doormat. Just then I heard a car coming down the track and straightened up. Too late to wipe the pot, too late to clean my hands, I surreptitiously wiped them on the back of my jeans, smiling as he walked up the steps. We went indoors together and I breathed a sigh of relief as he walked into the kitchen.

'Where's the water jug?' he called, 'I need to water the bonsai, it's not looking its best.' I hunted nervously through the cupboards. How did he do that? He hadn't even looked at it! I found the jug and he filled it at the tap.

'Put some water on for a cup of tea,' he said. Quietly I filled the kettle and lit the gas stove, listening all the while to what he was doing.

'Fucking shit, what the hell ...' He'd found out. 'Come

out here this minute.' He sounded as though he had his teeth clenched.

My legs were like jelly as I stepped onto the porch and looked at the bonsai. The glue hadn't held and the broken pieces of pot lay around the packed soil like petals on a flower.

'How did this happen?'

I told the truth, what else could I do?

'How many fucking times have I told you not to skip on the porch?'

I stared at him, he'd never told me not to skip on the porch. He'd told me not to skip in the living room, and I never did. He leaned down and picked the offending rope off the ground, holding it by the handles, the rope swishing back and forth.

'I asked you a question, how many times?'

'You never told me ... '

I never finished my sentence, he lashed out at my legs and I jumped back. Not far enough, the rope slashed round my legs, making a terrific thwacking sound, sharp pain bringing tears to my eyes. 'Go and tell your bloody friends they're never to set foot here again, smashing my things!'

I turned and fled and he struck me again across my back as I stumbled down the stairs. I didn't stop running until I'd climbed the barbed wire fence, tearing my jeans in my haste.

I reached Shona's house and knocked on the door. After a few moments I heard footsteps coming down the hall, then Shona opened the door. 'We're having dinner.'

I apologised, and started to tell her what my father had said.

'What's going on?' Shona's mother had come down the hall.

'She says her dad won't let us visit any more because we broke a pot.'

Shona's mum looked at me. 'Is that true?'

I nodded.

'In that case, you can tell him you're no longer welcome here.' And with that she firmly shut the front door.

Well, I thought, who needs friends anyway? I stopped halfway back, not wanting to go home, but not wanting to stay out after dark either, because of the dogs. My leg and back still stung and I had a huge welt curled round one leg, thick as my thumb. The skin had broken in one or two places, and tiny droplets of blood were beginning to crust over.

I climbed into my bedroom through the window, as quietly as I could. My bedroom door was shut. On my bed were the cut-up remains of my skipping rope. I wouldn't be doing any more skipping.

Chapter 13

It was nearly Christmas. My father arranged to go sailing to the Solomon Islands with a Swedish man who owned a huge yacht. He decided he wouldn't leave me with Lidia, saying he wasn't happy about the incident with the tropical ulcers, and he was upset about the time Lidia was taking off. Sometimes after three or four days of her absence, he'd have to drive to the village and talk to her father.

Lidia would be hiding, and her brothers would be sent to find her. Her father would talk strongly to her and eventually she'd get in the car. She was no longer playful, happy Lidia. Sometimes she didn't even undo the sleeping knots in her hair. Instead of combing her hair up into a cloud around her face, she'd wrap a scarf over her head. In the past, she wouldn't have been seen dead like that. My father said it was because she was lazy and didn't want to work, and it was true she didn't have the energy she used to have.

Staying with my mother was out of the question, she'd been to visit a few times, but we always ended up fighting. I could do nothing right, either I was too grubby, or my hair wasn't combed or I was too thin. I understood she didn't like me; I wasn't a loveable child.

My father arranged to leave me with Herr Schmidt and his wife, they had a daughter, Renate, a couple of years younger than me. We were very similar, both wild creatures. I didn't need to persuade her to climb trees or explore the jungle. At times, I had trouble keeping up with her!

Her family rented a run-down villa out in the country. My father drove me there, and as I opened the car door to get out, he took my face in his hands. 'I'm going to miss you,' he said. He leaned forwards and kissed me on the mouth, forcing his tongue between my lips.

I pulled free, got out of the car, and watched him drive away. Wiping my mouth on the back of my hand, I walked up to the house. I felt that kiss all day, and didn't like the feeling.

Herr Schmidt was very strict. The living room was his domain, where he kept his books and furniture he'd brought from Germany. Mrs Schmidt only went in to dust and put fresh flowers, and it was out of bounds. At night Renate and I slept on an old couch pushed up against the wall, while her parents slept in a huge double bed.

Outside there were dozens of aviaries. Herr Schmidt was an ornithologist, he worked for the Cultural Centre and was writing a book on birds of the New Hebrides.

Renate and I were kept busy. At sunrise Mrs Schmidt would shake us awake and send us to the bathroom, where we had to use the hand pump to fill the water tank. We took turns pumping until our arms ached, taking half an hour to fill the tank. Then we'd stand in the old iron tub, turning the water off as we soaped ourselves. After breakfast we'd clean the chicken run and bring fresh eggs back for Herr Schmidt's breakfast.

After the hens had been tended to, we moved to the back of the house, cleaning out the birdcages, gathering water bowls and food containers. Renate explained how to cut up the fruit correctly, which birds ate seed, which ones needed fresh grass seeds, and we made huge batches of Farex baby food for the chicks. Everything had to be done perfectly or Renate would receive another beating. Sometimes she did anyway. That would take us till lunchtime. Renate was happy though, it took her much longer when she had to do it on her own. Then if there were no other chores we were free to wander. We'd spend the rest of the day climbing trees, catching frogs and exploring the old war bunkers. At night, we'd sit at the kitchen table reading by candlelight.

The day after Christmas we had an unexpected visitor. My mother had come down from the Banks Islands and heard where I was staying. Her car was filled with presents. We sat outside, unwrapping them while Mrs Schmidt prepared coffee. Herr Schmidt had gone back inside, after an argument with my mother. She wanted to take me to lunch at the Rossi.

'You're not taking her anywhere. She stays right here.' His voice was very firm.

'But she's my daughter, you don't have any right to stop me taking her anywhere I want.'

'Her father left me with very strict instructions you were not to have her or even see her, but as it's Christmas I'm letting you see her.'

My mother began to cry. Why had my father done that? Why did he have to hurt her like that? I remember thinking it must be awful to have to beg strangers to let you see your own daughter.

'You can cry all you like, I know what sort of a mother you are, your tears aren't going to work on me.'

Amongst the presents were two beautiful dolls, life-size baby dolls with eyes that opened and shut. I think it was the most wonderful gift Renate had ever had. She took the parcel silently and clambered up onto a crumbling wall to unwrap it. She drew the doll from the tissue paper and hugged it close, rocking back and forth on her precarious perch. I politely thanked my mother, awkward under the circumstances.

At night, before we went to bed, Mrs Schmidt would boil up a huge cauldron of water and prepare a shallow bath. Herr Schmidt was very strict about personal hygiene, insisting we brush our teeth and wash behind our ears, pulling our ears painfully to check. One night he came into the bathroom as we splashed in the warm water by the light of a hurricane lantern. 'Make sure you wash yourselves properly, I don't want any dirty little girls in my house.'

'Yes, Papa.'

He grabbed the soap and pushed it between Renate's legs. 'And make sure you wash there properly.'

I sat there hoping he wasn't going to do the same to me. He didn't; he dropped the soap and walked out of the bathroom.

So all fathers did that.

Herr Schmidt had been invited to a government function and we were dropped off at Chinese friends for the night. There weren't enough beds and I had to share with one of the boys and Renate. Renate got quite aggressive with the poor boy, kicking him, and me when I got in the way. In the end I moved into someone else's bed. They obligingly moved over in their sleep to make room.

The next day I woke up with a terrible need to go to the bathroom, and it stung like hot needles when I urinated. The stinging itch between my legs had been developing over the last couple of days and was now unbearable. I changed my underwear, but in no time at all I was soaking wet. One of the Chinese ladies must have noticed because she took me into the bathroom and made me take off all my clothes. Then she put me under the shower and gave me a new bar of soap. The perfumed soap helped to clean me, but didn't stop the thick off-yellow discharge. She took my underwear away with a pair of tongs, to burn, she said, giving me some clean underwear, and placing a thick wad of material in the crotch. No one would come near me. When Mrs Schmidt came to fetch us, the woman told me not to give the pants back, she didn't want them any more.

I was no longer allowed to wash with Renate, nor was I allowed to use the tub, I had to use the rainwater barrel outside. I couldn't understand why. There were whispered conversations around me, but I couldn't follow what they were talking about.

When my father came back, Herr Schmidt took him into his living room and shut the door. They weren't in there for very long. The next day my father took me to see a doctor, for a routine checkup, he said. I sat outside while my father and the doctor talked. Then I had to come inside and undress. I felt embarrassed because he had to look down there. The doctor said it was nothing serious. 'A short course of penicillin and you'll be right as rain.'

He was right. After a week, the symptoms had all cleared up. I asked my father what was wrong with me. 'Wrong with you? There's nothing wrong with you. This is normal for young girls when they're growing up.'

Well, that was all right then, but I still couldn't understand why the Chinese woman had behaved so strangely. There followed a period of relative calm. My father didn't beat me and seemed to be much better tempered, but once I'd finished the tablets, he began calling me to his room again.

The barometer dropped dramatically during the morning. At lunchtime, the news warned of a hurricane due to strike North Efate at around six o'clock that evening. My father drove Lidia back to her village and I skittered round the house in high excitement. I loved hurricanes. I'd experienced a couple already, though admittedly they skirted the island, lashing the land with their tails. There was something about their savageness that excited me, howling wind whipping through the trees, darkness and driving rain. I studied the barometer, thrilling as it dropped lower and the wind began to pick up.

When my father came back we nailed down the shutters, preparing for high winds. The villagers were doing the same, tying down their roofs and weighing them down with concrete blocks, while children rounded up the pigs and chickens. By the time we finished, the sky was darkening and we felt the first savage lashings of rain. I could barely stand, lifting my face to the slashing rain, luxuriating in its stinging wetness, my hair whipping around my face.

I was completely drenched. I heard my father calling me, but ignored him. The chickens and the guinea fowls had to be brought in first. I chased round in the run after the sodden birds. The guinea fowls sensed my urgency and were particularly evasive. I struggled with them, two and three at time, carrying them into my bedroom. The rising wind forced me to crawl on my hands and knees, buffeting me in all directions. As I went out for the last three, I was horrified to see the henhouse torn from the ground and sent tumbling over and over until it smashed to pieces against the side of the house.

Panicking, I hunted through the grass, half blinded by rain, searching where the run used to be. Limpy Lola had to be somewhere; although she survived the pellet attack she could only use one leg. I knew she wouldn't have gone far. I found her underneath the hibiscus hedge, flattening herself against the wind.

Violent gusts tore at the roof of the neighbour's house, worrying it like a dog worries a bone. The corrugated iron flapped wildly, straining against the ropes, the sound drowned out by the unbelievable shrieking of the gale. With Lola stuffed down my top, I clawed my way back to the house. No further trips were possible but my father said the hens would find shelter. I hoped he was right.

Garbageguts disappeared under my bed, refusing to come out. It was as though the devil himself raged outside, destroying everything in his path. Shrubs and trees were torn out by their roots and debris flew through the air. As I peered through the crack under my bedroom shutters, I saw one of my bush hens hurtling past backwards, feathers blown the wrong way round, squawking as she was swept into the bamboo clump.

The savage gusts grew stronger, shredding the huts, sending people, pigs, chickens and belongings scattering. Pieces of housing catapulted through the air, slamming into trees with sickening force. As I watched, a sheet of corrugated iron sheared straight through a telephone pole.

Villagers began arriving at our door, banging urgently to be let in to the only concrete structure for miles. The wind was so strong that despite our combined efforts, the door would crash open and blast through the house tearing at the walls, ripping down paintings and knocking over ornaments.

The house gradually filled with people and livestock. Everyone was cold, wet and distraught and children cried incessantly in the half-light of our gas lantern. We eventually ran out of dry towels and hot drinks. People huddled under blankets and prayed. My father was very kind, making tea and doing his best to bring comfort where he could, but it finally became too much for him and he went to bed. 'It'll all be over in the morning,' he said.

I stayed with the villagers, we held hands and prayed. I prayed for my two hens and all the other animals in the devil's path. I think my father was the only one who slept.

Just after dawn the wind died, leaving an awful humming stillness and a peculiar dryness to the air. We knew it wasn't over, just the eye of the hurricane passing. We pulled open the door and went outside, surveying the overwhelming devastation. Trees were stripped bare and most of the huts gone. The absolute destruction was almost impossible to comprehend.

I found my bush hen upside down in the bamboo clump. Her legs were tangled up in, of all things, a wind chime. I needed a knife to free her and while she complained bitterly, she was unharmed.

After that night, my opinion of hurricanes changed. I'd never understood the terrible havoc they could create, now I saw them for the destructive force they were. The winds returned, sweeping in the opposite direction. We were better prepared this time, using the lull to stock up at the Chinese store, thankfully still standing.

I never did find my last hen, but that wasn't surprising; people had lost everything and were hungry.

Chapter 14

My father bought me a present. 'I thought you might like to keep a diary.'

I quite liked the idea. 'Are you going to read what I write?' I asked, wondering if there was something else behind this gift.

'Of course not, a diary is private.'

That night I sat in bed, my torch balanced so I could see what I was writing, thinking that one day it'd be filled with my writing, describing events that hadn't happened yet. I underlined the date and began. I wrote about Garbageguts, my chickens and my guinea fowls. I described how I'd caught them, and how much in love they were. When my writing began to deteriorate, I decided that was enough and slipped it under my mattress. So began my first diary. I faithfully kept it up to date, writing each night. In my innocence, I wrote about everything that happened.

One day I found the 'locked' door unlocked. I knew my father wouldn't be back for several hours so I went inside. The room was in a terrible clutter with artefacts stacked against the wall and wood shavings covering the floor. As I went to look at a half-finished carving, I knocked over a pile of books. They went scattering in all directions, knocking a folder off a small table. I knelt down, hastily stacking the books. As I picked up the folder a dozen or so Polaroid photos slid out, all of naked black women. They were posing, legs spread. Some were very young, breasts only just beginning to develop. I recognised some of them. One of the photos was of Lidia, blindfolded, tied to the bed. My father must have taken it that night. I wondered if Lidia knew. I left the room, carefully brushing the sawdust from my feet.

As a special treat, my father took me to the Solomon Islands. We flew to Auki in Malaita and booked into Mrs Lum's Guesthouse. I could tell Mrs Lum didn't like my father. She fixed him with a hard stare as he signed the registry book. 'I hope you won't be bringing any girls back to your room, Mr Plaat.'

My father looked up at her, slightly annoyed. 'No, I won't, though I can't see that it's any concern of yours.'

Then she spotted me peering over the counter. 'Who's this?' she asked, smiling down at me. I stared back at her, unsmiling.

'This is my daughter, Tanja.'

We walked into the township to rent a jeep, though you could scarcely call it a township, more a collection of corrugated iron huts lining a muddy street. I stared through the dusty windows as we drove off. 'Where are we going?'

'I thought we'd go and get Ama, the girl I picked up last time. You'll like her; she's very nice. I took her back to the hotel for dinner and Mrs Lum threw her out.'

Her village was some distance away and we drove past tiny settlements in jungle clearings. They seemed stark in comparison to my village, there were no flowers, just bare, freshly-swept dirt.

Ama was lovely; she chatted incessantly. She told me she was fourteen, she'd left school and was hoping to get a job in town. She giggled about her uncle. 'He was really cross with me for going with your daddy. He wanted to throw me out but my auntie wouldn't let him.

'Where are your parents?' I asked.

'They are bush people,' she said, 'they come from the Koja tribe, many days walk through the jungle. They don't believe in God, they still worship idols.'

'Why didn't you stay there?'

'I had to go, I played too much and was too much trouble so they sent me to the mission school, so I could understand the European way, but now I don't want to go back to my village. I don't want to marry a Koja. I want to marry a white man.'

'Do you want to marry Daddy?'

At this, she rolled her huge brown eyes at my father and giggled. My father laughed as well.

'No, she can't, her uncle says she's too young to get married.'

'Oh look, a river, Ronnie,' Ama suddenly exclaimed, 'please stop, let's swim.'

We followed it for a while and came upon a group of young boys, about my age, splashing about in the water. All completely naked, they were leaping from the trees growing over the water's edge and swinging from jungle lianas.

At first they stared at me wide-eyed, then called me to join them. I didn't need a second invitation. I tugged my dress off, and started to walk towards them. My father stopped me. 'Take your underpants off.'

'I don't want to, they're boys.'

'Take them off!' His voice had an edge, I bit my lip, and

pulled them off, then ran into the water, to hide my nakedness. I quickly lost my shyness and was soon clambering up the trees with them. We got quite rough, sometimes three or four of us at a time scrambling up the lianas, until our combined weight became too great and the vines would give way. We'd all go tumbling down into the water, laughing as soon as we broke through the surface.

Ama and my father stood on the bank watching, my father taking lots of photos. After a time, he called me to come out of the water. He and Ama wanted to walk further down the river. I didn't want to leave, and my friends were disappointed.

My father told me he wanted to make love to Ama and asked me to warn them if someone came past. Ama giggled as he pulled her after him into the undergrowth. I stood, waiting in the afternoon heat, staring up and down the river, narrowing my eyes against the brightness of the sun reflecting off the white stones. No one came by.

My father came back after fifteen minutes, straightening his clothes and Ama followed a moment later. Then it was time to take her back to her village, before her uncle returned.

The next morning we drove in another direction and when we came to a clearing my father decided to park. As we walked across scrubby grass, a huge butterfly sailed past, nearly touching my cheek, and alighted on a shrub nearby. It was one of the most beautiful I'd ever seen. As it rested in the brilliant sunshine, it fluttered its wings gently, flashing a shimmering of iridescent royal blue.

My father said, 'How wonderful, they're so rare. Hang onto my camera; I'll try and catch it.' Somehow he managed, waiting until its wings were together and trapping it between his palms. It was so large even his hands weren't enough to cover it. 'Quick, get the plastic bag out of the camera bag.'

'Why? It'll die if you put it in a plastic bag.'

'This is a rare butterfly, and worth a lot of money, just hurry up and give me the bloody bag,' he snapped.

'Get the damn bag yourself,' I screamed, stamping my foot. 'If it's rare, you should let it go.'

My father stared at me, shocked at my outburst, and the butterfly escaped, swooping off over the scrub. I chased after it. 'Shoo, shoo,' I yelled, waving my arms until it sailed out of sight.

My father didn't say anything for a long time. On the way back to the hotel he started. 'I'll probably never see another one, I'll never have the opportunity to catch one and it's all your fault.'

He went on and on, until I felt like screaming, but I remained silent. I knew that if I responded he'd get really angry. Back in our room, he continued. 'Even if we go back tomorrow, it won't be there. It was my only chance to catch one.'

He kept his voice down; the louvres onto the corridor were partially open. He slammed them shut. 'You fucking little bitch, I wish I'd left you in Port Vila.'

He'd raised his voice. I felt trapped, I couldn't leave the room, where would I go? I was staring silently at the floor when he swung at me, catching me across the chest and knocking me onto one of the beds.

'Fucking bitch,' he snarled, 'you can bloody well stay here and think about what you've done.' He left the room and locked the door behind him.

I sat on the bed crying. Later, when I needed to go to the bathroom, I knocked on the louvres until I attracted someone's attention and Mrs Lum unlocked the door. After I'd been to the bathroom she asked if I was hungry. I nodded and she sent me into the kitchen for something to eat. 'On the house,' she said.

The next morning my father was quite cheerful, 'I've been thinking,' he began. 'You were right about the butterfly. It would have been wrong to kill it. I'm glad you stopped me and I'm sorry I hit you.'

We drove to Ama's village. Ama's uncle wasn't happy to see my father, but after a heated discussion agreed to let Ama come with us, with me as chaperone.

Today my father wanted to buy artefacts. Ama knew of a custom village and we drove for hours, over winding tracks snaking though dark jungle, climbing high into the hills. As we bounced and rattled along I saw birds I'd never seen before, even a toucan amongst the branches of an ebony tree.

We reached the village shortly after lunch. As we parked, dozens of children ran over, chattering excitedly and crowding round. The bravest reached out, touching my long hair. We were offered green coconuts, the cool refreshing liquid sweet as nectar after the stifling hot drive. An older man was pushed forward. He spoke English, one of the few in this village. He was beginning to grey at the temples and had very few teeth, but the kindest eyes. We exchanged greetings, shaking hands and telling the villagers where we came from. The children gathered round my father, wanting to look at his camera. He slid the strap off his shoulder and showed them how to look through it. Then my father wanted to get down to business; he didn't have all day. 'Do you have any custom?' he asked.

One of the children was sent away into one of the huts and soon came back carrying a modern carving.

My father looked it over briefly and shook his head. 'No, custom from time before.'

There was a great deal of discussion then finally the old man translated. 'Yes, we have, but not for sale. You can look if you like.'

We spent the next hour looking at their treasured heirlooms, a dolphin-tooth necklace belonging to a long-dead grandmother; a club passed down through generations, and shell money necklaces; bride price, the pride and joy of a newly married woman. 'And how much is this?' my father kept asking, ignoring their insistence that nothing was for sale. Eventually the items were put away.

I played with some of the children and later we sat in the shade of a breadfruit tree and talked. 'Your daughter is lovely to watch,' the old man told my father. 'She reminds me of a heron dancing on the reef.'

He translated what he'd said for the others and there was a lot of comment. Then he turned to me, 'We will call you Dancing Bird.' He said the word in his language, and I'm ashamed to say I only remember 'manu,' which means bird. I liked the name. Dancing Bird.

As the shadows lengthened, they invited us to stay the night; they wanted us to go fishing in the morning. All around, women fanned smoky cooking fires and began preparing the evening meal. The children and dogs chased a chicken round the village, and it became part of the meal.

The old man left us for a while and when he came back, he had a present for me. 'I won't sell you anything,' he said to my father, 'but I have a gift for your daughter. I carved it myself.'

I took the comb from his hands, thanking him. It was a traditional long-toothed comb, ebony and highly polished, delicately carved in the stylised form of a frigate bird, its long beak curving down on one side.

We all looked up at the sound of a vehicle, approaching at

breakneck speed. Two vehicles. The old man laughed, 'We don't get many visitors, and yet here are more.' But it was no laughing matter, the jeeps contained police. One of the officers got out, but stayed close to his vehicle, his hand resting on the open door. 'Mr Plaat,' he called urgently.

I was very surprised, how did they know his name? My father and Ama walked over, while I stayed next to the old man.

'What's the problem?' my father asked.

'No problem, but I want you and your daughter to get in the jeep immediately.'

'Why? What have we done wrong?'

The officer was sweating profusely and seemed ill at ease. 'You haven't done anything wrong, just get in the jeep.'

'Not until you explain what's going on.'

'Mr Plaat, please do as we ask.'

I knew it was only a short time before my father lost his temper. He didn't like being ordered about. Around me, I sensed a stirring of anger, a low muttering. At a command, all the children scurried off, filing into nearby huts. Several of the men followed and came back carrying spears and clubs. I could feel the hair prickling at the back of my neck. What was happening? Again, my father insisted they explain what was going on.

'Mr Plaat,' the officer said, 'these people are cannibals, this is no place for you to have brought your daughter, or Miss Ama.'

As soon as Ama heard the word cannibal she leapt into the jeep, shutting the door behind her. I looked at the old man. 'Are you a cannibal?' I asked, unafraid, but very curious.

'We haven't eaten anyone for fourteen years,' he explained.

That was a long time ago, before I was born. Then a thought occurred to me. 'Who did you eat?'

'Some missionaries, they moved into our village. We kept asking them to leave, and in the end we told them they had to leave by sunrise. But they told us they wouldn't leave until their God was allowed to live in our village. We didn't want that, we have our own ways, so we took our clubs and killed them dead. Then we ate them. But that was a long time ago.'

Meanwhile my father was still arguing and Ama was trying to persuade him to get in. The crowd surrounding me slowly moved towards the jeeps, and the officers started up the motors, revving them gently. I followed the old man.

The old man approached my father. 'Don't you want to go? If these people are making trouble for you, we will beat them with our clubs and send them away.'

I tugged my father's hand. 'We should go. We can come back another time.'

I don't know if it was what I said, or whether my father realised he had no choice, but he finally got into the jeep, next to Ama. I shook hands all round then clambered into the other jeep, sitting between two Solomon Island police officers.

I waved out the back until we disappeared in a cloud of thick dust. On the long drive back, I asked them how they found us. It turned out Ama's uncle had heard where we planned to go and panicked. I told them I didn't think they were going to eat us, but they weren't so sure. Cannibals were cannibals, they said. They were still anxious, and from time to time, they looked behind as though they expected to see them charging after us with their cooking pots.

Ama's uncle was furious. He sent Ama running into the house with an angry slap and forbade my father to see her again. The police officers watched, in a hurry to drop us off at Mrs Lum's so they could go home.

Over the next couple of days we drove all over Malaita buying artefacts. On the last night, my father arranged the curtains until he was certain no spying eyes could see in. Then he lay down, pulling me onto him, while I went away in my head. He'd forgotten to bring the baby oil, but even so, he managed; lifting my light form up and down until he silently came inside.

It was too late to shower, but he'd brought a roll of toilet paper into the room, so I was able to clean myself before getting into my own bed and going to sleep. We flew back to Port Vila early the next morning; leaving behind butterflies and cannibals. My comb was packed carefully in my hand luggage.

I was playing on the monkey bars at school when the elastic of my underpants caught on something between my legs, I wriggled around, freeing the pinched skin and continued with my game, but it happened again. I went into the toilets to see what was catching. Crouched over I couldn't see anything, but there seemed to be something wrong, something that hadn't been there before. That night I told my father.

He got the torch, as the light from the gas lamp wasn't bright enough. He was silent for a moment, and then he said, 'It looks like some kind of growth, you'll have to see a doctor.'

He took me over to Iririki Island to see Doctor Bouden. On the way, he warned me not to say anything about our little games. 'I'll do the talking.' I nodded. I didn't feel much like talking anyway.

Doctor Bouden had a look, and asked me many questions, but I was too scared to answer. He called my father into his surgery. 'She has vaginal warts, I've never seen them in anyone so young. She'll have to have them surgically removed, they're too large to leave.'

On the way home my father was really angry with me, he said I'd caught them because I was dirty and didn't wash my hands properly.

A few weeks later I went back into hospital. Dressed in a hospital gown, I lay on the operating table, my legs apart. Doctors and nurses in surgical masks surrounded me and someone put a mask on my face. 'Count to ten,' she said.

I counted to six and dreamt I was back at Mrs Manaham's kindergarten, taking an afternoon nap. It was so real; I lay under a red blanket and pulled off pieces of fluff until Mrs Manaham woke me up. Then I was back in hospital and all around was the murmuring of doctors. 'She's not a virgin,' said a voice.

'They start younger and younger,' said another.

I hurt between my legs, badly. They told me I wouldn't have to come back to have the stitches removed because they'd used self-dissolving ones.

At school I sat on the porch during playtime. I hurt too much to play. Everyone asked about the operation, but I remained silent. I'd been forbidden to talk about it.

Sex became more painful, the stitches tearing apart as he entered me, reopening the wound. It took a long time to heal and the scar tissue caused problems for years to come, sometimes becoming inflamed, causing agonising pain.

My father started pushing Lidia to bring girls home for him, but she refused. From time to time he brought home a tourist he picked up in town, taking them into his bedroom for a couple of hours. He said they were easy, he only had to show them the pornographic circumcision shield next to his bed and they'd be hot for it. One of them, an American, wrote to him a couple of months later to say she was having his baby, but he didn't bother to reply.

Once, three women came to visit Lidia and he took them all into his room, locking the door. Lidia sat on the steps and refused to talk to me. Afterwards he told me it was the first time he'd had sex with three women. In fact, there was a constant stream of women, but whenever there was a lull, he'd call me to his bedroom.

Amidst all this he started an affair with a woman from Lidia's village. She frequently came and stayed the night, leaving early before Lidia arrived, as she didn't want to be recognised. I liked Susanna.

One time my mother came down from the Banks Islands. He took her into his room and shut the door, later telling me he'd slept with her as well.

In mid February 1973 we moved again, just up the road. It was new and had electricity but only two bedrooms. As soon as we'd unpacked and settled the animals, my father started to build a shed next to the carport, his locked room.

I had no free time, I had to run and fetch and pass him nails and hold the wood while he sawed. I frequently got punched if things went wrong. It was a relief to go to school. As soon as the shed was ready, he decided to make a smokehouse for ageing artefacts. When that was finished we started on huge aviaries for the parrots he'd started collecting. Herr Schmidt had given him three white cockatoos from the Solomon Islands, with blue around their eyes that looked like eye shadow. He also gave my father a pair of electus parrots. They didn't look like a pair, the female was deep red and blue and the male a most beautiful shade of green.

We also made crates so we could ship the artefacts he'd sold. I became quite skilled at thinking ahead, pointing out if a piece of wood was going to be sawn in the wrong place, or wire mesh cut too short, foreseeing his needs and ensuring I had the right tools to pass to him. I was always anxious in case I overlooked something, and careful to avoid anything that would make him think about sex. Which was difficult sometimes, especially when he was screwing wood together, and he'd say, 'A screw is always better than a nail.' I'd freeze, waiting for him to suggest a screw was a good idea and take me into his bedroom.

It wasn't always possible to foresee what would make him think of sex. We were making a display cabinet for his artefacts, to hang in the Hôtel Le Lagon. When it was nearly finished, he decided the interior wood finish wasn't a good backdrop for the artefacts and bought some covering material and latex glue. He cut the material to the correct size and opened the tin, smearing the glue over the wood. 'I've had a really sexy idea,' he said suddenly. 'I think it would be really sexy to glue you down with this and screw you.'

My heart sinking, I tried to talk him out of it, pointing out that the glue was probably poisonous. He read the instructions. It didn't say anything about it being poisonous, so he smeared glue all over a sheet of plywood and made me undress and lie on it. It felt horrible.

Because of the way he glued me down, it wasn't possible for him to enter me. The more he tried the more furious he became, and finally in his frustration he knelt awkwardly over me and forced me to open my mouth. It smelt faintly of urine.

He thrust back and forth, banging at the back of my throat, while the glue tugged at my skin on my back, buttocks and limbs. He moaned in the back of his throat, 'I'm going to come, and I want you to swallow.'

I had no idea what to expect, and when he spurted into the back of my throat, I gagged at the taste and the feel. It took forever to peel me free from the glue, and all the while I wanted to cry, I wanted to wash out my mouth and I wanted a shower. But I wasn't going to cry in front of him. If I cried, he'd put his arms around me and ask, 'Why are you crying? You know I only do this because I love you.' And that would make it worse.

Sometimes it seemed as though my entire life was sex, building crates and feeding animals. It was my job to feed my father's parrots. I cleaned out the cages, rinsed and refilled the water bowls and distributed the fruit and seeds. Then I had to feed my chickens and guinea fowls and make sure Garbageguts had enough to get her through the day. I'd go through the whole procedure again when I came back from school. I was no longer free to go to Colardo's plantation, with everything I had to do for my father, I didn't have time. My tree-climbing days were over and I sorely missed them.

Chapter 15

My diary was nearly full, I still faithfully recorded everything and hid it under the couch cushions in the living room. One day I came home to find my mother sitting stony faced on the couch, holding my diary. I snatched it from her, 'That's mine!'

'How dare you,' she screamed, 'how dare you write that I look ugly!'

I'd written a few days earlier that I thought she looked tired and her hair wasn't as tidy as usual. Looking back now, at all the things I'd written, it amazes me this was the only entry she read. If she'd turned one page back, she'd have read about the latex glue. Would that have made a difference to my life?

I told my father about her visit and how angry she was about what I'd written. 'Let me see your diary,' he said. He read the entire diary. 'We have to burn this. It's too private. It wouldn't be a good idea for people to read it, they would get the wrong idea.'

I watched, as the curling flames devoured everything I'd

painstakingly recorded. I couldn't understand why he had to burn it. It was a private diary, who was going to read it?

Port Vila was full of talk of the impending visit of the Queen of England. She would be stopping over for a couple of days, staying aboard her yacht. The Resident Commissioner came to visit my father. He told us the Queen had expressed an interest in seeing a rare angelfish, apparently tropical fish were one of her hobbies. We hunted through our books and found the fish she wanted to see. It was yellow with a black circle on each side and we remembered seeing them swimming off Lelepa Landing. We were asked to catch a couple and given several police officers to assist.

We snorkelled round for nearly an hour until I spotted a pair hiding under some coral. Six of us circled the coral outcrop with the tangle net slowly closing in. When the enclosed area was about a metre across, I was lowered in over the net. The fish watched me, their delicate fins frilling in the gentle current. I was careful not to startle them, I didn't want them to go crashing into the coral in panic, injuring themselves.

All the while, the men shouted advice and encouragement. I ignored them, concentrating on the fish, moving so slowly they soon got bored watching me and started swimming around, brushing against each other. Then my hands shot forwards and I trapped one between my palms. I stood up and the men realised they'd forgotten the container. I crouched back down, keeping my hands underwater while one of the officers splashed back to the beach. I deposited the first fish carefully in the bucket and then set about catching its mate, and after a few minutes it was also in the bucket.

We caught the launch over to the Resident Commissioner's house. I wanted to see the Queen when she came, but the Resident Commissioner told me children couldn't come to the reception.

My father came home hugely excited. 'I'm bringing a Chinese girl home tonight, I want you to stay in your bedroom. She works at the cinema, and I'm picking her up during the movie, so her boyfriend doesn't find out. Her boyfriend wrecked his motorbike and he wasn't insured properly. She said I could sleep with her if I paid the claim.'

I went to my room as soon as I saw his headlights turning into the drive. I was woken later when my light was switched on. I peered over at the door, where my father stood, behind him I caught a glimpse of the Chinese girl. I'd seen her before, she was about seventeen and very beautiful, but she looked nervous.

'Have you got a comb?' he asked. 'She needs to straighten her hair.'

I ran to the bathroom, gave my ebony comb to my father, and went back to bed. Behind me, I heard her soft voice as she stood in front of the hall mirror. 'It's a lovely comb.'

'If you like it, it's yours,' my father said, 'you can keep it as a memento.'

I was stunned. That was my comb.

My father and I were sitting at a table outside, and I was noisily sucking the last of my coke. 'Who's that?' he asked, pointing over at children playing on the swings. 'The girl in the jeans.'

'Oh her, just a girl in my class.'

'She's very beautiful, don't you think?'

I shrugged my shoulders. I hadn't really thought about it, but I suppose Diana was beautiful, her long ash blonde hair stark against lightly tanned skin.

'Is she a friend of yours?'

'Not really, I don't have any friends.'

He didn't say anything more and we left shortly afterwards.

My father bought a new Polaroid camera, an SX70, and on the weekend, while he was having sex, he stopped to go and get it. He re-entered me and took a photo of us. Just down there. He held the photo, waving it back and forth waiting for the picture to develop. Gradually the colours filled the white frame and he showed it to me; another picture joined the others in my mind.

A snapshot I will never forget. My hands were on my thighs as he'd arranged them, his dark pubic hair contrasting against the smoothness of my immature body. The sharp focus of the camera caught the diamond pattern of my gold ring and all the swollen veins of his penis, only half inside me. I guess it joined the other photos in his locked room.

On Sunday, he suggested I invite Diana to come and play. I was surprised, and a little shy about going to her house. 'Don't be silly, she'd probably love to.'

So began another friendship. On Wednesdays we'd walk to the movies and I stayed over at her house several times. She usually spent Sunday at my house, we'd play for hours in my room, reading comics and talking. Once we dressed up in some of my father's native grass skirts. When he saw us he told us it looked silly with our underpants on, so we took them off. We went up to Diana's house to show her mother, she wasn't impressed and threatened us with her wooden spoon if we didn't immediately rectify the situation.

When Diana slept over at my house we'd climb out my bedroom window, exploring the darkness and pretending we were white witches. Then we'd sneak back indoors and have midnight feasts. She loved coming to my house, we could do anything we wanted, and nobody complained about the mess.

I liked going to her house for exactly the opposite reasons. I guess the grass is always greener on the other side of the fence.

One Saturday my father suggested that the next day we go for a picnic and a swim at Eton beach. We set off shortly after ten. It was one of those glorious tropical days, clear blue skies, with only a few fluffy clouds. The limpid turquoise water beckoned, and we scurried down the powder-white sand and leapt in. My father sat on a rock watching as we frolicked in the waves; a thousand rainbows around us as the sun caught the water we splashed at each other.

My father wanted to go for a walk and called us to join him. He had his camera bag over his shoulder and we followed him along the path. Here and there, huge pink flowers lay on the ground. Picking one up, I twirled it under my nose, hundreds of stamens tickling me as I breathed in the soft sweet perfume.

Diana and my father were walking ahead. I hadn't been listening, but now I became aware they were talking about my mother. 'She used to be a famous model.'

'She must have been very beautiful.'

'Oh, yes, that's why I married her. But you're beautiful too, you could be a model when you grow up.'

'I could never be a model!'

'Of course you could, it's not so difficult, I could show you a few things if you like. You could pretend to be a model and I could take some photos of you.'

I didn't hear her reply, I'd spotted a piece of tunnel coral and was concentrating on brushing the sand out.

'Well,' my father continued, 'I take very good photographs and the light's perfect here. Don't move, I'll take a photo of you just like that.'

Diana stood still as he opened his camera bag and took the

camera out. 'That's good, really good, just move your chin a little higher ... perfect. Now look into the camera; give me a sexy look. Perfect, you're a born natural!' All the time he was talking, he was snapping shots. 'Now one with the two of you, come here Tanja.'

I stood next to Diana as he peered through the lens. 'Perfect Diana, just turn your face a little, excellent. Tanja, you can do better than that, why can't you pose like Diana? Try putting your arm around her shoulder.'

I slid my arm around her shoulder and we stood waiting for him to take the shot. 'No, the light's changed, it's no good. I have an idea, go over to that tree and hug it.'

Diana and I giggled but we clung onto the tree trunk while he took several more photos and then suggested we walk a little further along the track. We came to a grassy bank and he told us to lie down. 'No, it's not quite right,' he said. 'You'll both have to take your swimsuits off. That would be the most amazing photograph.' Diana wasn't so sure that was a good idea.

'Don't be silly, I'm not going to take pornographic photos, I'm an artist! I only take beautiful photographs, you'll see for yourself when they're developed. I guess you're too young to understand the difference between pornography and art.'

He was most persuasive and I knew better than to dissuade him, so I drew off my swimsuit, as did Diana. We lay together in the hot sun while he moved round posing us, brushing Diana's hair away from her face, moving a twig that detracted from the composition. He took about ten shots of us lying there.

The sun burned down and it was a relief when my father finally suggested we move into the shade. He wanted us to climb onto a low hanging branch, still naked, and sit hugging each other. Sunlight dappled between the leaves, and he said the effect on our bodies would be stunning.

We climbed up and sat on the branch. He took a few more photos and when Diana insisted, we returned to the beach to eat lunch and cool down.

Chapter 16

G od answered my prayers, just as Opa said he would. My father fell in love. Her name was Moira. He couldn't eat, couldn't sleep and best of all he left me alone.

Moira was about twenty-four, with thick curly ginger hair that reached her bottom. I adored her – she'd grown up in Santo and in some ways we shared the same wild streak. She had a Zodiac and we spent weekends on the water, fishing, swimming and exploring the coast. She was always laughing, smiling and putting her arms around me. Within a couple of months Moira was pregnant. We met her parents and although her father was a little reserved about her new living arrangements, Jean welcomed us warmly and became my grandmother. In my heart she still is.

Although my father was in love with Moira, he still spent time with Susanna. Not as often as before, because it was a little difficult to meet her without Moira finding out.

Lidia left us and I rarely saw her again. I missed her terribly. Moira replaced her with an older woman. Because Moira was allergic to cat hair, Garbageguts was banned from the house. This didn't stop me sneaking her in through my bedroom window and she became very proficient at lying flat under the covers if someone came into my room.

As 1973 slowly drew to a close, I sat the primary school leaving exam. My father told me it was important I passed the exams with distinction, it was the only way I'd get into the local British Secondary School, or BSS. I only half listened – I knew I didn't have a chance.

I told my Opa one night, worried about what would happen if I failed. He cupped my chin in his shadowy hands and told me not to worry, he'd be there to help.

The day of the exams finally arrived. I was apprehensive as I sat in the exam room, the walls bare apart from a large clock. The examiner came in and walked round the room, issuing new pens and lying the exam papers face down on our desks.

I was so nervous I kept wiping my sweaty hands on my jeans. The room seemed to be overly bright, noises too loud. Finally, he said, 'Turn your papers over.'

I turned the sheets of paper over and began to read. Once I could get the print in focus, I froze. I didn't know any of the answers. How was I to know when Columbus discovered America? I'd never heard of him. All around me my classmates were ticking boxes, heads bent with concentration. What was I going to do? Then I heard my Opa talking to me in my head. 'It's all right, I'm here.' Together we read the questions and he told me which box to tick. We completed it with half an hour to spare.

One night, when Moira was about three months pregnant, she went out for the evening. A friend of hers was getting married the next day. While she was out, two women from Pango village arrived at our kitchen door asking for my father and the three of them drove off in his car. The next day I managed to get him alone. 'What did those women want?' I asked.

'They took me to see Susanna, she's pregnant and they wanted me to take part in a ceremony. I think she wants me to be the father.'

'Are you the father?'

'I doubt it, Susanna sleeps around, anyone could be the father.'

I was surprised; I'd always thought her to be very shy and modest.

I was still firm friends with Diana and would often go to her place after I'd finished my chores. She didn't come round to my house very often, and had sworn me to secrecy about the photos, afraid her mother would find out. She'd been in serious trouble when her mother discovered she had a sunburnt bottom and covered up by saying we'd been sunbathing in the nude. Just the two of us.

When the holidays finally arrived and I left primary school we spent even more time together. However, it wasn't for much longer. Her parents were sending her to school in New Zealand. I was staying in Port Vila, I'd been accepted by BSS. When my school-leaving certificate arrived I was stunned. I'd received ones in all four subjects. The exams were graded one to six with one being excellent and six, well, six meant really bad.

Yes, those were wonderful times, but all good things have to come to an end. Isn't that how the saying goes? I woke late one night with a sharp pain between my legs and my father lying heavily on me. I struggled beneath him, trying to push him off in my panic. 'Moira will come in,' I pleaded.

'It's all right,' he said, 'she's gone to visit friends, she won't be back for hours.'

When he'd finished, he left me alone in the darkness with his stickiness. I didn't get up and wash as I normally did. I lay there amongst the tangled sheets, my world dissolving around me. I'd nearly forgotten that part of my life. He hadn't touched me for months and I truly believed it was over. I knew it wasn't right. I was betraying Moira. After that night, every time Moira went out he came into my room. I began sleeping under my bed, pulling the pillows and bedding into the narrow space beneath.

When Moira became heavily pregnant she no longer went out in the evenings and my father bought a foam-rubber mattress, which he kept in the boot of the car. 'For picnics,' he told her. He put it there so he could take me to Malapoa Point, to a piece of land he'd bought. I hated going for drives with him; I hated getting into the car waving a cheery goodbye, knowing where we were going, and why.

Moira's parents also bought land there, further up the hill, where they were building a house. One afternoon after the builders left he carried the mattress into the half-finished building. He told me it was a really sexy idea, knowing we were the first ones to have sex in the house. I hated it, and when the house was finally finished, the ghosts of that memory followed my every footstep.

My mother and Maurice were now living in a house at Mele Beach and Moira encouraged me to visit, it gave her time alone with my father. At first I really enjoyed it. I think my mother did as well, she'd taken up painting, and we'd sit outside with our easels and oil paints, sharing companionable silences as we worked. I entered a painting competition, held by the Cultural Centre. The subject was 'Your House'. I painted my mother's house, surrounded by jungle and pandanus trees. I ran out of canvas, but my mother found a piece of plywood and I used that. It had a crack running halfway down one side, and I incorporated that into the painting, using it to accentuate a branch. I was overwhelmed when I came first, sure someone had made a mistake. My father confiscated the painting and the certificate and put it in his locked room. That way it wouldn't be damaged, he told me.

My father became more and more bad-tempered with me. One day when we drove back to the house he started shouting; I can't remember what I'd done wrong. As we pulled into our drive I shouted back, I couldn't contain myself any more. He punched me furiously across the chest. I yanked open the front door, crying loudly, and raced for my bedroom.

I was horrified to see we had company. Our friend Alastair began to get up to greet me, then he saw my tears. As I rushed out of the room, I heard Moira apologising. I sat in my room crying, listening to my father tell Moira and Alastair what a complete bastard I was, his words hurting more than his blows.

I would have liked to talk to Alastair. Many years before, when he'd been living in Port Vila, he'd painted a life-size portrait of me. I stood for hours in his attic, which smelt heavily of oil paints and turpentine, in a new blue dress while he sketched. It was stuffy and hot, the sun burning through the skylight. He talked all the while and I decided I liked him. I certainly liked the way he painted, his colours dabbed on thickly. After four hours of standing in that stuffy room, I fainted. I woke up with Alastair splashing water on my face. He was most gentle and terribly concerned but I was fine after a drink of water.

The finished painting was striking. Although it was impressionistic, it could only have been me. I stood against a blood red backdrop, a yellow balloon hovering over my head and later, when it hung in the Hôtel Rossi, I heard people arguing that it represented the sun.

But it was my eyes that caught the most attention. They watched you, following your every move. Eventually they took it down because people complained about the eyes. I heard one woman criticising the painting at the original showing. 'It's supposed to be a painting of a child, whoever saw eyes like that in a child?' Then she turned and looked at me, she knew I was the subject of the painting.

I think I unnerved her, she looked back at the painting and muttered to her companion that Alistair had caught a certain something.

Chapter 17

One day I saw my father working on something in the carport. He was taking the metal eyes off the end of a fibreglass fishing rod. 'What are you doing?' I asked.

'I'm preparing a stick to beat you with. I'm sick of your attitude and I'm going to beat it out of you. It's about time you had some discipline.' I stared at him, his tone was level, as though we were talking about the garden. He didn't seem to be joking.

He wasn't. The following Saturday, when I was playing with Garbageguts, I heard him screaming for me. I ran to the carport, where he was standing in front of the parakeet cage. 'What have I told you about playing around before you've fed the animals?' His face was apoplectic. In his hand, he held the fibreglass rod.

My stomach tightened. 'But I did feed them, I gave them fresh pawpaw, you can ask Moira.'

He grabbed me by my hair and shoved my face against the cage. 'You fucking liar, anyone can see they haven't been fed, there's no food in their cage! I warned you about your bloody attitude.'

I couldn't understand it, I really had fed them, Moira had helped me cut up the pawpaw. Nevertheless, there was no fruit in the cage.

He slashed at my legs and I howled in pain. It was worse than I could imagine. I'll never forget the sound of the fishing rod whipping through the air while the parakeets shrieked in their cage. I crawled on my hands and knees towards the kitchen door, howling and screaming the whole time, and still he kept beating me, slashing my back and buttocks. I could hear Moira washing the dishes. I tried to stand up, covering my face, begging him to stop.

He hit me so hard he shattered a clamshell bracelet I was wearing. He went berserk, his face scarlet with rage. 'You fucking bitch! That was really rare. I'll never be able to get another one!' He lashed me with all his strength and I staggered to my feet and pulled away, running around the house, my body on fire. He ran after me, but I streaked out of the garden and went tearing up the neighbour's driveway, looking for help. I decided to climb the wall between our homes and get to my room before my father. Then I could lock the door.

I ran amongst a family standing in their carport, someone doing laundry, the tubs filled with soapy water. I sprang up, trying to get over the wall. Someone tried to pull me back, offering to help, but I was too terrified. I scrambled free and leapt over the wall into the laundry tub on our side. My feet were soapy and I slipped on the smooth surface, smashing onto the ground, smacking my head on the concrete. I saw stars and everything went black. Then my father was on me again, screaming abuse, beating me for the parrots, for the bracelet and for running away.

Above: Me, aged around two months, with my mother.

Below: My father, Ronald van der Plaat, Wellington, 1961. (*Courtesy of Ans Westra*)

Above: The *Lolita* photo. (*Courtesy of Ans Westra*)

Below: My mother and I at a family gathering in Holland in 1963.

Me aged eight.

Above: Our first house in Port Vila, Vanuatu.

Inset: One of the photos taken of me swimming with other children in a river in the Solomon Islands.

Below: Me and my maternal grandmother, on a visit to Holland in 1976. The photo in the background on the left is of my Opa.

Above: The house my father was renting when we were deported from Vanuatu.

Below left: Me on the 'balcony'.

Below right: At Pango Point, Vanuatu.

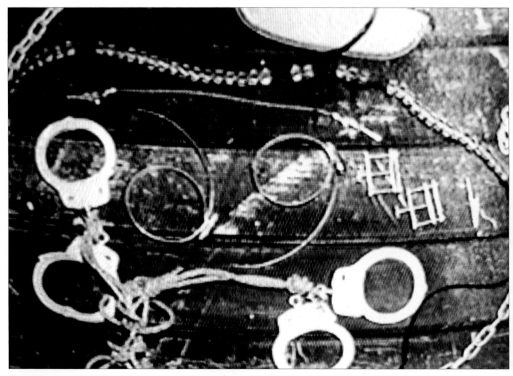

Above: Some of the items found during a police search of my father's house.

Below left: My father and I in New Caledonia.

Below right: At Eton Beach, Vanuatu, in the early 1980s.

Above left: Bill and I were married in Auckland on 24 April 1994.

Above right: On that fateful Sunday walk with Bill when we talked about flying free among the clouds.

Below: Demonstrating my gem-cutting skills at a trade fair in Germany in 1998.

Contemplating the future, in Bora Bora.

Moira swung open the screen door. 'That's enough, Ronald, stop it.'

He didn't stop, he'd gone mad, I finally curled up in a ball and covered my head with my arms trying to protect myself. I didn't scream any more, I couldn't, the pain was too bad; I thought he was going to kill me. Eventually he stopped, kicking me before he walked away.

The beating had gone on for more than half an hour; he'd even cracked the glass of my watch. I lay curled up for a few minutes, agony wracking my body, half expecting him to come back. However, he'd gone into his locked room, and I heard the key turn in the lock.

I staggered to my feet, dizzy with pain. Once I was in my room I locked the door and collapsed on the bed. My body was covered with raised welts, criss-crossed over each other, broken skin leaking blood. I counted more than fifty on my legs and arms; I couldn't count the ones on my back or bottom. I was on fire with every move, but the worst pain came from my little fingers, swollen to twice their normal size.

At around six Moira knocked on my door. 'You can come out if you want. Your father isn't angry with you any more.' I refused. I didn't want to see him. A few moments later she returned with a meal. I opened the door a crack, expecting a trap. She stood there, with a bowl of spaghetti bolognaise. I took it from her and locked myself back in my room.

The next time we went to the beach, he wouldn't let me go swimming. I sat in my jeans and long-sleeved blouse while they walked along the beach picking up shells. He said it was too windy to go swimming. I knew it was because he didn't want her to see the bruises. They'd begun to fade, and were flecked with yellow, but they were still obvious. I had to wear jeans and long sleeves all week.

My hens stopped laying; Moira said it was because they were getting old. I thought it was because they weren't happy in their tiny run and persuaded my father to let them roam the garden. At night I'd round them up and lock them in. The guinea fowls stayed loose, flying up into the treetops to roost and making it very clear they weren't going back in the run.

Shortly after Christmas I woke up to the guinea fowls making the most horrific racket. I ran outside to find the male on the roof, wings spread out, making a noise that could've been heard miles away. I hunted high and low, but I couldn't find the female anywhere. The neighbour called out to me over the fence. 'Are you looking for your guinea fowl? I think Man Mosu has it, he was in your garden a while ago.'

Man Mosu was the nickname we gave to the local odd-job man. He was sly and no one really trusted him, but he was very pushy and sometimes it was easier to employ him for a day than to try to send him away.

My heart froze. If Man Mosu had my guinea fowl, chances were she was already dead. When my father heard what had happened we drove to Man Mosu's village. We found him sitting outside his hut, with my guinea fowl. She was still alive, but he'd already plucked her. I stared in horror at the naked bird, lying on the ground surrounded by her feathers, beak open, gasping in terror. After a heated exchange, Man Mosu gave her back. She didn't make it home – she gave a final gasp and died shortly after we got into the car.

We buried her under the banana tree. All the while the male shrieked from the top of the roof, flapping his wings and twisting his head from side to side in his anguish. He kept it up for three days and three nights, calling for his mate. On the fourth day, he fell off the roof, stone dead. I buried him with her, under the banana tree, hoping they'd be happy in heaven.

Chapter 18

In February 1974, I started secondary school. Not long afterwards my father flew to Australia. When he came back he smuggled two Major Mitchell parrots in his briefcase, but one had died. He was in a terrible rage, screaming about the taxi driver. Both parrots had been fine when he landed, and he'd caught a taxi, putting the briefcase on the back seat while he went to collect his suitcases. When he came out the taxi had gone. Another driver told him the first taxi had taken a passenger to the Hôtel Le Lagon. They chased after him, finally catching up with them in town. He snatched the briefcase back and opened it, but the male had suffocated.

She was beautiful, pink and white, preening herself on the edge of my bed. The next day he cut off the dead bird's wing and posted it to the pet shop, saying the parrot died two days after arriving in Port Vila and he wanted a refund. In due course, he received a cheque for three hundred and fifty dollars.

That weekend we built her a large cage; it took up about a third of my bedroom. My father named her Fred. Within a few weeks she'd made a large hole in the wire, where she'd sit whenever she wanted attention. Sometimes she'd fly out and sit next to me while I was reading. We'd sit together, sharing sunflower seeds and almonds. From time to time she'd waddle backwards to the edge of the bed, lift her tail and poop on the floor. Occasionally she'd sit on my shoulder, preening my hair.

We didn't go out in Moira's Zodiac any more. When she was three months pregnant she'd gone off for the day and my father went half-crazy, certain she'd decided to have an abortion. She came home well after dark. As she walked up the gravel path, my father flew out the door screaming at her. 'Where the hell have you been?'

Moira laughed, 'I went out in the Zodiac.'

'Are you completely crazy?' my father yelled, 'You're pregnant – the time for gallivanting around is over.'

Moira stood defiantly in front of him, not realising how angry he was. 'I'll go out whenever I please. You're not my master.'

'You damn well will not,' he snarled and grabbed her by the shoulder. Moira struggled to free herself as he belted her several times on her behind.

'Don't you ever hit me again,' she yelled.

'Then don't be so bloody selfish,' my father retorted.

The boat was sold a couple of days later.

At 6pm on 19 May 1974 Moira felt the first contraction, both of us running to the bedroom when we heard her call out and an hour later they left for the French Hospital. Just after two my father came home. I woke up when he came into the room, turning on the light. 'You have a brother,' he said. 'He was born at ten to one, he was completely blue, he had the umbilical cord around his neck, so they've put him in an incubator.'

I wanted to know when I could see him, and he promised to take me the next day, then he left, turning off the bedroom light. I was nearly asleep when he returned. He took longer than usual. I went away in my head, thinking about my new brother.

The next day we drove to the French Hospital and I saw my brother for the first time. He was so tiny, so adorable. They didn't name him for a week, debating for hours while he kicked and gurgled in his cot. Names flew back and forth, from the common to the ridiculous. In the end, Moira flung herself down on the bed and picked up the book she was reading, Captain James Cook in the Pacific. As she turned the pages, my father and I kept thinking of new names. My brother stared at us through the bars of his cot, happily sucking his fists. Suddenly Moira looked up. 'What about James?'

'James, what ... like James Cook?' exclaimed my father. 'Absolutely not.'

In the end, they compromised and my brother was named Ronald-James. Susanna's son was born a few days later and she named him Robert.

Moira found me a job babysitting on Saturday afternoons, for the postmaster's sons. Their mother had died and their normal babysitter couldn't come on Saturdays. They were adorable, and very well behaved.

I read to them, played hide and seek and helped them with their railway set. Sometimes they'd ask me if I knew their mummy, and did I think she was happy in heaven? I'd tell them she was very happy and could see them from heaven.

One Saturday I heard a car pull up into the drive. I wasn't expecting anyone, and putting Matthew down, I walked over to the window and pulled the curtain back. It was my mother and I could tell from her face she was going to make a scene.

I ran to the door, telling the boys to stay indoors. I walked down the wooden steps towards her. 'I've just been given the date of the divorce and I wanted you to be the first to hear,' she spat, not giving me time to speak. 'I tried to arrange it for your birthday, so you'd never forget you're the bastard who broke up my marriage.' She paused for breath. 'But the closest they could give me was 2 October. Remember that date, you little bastard, the day your parents are getting divorced.'

She stepped towards me and I turned and fled up the steps. My hands were trembling so much I could barely turn the key in the lock. What if she tried to break in? What would I do with the children? What would their father say if he found out? I stood there, not knowing what to do, and finally burst into tears.

My mother got her wish – I'll never forget the day my parents were divorced. I had to go to court while they fought over me. Neither of them wanted me, they just didn't want the other to have me. My father won; he carefully coached me in what I was to say to the judge and secretly paid my mother's lawyer to work against her. I was awarded to my father; my mother had no access at all. My mother walked up to the judge and slapped him across the face. He did nothing, saying he understood she was under a lot of stress.

My father went to Holland to visit his family as his mother had cancer. He also flew to England to see my half-brother Richard and his mother, but Moira didn't know that and I wasn't going to tell her.

While he was gone, Moira gave my chickens away. I was stunned when I came back from school to find the run empty. 'Where are my chickens?' I screeched as I raced into the house.

'I gave them to the Wilsons, I was fed-up with the noise. It was your father's idea.'

I cried for hours, they'd been part of my life for nearly five years and I didn't even have the opportunity to say goodbye.

My father returned laden with presents. My Oma had bought me the most adorable stuffed toy, a beautiful white fluffy cat, with huge blue eyes. She also gave my father her diamond engagement ring to give to me, for when I married. My father wouldn't let me keep it, he said I'd lose it. He gave Moira a beautiful necklace and James was lavished with toys. He also smuggled in four tiny turtles.

He bought a deep green bath with a few chips in its finish, part of an insurance claim. We set it up in the garden and filled it with water, putting a large rock in the middle for the turtles to sunbathe on.

James had begun to crawl and they decided to move him into my room, putting his cot at the end of my bed. Garbageguts was permanently banned, yowling for weeks under my window. At night when James woke, I'd go into the kitchen, make up his milk formula and feed him, letting Moira sleep. Fred was also moved out of the house, and I spent another weekend passing the hammer and nails, as we constructed another aviary.

It was a very lonely time. When I returned home from school I'd eat dinner and then go into my room. I'd sit alone on my bed and listen to them playing with James. If I went to sit with them, silence would fall and Moira would ask if I had any homework. When it was James' bedtime, Moira carried him into my room and tucked him up in his cot, gurgling and cooing, rarely looking in my direction. I was practically forgotten, except when Moira went out and my father came into my room.

One night I heard her talking with my father. 'She should go to boarding school. We need to have our own life, and I don't have time to be looking after her.'

That really hurt, not that I'd be going to boarding school, in a way I was quite excited by the prospect. I didn't think about it in terms of escaping from what was happening to me, it didn't seem something I could escape from. I was hurt that my father was willing to send me away. Why was I such an unlovable child? I'd lost everyone I loved. My mother, Lidia, even Moira had turned against me and now my father. I guess he didn't need me any more; he had Moira and James.

The next morning he took me for a drive. 'Moira wants to send you to boarding school,' he began.

'I know.' It had gradually dawned on me that he couldn't come into my room if I was in another country.

'Well, I can't afford it. Moira takes all my money and I'm already having trouble paying your fees at BSS. When she talks to you about it, say you don't want to go overseas. Do you understand?' I nodded, a little regretfully. My father noticed my expression. He put his arm over my shoulder. 'You don't want to go away and leave me all alone, do you? It's hard enough having to put up with Moira and her nagging all the time.' I shook my head. 'Then you'd better be convincing, otherwise I'll have to send you away from all your animals. Who would take care of them? You know Moira hates your cat.'

I thought about that and decided to be convincing. Sometimes I could be really stupid. Moira and I ended up having a screaming match. I stalked into my room, slamming my door, shaking with anger as I heard my father telling her not to get so upset, it was probably all just hormones, after all I was fourteen now.

Moira and my father were drifting apart. Moira went out

dancing with her girlfriends and I'd look after James. On Sundays he no longer wanted to go swimming or fishing, instead he'd sit in his locked room, carving. Moira began going to the beach with James, but she never asked me to come.

One particular Sunday, I was in the kitchen, making myself a Milo milkshake as she left. As soon as her car turned out of the drive, my father came into the kitchen. 'Come into the bedroom.'

I knew what he wanted. 'No.'

He ignored me and pulled me into his room, pushing me onto the double bed.

I sat up. 'No,' I said, 'I don't want to. Moira could come back.'

'She won't be back for hours, take your pants off.'

Something strange had been happening in my head. I think the idea of boarding school, the opportunity to stop what was happening, had been circulating in my mind. It gave me strength to refuse him. 'No,' I said again, 'I won't.'

It was as though I'd said nothing. He pushed me back on the bed and tugged my pants off. 'I'll be very quick, just count to ten.' He pulled his jockeys down around his knees and smeared baby oil all over his swollen penis. I shut my eyes. It would soon be over.

'What the hell is going on here?' Moira stood in the doorway, the image of her standing with my baby brother on her hip, her face contorted with shock and anger, burned into my mind for eternity. My father stood stock-still, total shock on his face, the plastic bottle of baby oil in one hand and his penis in the other. He whipped his pants up and I fled from the room, pushing past Moira.

I hid in my room as they screamed at each other. 'Just explain what the hell was going on!' Moira shrieked, nearly hysterical.

'What did you think was going on?' My father lowered his voice, to a calming, even tone. 'Surely you don't think ... how could you even think that of me?'

'But I saw you,' Moira yelled. 'You had your penis out!'

'Don't be silly,' he said, his voice still calm, 'you must have had the sun in your eyes, I had the baby oil in my hands. Tanja asked me to look at some sores, I was just putting some oil on her.'

'Why didn't she ask me to look?' she asked, lowering her voice, grasping at this opportunity to be mistaken.

'Come off it, she hates you. How could she turn to you about something so personal?'

I didn't hate her, but how was she to know? He'd efficiently turned the tables to his advantage. It amazed me he could be so convincing, and that Moira could be so gullible. Then there was silence and my father came into my room. I scrambled back on my bed. 'It's all right, she's gone shopping, she'll be back shortly.'

I felt relief flooding through me; I'd been terrified Moira would leave, then I'd have to have sex all the time.

When Moira returned she came into my room and hugged me. 'It's all right, Tanja,' she whispered as she rocked me back and forth. 'I'm not going to leave.'

The next day Moira went to the pharmacy and bought some medication and told me I had to douche myself twice a day.

A few days later she moved James out of my room, angry with me for changing his nappy the night before. He'd woken me with his crying; when I went to see what the matter was, I found he'd soiled his nappy. Moira said I was interfering with his sleep patterns. I remained silent, thinking it was the other way round. But there was no point in arguing.

Chapter 19

The thought of boarding school opened doors in my mind to the idea of escape from my private hell. When Moira saw us, I thought my father would stop, believing he'd had such a fright he'd never touch me again. What foolish ideas children have. Within a week he drove me out to his piece of land and the doors in my mind slammed firmly shut. I was now fourteen and sometimes it seemed too terrible to deal with, the secrets, the beatings and the loneliness.

While the court denied my mother access, legally things were quite lax in the New Hebrides. She insisted on seeing me and my father made no effort to stop her. I resolved to tell her what he was doing the next time she came to pick me up. As we drove through the main street, I began telling her about Moira walking in on us. I didn't get very far.

She slammed on the brakes. 'What are you telling me?' she shrieked. I thought she was angry with me for saying something against my father. Cars behind us began tooting, and I couldn't finish what I'd begun.

I felt more and more awkward, so I shrugged and said, 'Nothing, nothing at all.' I'd been foolish to talk to her, taking a terrible risk, if she was that angry she'd tell him and the fishing rod was more than I could bear.

I woke late one morning, burning hot with a splitting headache, and went to find my father; he was still in bed. Moira and James were away for the day. 'I don't feel well,' I said, close to tears.

He reached over and felt my head. 'You have a temperature, you'd better get into bed.' I climbed in, moving carefully. My whole body ached and the fever was starting to make me feel lethargic. He put his arm over my shoulder. 'What would make you feel better?'

'I want to see my mother.' I'd visited her a few times over the last couple of months, and things had improved between us.

He agreed to take me, but only if I'd have sex. He ran his hands over my stomach, his erection pressing against my hip. 'You look so sexy, your skin is so pink.' I looked down at my body, which was flushed with fever. It had betrayed me again. He rolled on top of me, reaching for the baby oil, and as he entered, he groaned. 'This is such a sexy feeling, you're so hot down there.'

Afterwards he drove me to Mele Beach. My mother and Maurice took one look and decided I should see a doctor, Maurice suggesting I might have dengue fever. My father refused to accept I was that ill, but they insisted and we drove to the French Hospital.

My temperature was 40°C. The doctor stood in front of me, 'Does it hurt when you move your eyes?' I nodded. 'And do you feel nauseous?' I shook my head, then promptly threw up. Maurice had been right, I had dengue fever.

I spent six days in hospital and it was nearly two weeks before I returned to school. A glass wall surrounded me. No one could see or touch it, but I knew it was there, surrounding and isolating me, dulling the sounds of the world, fading the colours. Nothing could touch me any more. I rarely cried, not even when Moira took Garbageguts to the vet and had her put to sleep. I had no more tears.

The rainy season brought a new era of terror. One night my father shook me awake, outside I could hear a torrential downpour. 'Go and check the turtles, the bath might overflow.'

Still half-asleep I stumbled in the darkness to the bath, which was overflowing. I felt round in the cold water for the plug, rain streaming into my eyes. My fingers closed on the chain and I tugged it out. As the water level dropped, I frantically searched for the turtles, feeling blindly through the water, desperate to feel their shells. Over and over, I only counted two.

Eventually I had to tell my father. He told me to go back and not come in until I'd found them. I found a torch and searched for hours. It would have been a miracle if I found them; they were only three centimetres across. Finally, cold, exhausted and too afraid to return indoors, I slept on the side steps.

My father found me in the morning. I wasn't allowed to go to school until I found them. I spent a week walking around the neighbourhood, asking everyone if they'd seen a turtle. When I returned empty-handed on the second day, my father took the fibreglass fishing rod to me, to teach me a lesson for being so irresponsible. This beating was even more savage than the last.

On Friday, there was a knock on our door. A New Hebridean stood there, one of the turtles balanced upside down on a piece of plywood. I was overjoyed, but my father said if I hadn't been so stupid, it would never have wandered off in the first place. The other turtle was found two days later and I was allowed back to school.

But that wasn't the end of the turtle saga. Every night I'd scan the skies, seeing if it was going to rain. If there was any chance, I'd half empty the bath. When it rained, I'd wake up terrified, running out to check the water level. It became an obsession and it only took the slightest patter of raindrops to rouse me. Moira finally got angry with my father. 'Why don't you just cover the bath with netting? That'll solve the problem.'

My father would have none of it. 'That'll look ugly and I can't see why it's such a bloody problem for her to make sure it doesn't overflow.'

And that was the end of any discussion.

Moira and my father were fighting again, this time because Moira wanted to move. 'Well it's far too bloody small!' she screamed.

'There's nothing wrong with this house, you're always bloody complaining, nothing's ever good enough!'

'It's too small! James needs his own room, he's old enough to understand what's happening and I don't like the idea of making love with him watching.'

'Well, put him in Tanja's room!' So he can watch my father and me instead, I thought cynically.

'Don't be ridiculous, we need a bigger house, either that, or send your daughter to boarding school.'

'I'm not sending my daughter away and I've had enough of your bloody interfering, trying to break up my family.'

The argument ended abruptly, with the slamming of the bedroom door.

At Christmas we were invited to lunch at Moira's parents' new house. After lunch, we exchanged presents. Moira gave me a training bra, I was horribly embarrassed and rewrapped it hurriedly. Her parents, Jack and Jean, gave me a large tin of English toffees and everyone else gave me Rubik cubes – four in total, in three different sizes.

At two Moira announced we were leaving; James needed a sleep. As we drove home Moira and my father argued about Jack. He was still upset they weren't married and his only grandson was a bastard. I sat in the back playing with one of my Rubik cubes, not really paying attention.

We turned into the drive. In silence, Moira got out with James and went indoors. I gathered the presents and awkwardly climbed out of the car, banging the car door shut with my hip. I heard my father slam his door. 'Oh fucking shit! The fucking keys are locked in the car. How could you have been so bloody brainless as to lock your door?'

I took a step backwards, nervously. 'But you told me I have to lock the door when I get out.' I should have remained silent.

He grabbed me roughly by the arm, sending the presents scattering and dragged me to the carport where he snatched up the fibreglass fishing rod. I was so afraid I lost control of my bladder, the warm wetness soaking into my pants as I waited. I howled and screamed for him to stop as the rod flailed at my back and legs. In my panic, I tried snatching at it but this infuriated him even more. Through the open bedroom window I could hear Moira singing to James. Couldn't she hear me, my pain-befuddled mind asked, as I attempted to shield my body with my arms? Finally he threw down the rod and walked away.

Painfully I got to my feet and picked up the fallen parcels, carrying them into my room. Next thing the door was flung open and my father stood there. 'Give me the key!' he screamed, his hand out.

I stared at him. 'But I don't have the key.' Had he finally gone crazy?

'I want the key to this door.' He emphasised the word by slamming it back against the wall. I found it on the windowsill. He snatched it out of my hand. 'If I can't beat stupidity out of you, you can bloody well stay in here, I can't stand the sight of you.' And with that he slammed the door and locked it.

I stayed in there for two days and nights. Sometimes I'd see Moira drive out with James. At other times I could hear them playing with James and talking. I thought Moira would bring me something to eat but she didn't. I slept, read and ate the toffees her parents had given me.

At night I crept out the bedroom window to go to the toilet and drank from the tap. On the third day, my father unlocked the door. The parrots needed feeding.

Chapter 20

In February 1975 we moved to a two-storey house directly across from Vila Base Hospital. We started shifting one Saturday and as darkness fell my father suggested Moira stay with James in the old house, in case of burglars. While Moira didn't like the idea, he was persuasive – he said I'd unpack the kitchen so everything would be organised by the morning. Shortly afterwards, my father and I drove to the new house.

I went into the kitchen and started unpacking. After a while, I asked if he'd like a cup of tea. He came into the kitchen and stood behind me. Lifting my skirt, he pulled my underpants down. I tried to turn but he pushed me back facing the bench. 'I've locked the door and turned the key sideways so Moira won't be able to use her key.'

My pants were around my ankles and he bent his knees, trying to enter. I was too dry, so he reached over and picked up the butter. I wondered what he was going to do with it. I soon found out when he thrust his buttered fingers between my legs. 'You can't put butter there!'

'Of course I can! Don't you think it's sexy?'

I thought it was disgusting. It melted rapidly and he pushed his way inside. I closed my eyes, at least this way I didn't have to look at him and it would soon be over. He stopped. 'I've had a really sexy idea, let's make love in every room.'

Over the next two hours we went from room to room, having sex on the floor, over the edge of the bath, sitting on the toilet seat.

Every time he came close he withdrew and we moved to another room. He made me undress and led me through the garden and into the flat downstairs. He didn't seem to care that Moira might catch us, saying both the gates squeaked and we'd hear if she turned up.

Finally he took me outside to the entrance. He pushed me back on the steps, which dug into my back as he thrust inside. It was cold, and I expected to see Moira appearing in the shadows at any moment. At last, he came and as he withdrew, stickiness ran between my buttocks. 'Yuck, I'm all sticky,' I complained.

He reached down and took the hose in one hand while he turned the tap. Water spurted out, splashing my legs. 'Then clean yourself,' he laughed as he began hosing me. When he turned the tap off I was soaking wet. As I dried myself I tried to ignore the burning between my legs, grateful it was over. Till next time.

The next morning my father and Moira had a terrific argument. Moira had come round the night before, but was unable to get in. She wanted my father to explain why he'd locked the door from the inside. She moved out a couple of months later, taking with her my last hope of escape and another phase of my life began. An even more terrible one.

The night Moira moved out my father moved me into his bed. My bedroom became his locked room, a door he waved at to visitors, 'That's Tanja's room.'

James was nearly two and beginning to talk. He still couldn't manage my name and called me Tanjas. I much preferred it and no longer answered to Tanja.

Moira escaped from my father's control, falling in love with an Australian. I understood her leaving. Over the two years she was with us she changed from a wild, happy, carefree girl to an unhappy woman. Once she'd settled into her new life James moved back and forth between his parents.

My father steadfastly refused to refer to Moira by her name; he now hated her with a vengeance, calling her 'The Whore of Port Vila'. It was left to me to care for James, who became confused, telling people I was his 'other mother'.

Moira took the housegirl with her, so I had to find another one. I employed an unattractive, older woman with her own children, I figured she'd be safe from my father and experienced with children. During the week she looked after James during the day. I'd bathe him, change him into his pyjamas and cook him dinner on my return from school. Then I'd tuck him into bed and read him stories until he fell asleep. I was up again before daybreak, feeding the parrots and organising his breakfast before I went to school.

One day my father brought Dylan home. Moira had introduced them, as they both liked to scuba dive and they quickly became friends. They shared another interest, jujitsu, and often trained together. One time he kicked at James, stopping millimetres from his nose. Even so I liked Dylan and loved listening to him talk about his home in South Africa.

I turned fifteen and dealt with becoming a woman on my own. I didn't run screaming in terror the first time I found spots of blood on my pants. I knew about menstruation from hand-me-down copies of the Woman's Weekly. Of course, my father found out within a day or two. From then he only came inside during my menstruation. The rest of the month he withdrew at the last moment and came on my stomach. He used a condom a few times, but told me it didn't feel as nice and threw the rest out. I lived in permanent fear of pregnancy, counting the days, suffering hell whenever I was a few days late.

My breasts had grown to the size of small apples. How I loathed them. My father loved fondling them during sex and pinching my nipples. I hated it when he told me how beautiful they were, just the right size he'd say, a handful. He compared my breasts to Moira's. 'She had ugly breasts, too big and they drooped, especially after the baby.'

The feel of his hands on my breasts sickened me. He was proud of his soft hands and his long, perfectly manicured fingernails. The feel of his beard against my body revolted me, I could close my eyes and go away in my head, but his touch was still there, his smell still lingered.

He wouldn't let me wear a bra and I went through months of anguish, my nipples poking through the thin cotton of my school blouse. Eventually a letter was sent, requesting that he buy me some brassieres. He refused, buying cotton singlets instead. He told me I wasn't allowed to eat taro, the local root crop, as it had something in it that made breasts grow, pointing out the well-endowed native women. I decided that if he didn't like big breasts, I needed to develop them, eating as much taro as I could. It didn't make the slightest difference, they remained pert and round as apples. He became obsessed, photographing them at every opportunity and making me walk around naked. I don't know what James thought, I hoped he was still too young to be able to remember it when he grew up. On the weekends, my father wouldn't let me get up until we had sex. Sometimes James came into the room, and my father would continue while James sat on the floor and played with his toys.

At Christmas we were invited to Moira's parents. Moira was there with her new boyfriend and the usual crowd. As I sunned myself on a banana chair, the adults talked to James. The usual silly question's adults ask children. How old are you now? And what's your name? And where do you sleep? Someone asked, 'And where does Tanjas sleep?'

James innocently replied, 'In Daddy's bed.' There was an awkward silence then several people spoke at once, asking if there was any more of that lovely punch, and wasn't the garden lovely. My father didn't bat an eyelid.

After this, our bedroom door stayed locked, my father hanging a cloth over the keyhole, so James couldn't look in. James wasn't stupid, he knew where I was. He'd stand outside the door begging to be let in. My father would forbid me to open the door, even when he started to cry. I couldn't bear it, I'd put my hands over my ears; frightened it might have a long-term effect on my brother, being shut out like that.

Chapter 21

Two American women saw the display in the Hôtel Le Lagon and rang my father, interested in purchasing artefacts. Shelley and Ada were sisters, both married to rich men too busy to travel. They asked my father if they could accompany him on one of his bush trips. He decided to take them to Ijapkatas village, home of the Small Nambas, in the interior of Malekula. I'd been to Malekula before, but always stayed in Butin village, where he would leave me while he continued into the mountains. I loved tribal life, running wild with the children, watched over by many mothers.

I made friends with two girls my own age. I couldn't speak their language, they couldn't speak mine, so we communicated with sign language and laughter and that was enough. It was special being there, seeing another way of life, a different concept of what was important. Their universe was their village, growing up surrounded by family and friends, in the security of knowing everyone. I didn't see the men for most of the day, they were hunting birds and wild pigs.

During the day, as I played in the village, I could hear the women up in the hills, calling out to each other. Every so often they'd come down to feed us the food they'd gathered – sometimes fat white grubs they roasted over a fire, or strange fruit I'd never seen before. There were also wild grass seeds, sweet as peas. Most of the time I had no idea what I was eating, but I didn't care.

Late in the afternoon we'd gather against the wall of a hut. Mothers would search our hair for lice, talking and laughing as they crushed them between their nails. I felt enveloped in their cocoon of contentment. Around us, scrawny dogs lay in the dust, ignoring the chickens scratching at the roots of trees. Smoke from the cooking fires drifted up amongst the breadfruit trees, making swirling patterns in the sunlight.

When night fell, we'd feast on fat wood pigeons, parakeets, breadfruit, yams and taro. The women, children and domestic pigs slept together on soft woven mats and the men would go to their own huts. The first night I awoke to a huge black sow settling against my back, trying to get comfortable.

This time my father said I was old enough to accompany him, and we arrived late in the afternoon. The Americans had gone up in my estimate, they hadn't complained once during the long drive in the back of a dilapidated utility. We sat on the luggage, bouncing and jarring over the bumpy road jammed in amongst a dozen curious Malekulans. Shelley and Ada admired the wild jungle, taking photos and talking to the Malekulans, not realising they didn't understand a word!

As soon as I jumped down from the truck I saw my two friends pointing and giggling. It was several years since I'd been here and we weren't children any more. We saw the changes and realised how different our lives were. We sat together that evening and ate dinner served on laplap leaves. Occasionally, we'd look at each other, smiling shyly, there were things we wanted to say, but language had become a barrier.

Poor Ada struggled with her food, nearly dying when she discovered she'd been chewing on a chicken head in the half darkness. Laughter filled the hut at her horrified reaction – she didn't realise she'd been given the best part.

The next morning word came that it would be taboo for us to go up the Small Nambas' village, they were in the middle of tribal ceremonies. Instead we decided to go to Brunwick, a coastal village, and then on to Amok, a village where the Big Nambas lived. They were said to be cannibals and lived as they had for hundreds of years, their tribal system unchanged. There was a strange atmosphere in Brunwick, although the inhabitants were friendly, offering us a hut for the night. As the evening wore on, we learned Brunwick was going to have a battle with the neighbouring village the following day.

We gathered it had something to do with missionaries. The villagers were angry because they felt the missionaries, who'd been there more than seven years, were draining their resources. They suggested that under the circumstances we should return to Port Vila, but after a lengthy discussion it was agreed that guides would take us on a day trip to Amok.

In the morning, as we were about to leave, we were told that Verembat, the Chief of the Big Nambas, was visiting Brunwick. As we settled down to wait, I took my shoes off and put them in my bag; it was easier to walk barefoot. The Americans were horrified, not realising the tracks were as smooth as a tiled floor.

After a time, Chief Verembat arrived with his lieutenants. He wore a penis wrapper and a thick bark belt, and smiled as he shook hands with us. When he heard the sisters had come from America, he offered to guide us to his village. His lieutenants could bring us back before evening.

We set off under the burning sun. The Americans slowed us down and I became frustrated, as it's tiring to walk slowly. At one point, we had to wade thigh-deep through a river. My father refused, he didn't want to get his shoes and socks wet, nor did he want to take them off, as he'd cut his feet on the riverbed. Chief Verembat and I had already crossed.

'Come, we go ahead,' he said. He spoke to his lieutenants, telling them to look after my father and the women. As we rounded a bend I looked back and caught a glimpse of my father being carried over the river.

Chief Verembat walked at a fast pace and I trotted to keep up with him. Whenever the track widened, we'd walk together, talking. He told me about his daughter. He was very proud of her; she was famous as one of the most beautiful women in the New Hebrides.

Soon we were far ahead, surrounded by jungle and the sound of insects. What an incongruous pair we made, the Chief of the Big Nambas, a wild man by any standards, and me, a skinny little white girl. Once he stopped to help me climb over a fallen tree trunk. 'Normally I wouldn't help, it's against custom to help a woman, but you are like my daughter.'

I smiled at this, feeling a warm glow. A little further on, we stopped. 'Wait, I will get us a pawpaw,' he said, disappearing into the undergrowth. Returning with a small, perfectly ripe fruit he cut it in half and scraped out the black seeds, handing me a slice; it was warm, almost hot, from the midday sun and smelt of the jungle.

In places the path had worn into channels that were nearly knee-deep, with the passage of thousands of feet over hundreds of years.

It was unbearably hot and I was dripping with perspiration, envious of Chief Verembat's cool attire. We talked about the tribal war. 'It's because there isn't enough food at the moment, there hasn't been enough rain and the root crops failed this year.'

He was walking rapidly as he spoke and I was trotting behind trying to hear what he was saying, 'They've been surviving on wild yams. And a man with an empty stomach is a man looking for problems... ' he was saying, when suddenly he stopped. I nearly walked straight into him.

'Don't move,' he hissed, 'maybe he doesn't see us.' He pointed up the track. About six metres ahead stood a huge black wild boar, with vicious looking tusks. I froze; wild boars were the most dangerous animals in the jungle, known to gore people to death.

The pig had his head up, sniffing the air, his beady little eyes searching for us. We were on a section of path sunk into the ground and it was impossible for the pig to disappear into the undergrowth, his only options were to walk backwards in the narrow confines of the track, or charge us. He did a mock charge, his bristles raised along his back, giving a short bark and then stood still.

Chief Verembat motioned that we should move into the bush and circle round. We clambered up out of the ditch and once we were back on the path, he explained it was the safest thing to do, as he didn't have a club with him. I was rather glad he didn't.

I began trotting again, feeling cooler after the short stop. 'You walk good for a white man,' he suddenly said. 'You got good legs.' We'd stopped for a moment and as he spoke he lent down and felt my lower legs. 'Good walking legs, and strong ankles,' he nodded approvingly. 'You are Walk Far Woman.'

When we finally reached his village the sun was high; we walked amongst huts with steep roofs reaching to the ground, the baked dirt of the compound swept clean. Children peered round the corner of a hut, staring wide-eyed. Chief Verembat called something to them and they scuttled off, returning with green coconuts. He opened one with three cuts of his bush knife. I was most impressed. Usually people just hacked the top off, but Chief Verembat had made a neat fitting lid. The liquid was deliciously cool and slightly fizzy, the husk insulating it from the heat.

The others arrived twenty minutes later. My father was angry, but he couldn't say much in company. Shelley had stayed behind on the track, I suspect she was still jet lagged.

We only spent an hour in the village. Ada was worried about her sister and the lieutenants wanted to take us back before the battle, unhappy about the slow progress coming up. They said something and Chief Verembat laughed and answered them. Then he translated. They were surprised to hear we'd already been here a long time. 'I told them you know how to walk, and your name is now Walk Far Woman.'

The trip back was fairly uneventful. We were hastened out of Brunwick and across the river; they were in a hurry for us to leave, politely waiting until we left so they could go to war. Later we heard it wasn't the usual inter-village squabble – fourteen people were killed before Verembat put a stop to it.

Chapter 22

My Opa came to say goodbye, waking me one night while my father was asleep. He was leaving, he said, but I wouldn't be alone; my Oma van der Plaat would look after me. In the morning, I asked my father if my grandmother had died. He looked at me strangely, 'No she hasn't, why do you ask?'

I told him I'd dreamt she died. 'I can assure you my mother is alive and well,' he exclaimed. I knew she wasn't well, she had cancer.

That weekend I stayed with my mother, Maurice was overseas. Neither of us could sleep, so we sat on the beach, waiting for the sun to rise. We sat near the water's edge, a thick blanket around us against the chill night air. My mother arranged the gas lamp and poured some wine, while I opened two tins of chocolate pudding. The stars were out in all their glory, and the moon trailed across the stillness of the ocean. We sat; the mother and daughter we so rarely were, talking in easy companionship. She told me about her life with Maurice and about a book she was writing. Why couldn't life always be like that?

An occasional wave lapped gently at the shore and night birds circled and cried mournfully overhead. I dug my feet into the sand, surprised at the warmth beneath the surface. It gradually began to get lighter. Small strands of pink and orange began to stretch across the sky and the shadows of the night began to dissolve. We leaned against each other lost in thought. Suddenly my mother prodded me. 'Look, a shark.'

I stared in the direction she was pointing and saw a fin rippling the water, only metres offshore. It slipped beneath the surface to our right, then we spotted it again, on our left, some distance off. It's strange how the sight of a shark can unnerve you, even when you're sitting on dry land. We were about to return indoors and make breakfast, when suddenly it was streaking towards us. He came half out of the water, a metre from our feet, thrashing for a half second on the sand and then he was gone, leaving a memory of white teeth in a half moon mouth, round staring eyes and water streaming off his sleek, grey body. We decided to move further up the beach and see if he'd come back. 'I'm going to write and tell Oma van der Plaat,' I exclaimed, 'she'll be amazed.'

My mother stared at me. 'Oma van der Plaat is dead, didn't Ron tell you?'

'I don't believe you!' Why did she have to spoil it all by lying?

'If you don't believe me, I'll show you the letter my mother wrote.'

She went into the house, returning with a light blue aerogramme. It was in Dutch, but I could understand the gist of it, and she translated the rest. 'Why did Daddy lie to me?'

'I don't know, perhaps he has trouble coming to terms with it.'

I confronted my father when I returned home. 'Oma is dead, why did you lie to me?' I was really upset. My mother had gone cold again, because I hadn't believed her, telling me I had nasty eyes and it was only because I was her daughter that she could stand me at all.

'I didn't want to talk about it,' he snapped.

I went out and stood on the balcony. I wished I had my own room to go into, my own door to slam. My own space to sit in and think.

Some of the day boarders decided to get together one Friday night to go to dinner and a movie. They planned it for weeks, while I sat on the edge, listening. They paired off, no one offered to be my partner, although I was invited to join them. I wasn't upset, I could understand why no one wanted me – I didn't seem to be the sociable type.

I plucked up courage to ask my father. At first, he said no; I had to study, but I persisted and he finally agreed. There was however, a condition. On my return, he'd be asleep and I had to 'seduce' him.

He wanted to wake up inside me. I was desperate to go, to be a normal teenager, so I agreed.

After school I changed into green slacks and a tank top. I brushed my hair loose; happy with the way it curled after being in plaits all day. There was nothing I could do about my glasses. I was as blind as a bat without them, but then, who was I trying to impress?

We had dinner at the Hôtel Solaise and walked to the Cinéma Pacific. The movie was *Tora! Tora! Tora!* I sat in the flickering darkness, while the others passed popcorn, my stomach in knots at the thought of what I had to do when I got home. The sitting and waiting was so unbearable it was a relief when I discovered the others wanted to leave; Jenny and her sister, Karen, couldn't stand the film. Out in the cool night air we debated what to do next.

Garry and Jenny wanted to go to the Hôtel Le Lagon; I wanted to go to church. The others laughed. 'Are you crazy?' I was insistent. I suddenly needed to sit in the calm, sane environment of a church. I wanted to feel close to God. In the end we walked to the British Paddock, to the Presbyterian Church and I was shattered to find it locked. Whoever heard of a church that locked its doors? The others were larking round in the trees, calling out and giggling. I crouched on the top step and prayed. I needed strength for what I had to do. There was no question of not doing it. It didn't work like that in my family.

Afterwards we walked to the Hôtel Le Lagon, me feeling like a wet blanket. When we arrived I told them I was going home. 'Nightclubs aren't my scene,' I said, me who'd never set foot in one. 'I'll see you on Monday.' I turned and walked towards the taxi stand before they could change my mind. There was something I had to do.

I fulfilled my duties as soon as I arrived home. I wondered what the others would say if they could see me. I imagined them sitting in the nightclub, dancing and laughing; having teenage fun. How different my evening was from theirs. It had been such an ordeal, knowing what I had to do when I got home, that I never asked to go out with friends again.

Chapter 23

It was the middle of the hot season, and the school holidays were slowly drawing to a close. Early one morning the *Tokelau*, a mission boat, hit a reef off the coast of Malekula and sank.

As the Lloyds Insurance Representative, my father was sent to investigate. Dylan and I accompanied him; Dylan for the adventure it promised to be and me because there was no one to look after me.

Arriving in Milip village, we walked two kilometres to the site of the sinking. We found the missionary and his crew huddled on the beach, trying to warm themselves around a small fire.

The missionary had recently completed a navigation course. As night fell, he sent the captain to his bunk and said he'd navigate. He plotted the course, then went below to sleep, leaving the vessel on autopilot. He'd calculated they'd arrive at eight o'clock in the morning. Unfortunately, they arrived at six. They struck a rock, a hundred metres offshore, which ripped out the side of the hull, throwing everyone into the sea.

My father and Dylan swam out to inspect the wreck and I fell asleep on the beach, waking up when Dylan dripped water on my face. I'd forgotten to bring towels and they weren't amused so I made a fire. As they sat drying themselves, they told me about the underwater trail left by the sinking, drifting Tokelau and Dylan gave me a tin mug he'd salvaged. Once they were dry, we walked back to Milip village.

It was a terrible night. It rained endlessly and the wind strengthened, threatening to tear away the thatched roof. We planned to leave the next morning, but as I lay listening to the sea pounding, I wondered if our launch would come back to collect us.

I awoke the next morning to the sounds of a chicken scratching near my head and someone grating coconut. I crawled out, leaving the others to sleep, and went to the water's edge to brush my teeth. The sea looked hostile and the beach was cold and wet. I was overjoyed to see the launch, a dot on the horizon, but getting closer.

At eight o'clock the chief came to invite us to breakfast. It was wonderful, French bread, boysenberry jam and smoky tea. My father refused to eat, afraid of being seasick later.

He turned a sickly colour the moment he clambered aboard, although he'd already taken three seasick tablets. The boat was tossing horribly and we all had to sit below, with the diesel fumes. The next two hours were appalling. We battled against the wind, the motion becoming increasingly violent, the small launch crashing into each wave with unbelievable savageness, jarring our bodies and numbing our minds. Water sloshed around our feet, gradually getting deeper. 'It'll improve once we get round the point,' the captain yelled, barely audible over the rain and the sea.

The water was covering our ankles, and we were soaked. The waves grew higher and higher. We'd be caught up by each foam-capped mountain, balancing precariously for a few seconds, before plunging into the trough, with a spine-wrenching thud. Then we'd be swept up by the next and hurled skywards again.

Nobody spoke, we just held on for dear life. The wind had reached an incredible state of fury. The crew wanted to go back to Milip. I wanted to go back as well, but my father and Dylan wanted to continue. The point was relatively near and Milip was a good two hours downwind. I was fed up with the horrid stinking boat.

Then the pump broke down. The water level kept rising and the captain began to worry about the engine flooding and there was general agreement that we return to Milip. I stared at the tiny sliver of land on the horizon. It was so far away.

The captain set about the tricky business of turning the launch. Everybody was shouting, no one could agree on the best tactic, not that anyone was playing the slightest attention to anyone else anyway. The captain put the helm over, putting the side of the vessel directly against the waves. We were turning slowly, and just about round when I saw an enormous wave, towering above the others. It came at great speed, striking before I could scream. The launch lifted high into the air, and my stomach did terrible things as we slammed down into the trough.

We were thrown against the side and scrambled desperately up the floor, which was now nearly vertical. My nails scraped at the wood as I tried to get a grip on something, anything. The boat seemed to stand on edge forever. Then a cross-wave struck, saving us. The vessel slowly but surely righted itself, and we started the roller-coaster ride back the way we'd come. The waves were now coming from behind, and the motion somewhat easier.

We returned to Milip, dried ourselves around a cooking fire, and drank cups of sweet smoky tea. We decided to walk to the airport. Dylan dug out his map and worked out it was about forty-five kilometres. The chief tried his best to talk us out of walking. It was definitely too far, the weather was too bad. The tracks would be too muddy. 'No, no,' he continued, 'you should wait until the weather is better, then try again on the launch.'

There followed a heated discussion about walking. 'Don't you think we can walk it?' asked my father.

Laughter rippled round the hut. 'No, you are European, maybe we could walk it, but white people can't walk, your legs are too thin.' It seemed hopeless, it wouldn't be possible to walk without guides, and unless the chief agreed, we weren't going to get any. A young man pushed forward and stood next to the chief, gesturing towards me, speaking rapidly. There was a sudden silence. The chief turned to me. 'This man says you are Walk Far Woman.' I nodded.

'What's he talking about?' asked Dylan. I briefly explained how Chief Verembat had given me the name. As I spoke, the Chief followed my account with interest, and agreed to give us guides, but only to the next village. Then it was up to the next chief.

I was given the two bottles of Evian water to carry and without further delay, we set off at a torrid pace. I felt as though I were trotting most of the time. My legs seemed very small in comparison to everyone else.

After we'd been walking for about twenty minutes the sun

broke through and the dense jungle turned into a steam bath. I took off my jumper and tied it around my waist. In no time at all we were perspiring heavily, the water bottles becoming heavier as I struggled to keep up.

After what seemed a very long time, the men stopped. I tried to persuade everyone to drink lots of water, pleased my load would be lighter. Before I caught my breath, they were off again. At least I didn't have to carry so much, and the going was easier, but the result of so much water was a stitch in my side. I dug my finger in, trying to relieve the pain. I slowly fell from second in the column, to third, to fourth. It wasn't long before I was struggling to keep up. We came to a river with a steep muddy track leading into the jungle on the other side. The men hurried up the bank with the greatest of ease. I managed to trip halfway up and slid all the way back down into the river.

When I managed to get back up, it was very still at the top. There was no sight or sound of the men; they'd gone on without me. I hurried down the path until I came to a division in the track. Which way? Left or right? I checked the paths carefully, but couldn't tell. I called out, but there was no reply. While I was wondering what I should do, I spied a cocoa bush. I went over and picked two of the yellow pods. I sat down and cut one open, deciding they'd eventually notice they'd mislaid me, and come back.

I sucked the white flesh off the beans, the slightly sour taste very refreshing. I was just about to start on the second one when I heard a whistle. It was my father's 'where the hell are you?' whistle. I whistled back. In no time at all I was back in line. I'd been thoroughly berated.

Mud aside, it was a beautiful hike. Hundreds of butterflies danced out of the undergrowth into the sunshine. Everything was so green. Occasionally flocks of screeching parakeets flew high overhead. Several times the way led over incredible beaches, kilometres long, lining crystal clear blue water. Finally we stopped for a rest. The sand was a glorious rosebud pink, marred only by six sets of footprints marking the way we'd come and a few crab tracks ahead. We sheltered under the shade of some coconut trees and shared the remaining cocoa pod. The chief told us we were the first Europeans to walk on this beach and I felt suitably honoured.

Much later we crossed another beach, which sparkled so much it hurt my eyes. It wasn't sand, it looked like polished glass, pale blue and pink, with pebbles as big as bush fowl eggs. It was very difficult to walk on and felt strange to my bare feet. I gathered stones, each more beautiful that the last, and carried them in my drawn-up skirt. They were heavy and everyone kept telling me to put them back, I wouldn't be able to carry them for long. I ignored them. The chief laughed at this crazy white girl carting rocks through the jungle. In the end I kept ten fairly small ones, perfectly shaped and clear.

One day, I promised myself, I'd make a necklace out of them. At the time, I had no idea where those stones would guide me. How could I have known the extraordinary chain of events I set in motion with the simple act of picking up pretty pebbles?

We reached the next village and bid farewell to the chief and our guides. We zigzagged up the coast, changing guides at each village. At the fourth village they told us it would be impossible to walk any further; the track was too muddy.

It wasn't a track; it was a knee-deep bog. An uphill mud climb, it was perfect if you were a pig and you didn't have to catch a plane, kilometres away, at nine the next morning.

Our guide suggested we go by canoe to the next village. The idea seemed dreadful at first, but the track was clearly impassable, so we agreed.

We went back down to the shore. At least the water was calmer on this side of the island. The canoe was a large outrigger with room for twenty people.

It was now ten to six and the light was fading rapidly. We helped the guides shove the canoe into the water and leapt in. The men began paddling; two at each end with me in the middle. The canoe had been made from a narrow, hollowed-out tree trunk, only as wide as an average bottom, the slender outrigger lashed in place with intricate native weaving.

At first it was very pleasant. We were close to shore and the water was calm, with only an occasional ripple. We sped past glistening beaches, slowly turning pink with the sunset. A solitary seabird cried out as the sun slowly sank lower. The sea turned from brilliant azure to soft pink, then grey, and as the sun slid beneath the horizon, just for a moment, beaten silver. The sun slipped completely out of sight and the water became a dull, cold grey. Within minutes, the sea and sky had blackened and it became so dark I was unable to make out my father in front of me.

I developed cramp in my left leg and then my bottom went to sleep, but I didn't dare move, sitting motionless. If it hadn't been for the phosphorescence stirred up by the paddles, I might have thought we weren't moving at all. I could no longer hear the waves breaking on the reef so I knew we were a long way off shore.

Stars appeared one by one. The sound of the paddles was almost hypnotic and I felt as though I'd always been in that canoe, paddling in the darkness. I slowly shifted my weight and blood rushed back into my leg. A gentle wind sprang up, the sea began to get a little choppy and water splashed into the canoe. I was very cold, my nose hurt and my fingers were stiff. I seriously began to believe I'd been born in that canoe. It seemed as though I'd been there through all eternity. Suddenly the stillness was broken by three or four loud thumps on the side of the canoe. A terrified yell came out from the darkness ahead, followed almost immediately by relieved laughter and the words 'flying fish'. My teeth were chattering and I wondered if I'd ever been so cold.

I nearly had heart failure when one of the men behind me let out a piercing whistle. The others joined him and after a time, their whistles were answered from the darkness where I could just see a figure making his way down a beach with a flaming torch. The canoe altered course slightly and we headed for the light. By the time the canoe slid up onto the sand, it seemed the entire village had been roused, and everyone was there to greet us. It was already past two in the morning – we'd been eight hours in the canoe. We were taken into the village, to a cosy hut lit with several hurricane lanterns and everyone crowded in. I was so tired. I just wanted to sleep, but our hosts were keen to hear about the rest of the world. It was hard to imagine that less than twenty minutes before they had all been asleep.

They were very interested in the sinking of the *Tokelau* and everyone roared with laughter when we came to the part about the missionary's swim to shore. An old woman pushed her way in with a pillow for my father. She'd heard white people needed pillows to sleep on. We began arranging our bedding and the villagers were very impressed with our airbeds. I was just wondering how I was going to stay awake any longer when a girl came in carrying a huge pot of steaming fluffy white rice. Several others followed with plates, cups and a large pot of tea.

All the men sat in a circle and dinner was served, the women sitting against the walls of the hut while the men kept us company, eating large bowls of rice and drinking smoky tea. I fell asleep in the middle of dinner and awoke with my father shaking me. 'Get up, you have two minutes to get ready.'

It was still dark, I just wanted to turn over and go back to sleep. Five minutes later I was on the beach wading knee-deep in the incredibly cold water, struggling to push the canoe out. I dug my toes into the gravel bottom but the current was too strong and I lost my balance. I must have looked stupid, everyone went into hysterical laughter and nearly let the canoe go.

It got lighter by the minute and after a time we left the safety of the reef and crossed a choppy stretch of sea. Water began slopping into the canoe and I was promoted from chief nervous wreck to chief bailer. All went well, they paddled, and I bailed. I bailed and bailed and they paddled and paddled. I took on robot-like actions. Dip the bailer, scoop up, hurl out the water. Dip the bailer, scoop up, hurl out the water. Dip the bailer, scoop up, hurl the bailer overboard. I nearly choked trying to tell the men to turn the canoe round so I could rescue the bailer, which bobbed up and down in the waves. It sank just as I reached out to snatch it back. I felt awful. It had been a beautifully carved bailer, but the owner just laughed.

At about seven we entered the Maskelynes, dozens of tiny islands, scattered across what must be the most beautiful stretch of water in the world. I never want to forget how it looked that morning. The islands, averaging a hectare or so, were ringed with pink sand and edged with elegant coconut trees and the occasional breadfruit tree. They were shrouded in early morning mist, mingling with the smoky fires and reflected in the glassy, almost emerald green waters. A flock of parakeets swooped from one islet to another and for a moment I wished I had a camera, but even if I had, I would never have been able to catch the beauty. I wouldn't have been able to catch the sounds and the smoky smell of island cooking.

It was half past eight when we finally rounded the point. Fortunately the tide was in and the canoe brought us right up to the beach. We paid our guides and hurried up the beach and along the track to the airport. Quarter to nine. Fifteen minutes before our plane was due to take off. There was still a chance we might catch it.

We reached the edge of the airstrip just in time to see our plane take off. We'd missed it by seven minutes. Of course, my father and Dylan were very quick to point out that it was entirely my fault. If I hadn't dropped the bailer ... We walked the remaining couple of hundred metres to the ticketing hut. An Air Mélanésie agent was waiting. He didn't seem to notice our bedraggled appearance. 'You've missed your plane,' he said cheerfully.

It was Sunday, James was with Moira; she and her boyfriend were spending the weekend on the other side of the island. My father and I sat in the living room, eating breakfast. Fred was waddling around on the tiles, nibbling crackers and preening her feathers. There was a knock at the door, so I hurriedly pulled on a top and went to open it. It was Dylan. 'It's a lovely day, we should be diving,' he laughed as I led him into the living room.

My father smiled. 'Be careful where you walk, Fred is loose.'

With the foolishness that overtakes us all sometimes, Dylan's response was to leap high in the air over Fred, in a perfectly executed jujitsu leap.

Fred squawked in terror and rolled on her back. Dylan had made no allowance for her sudden movement and landed on top of her, even though he twisted in a desperate attempt to avoid her. Fred rolled over, screeching in agony, flapping one wing. My father leapt from his chair like a mad bull and charged at Dylan. 'You fucking bastard,' he raged, knocking him to the floor.

'Stop it,' I screamed, as my father dragged Dylan to the door, 'Fred needs help!'

It was chaos, with my father screaming, 'Get out of my house, you fucking bastard!' his face distorted with rage, and the parrot screeching.

Dylan tried to calm my father, but no one can do that. As I watched, my father dragged him to the top of the steps and threw him down. I ran back indoors as the men exchanged threats and abuse. Poor Fred was still alive, but her wing seemed to be broken.

We wrapped her in a towel and carried her down to the car. The car wouldn't start, and eventually we started walking. It took us nearly half an hour to reach the vet's house. He rushed us to his surgery where an X-ray confirmed Fred had a broken wing, the bone so badly shattered it was irreparable. My father was beside himself. There were times when I felt that Fred was the only living thing he ever truly loved.

'There are only two options, either we put her to sleep or we amputate her wing. The chances of her surviving are very slim, she's had a terrible shock, and shock isn't something a parrot handles very well,' the vet said.

My father asked him to amputate. After an hour they came out to tell us the operation was a success. 'She's still anaesthetised, it's simply a question of her waking up. If she wakes, her chances are very good.'

He dropped us back at the house. I held the cardboard box, peering through the gauze cloth. The poor darling was bandaged all down one side. I watched her breathing, praying she'd wake up.

I crooned gently to her, as I did when she was preening my hair; she looked up at me, her black beady eyes seemed alert, and she crooned back. I was overjoyed. Fred had survived!

She died less than five minutes later. The only thing I can say is that she didn't appear to be in any pain. 'That fucking bastard,' my father yelled, throwing the book he was reading across the room, 'I'll kill him.'

He stood up, and I grabbed his arm, trying to stop him from leaving the house. He was in such a rage; I felt he was quite capable of killing Dylan. He shrugged me off and went into his workroom, slamming the door. I sighed with relief. We buried Fred the next day, in a large Chinese pot, on the land out at Malapoa Point.

He talked of revenge for weeks. I listened to the dozen ways he planned to get even with Dylan. Then suddenly he did a complete turn around. 'He was a good friend, and it was an accident. I should talk to him, apologise for throwing him down the stairs.'

A few days later, Dylan began coming round again. It seemed as if everything was as before, apart from an empty cage in the corner of the living room.

Moira's mother had given us a huge pile of magazines and one evening, we read each other snippets that caught our attention. My father came across an article on asbestos.

'Listen to this,' he said, reading the whole article to me. 'Don't you have asbestos mats in your science laboratory?'

'Yes, but I don't think it's the sort they're talking about.'

'How can you be sure?' he persisted. 'I think I should check it out, bring me one home tomorrow.'

The next morning before I left for school he reminded me about the asbestos mat. 'I'll be really angry if you forget.'

It was one thing promising to bring one home, it was another thing getting one. During recess, I sneaked into the lab; my heart in my mouth, terrified of the very real possibility of being caught. We were absolutely forbidden to go into the science lab outside of lessons, because of all the poisons stored there, but I was more terrified of my father's anger if I returned empty-handed.

I took one of the mats, sliding it in my basket between two large folders. I spent the rest of the day on edge. They were bound to notice it missing and search for it. I'd be accused of stealing. I wasn't really stealing it, only borrowing it for the night. Nevertheless, who would believe that?

As I walked in the door, my father greeted me with, 'Have you got the mat?' I nodded and handed it to him. He took it away into his room. 'To do some tests,' he said as he shut the door in my face. I couldn't imagine what sort of tests, but didn't really care. He gave it back the next morning. 'Don't worry, it's perfectly safe, not the dangerous sort at all.'

As I slid it back under the burner, I noticed one of the corners had broken off. I hastily searched through my bag looking for the piece but couldn't find it.

On Friday, my father took me to a Chinese restaurant that had opened at the back of the Hôtel Vate, where we were surprised to see our old landlords. They beamed when they saw us and insisted on giving us the best table. They'd sold the store and were now living in town, and asked if I'd like a kitten, remembering that I liked cats. He returned a few moments later with an armful of kittens, as he put them down on the floor they fled in all directions. All except one, a ginger male.

He circled under my chair, tail up, rubbing against my legs. I picked him up, cuddling him on my lap during the remainder of the evening and feeding him pieces of spring roll. My father agreed I could keep him and so I had a cat again. I named him Mousecat, because he was so tiny. The first week he disappeared under the fridge, only coming out at night to eat when the house was quiet.

Next time Dylan came round for lunch, my father asked me to prepare my meatball dish; it was one of Dylan's favourites. When I started to serve lunch, my father shooed me out of the kitchen. 'Go and sit down, it's about time I did something to help. I'll dish up.'

My father served us with a flourish, pretending to be a swish waiter, with a tea towel over his arm instead of a white napkin. Then he went back into the kitchen. 'Hey, that's not fair,' grinned Dylan, 'you have more than I do.'

I looked down at my plate and then at his. There really was no difference. He was always teasing me. I picked up my plate, laughing as I handed it to him, 'Then you'd better have mine. Start eating,' I said, 'before it gets cold,' as he handed me his plate in return.

After Dylan had gone I stacked the dishes and carried them into the kitchen. My father seemed to be bursting to tell me something. 'I got the bastard,' he exclaimed gleefully. 'Now he's going to pay.'

I didn't understand. 'What bastard? Who's going to pay?'

'I sprinkled his food with asbestos, now he's going to get stomach cancer and die.'

My blood turned to ice in my veins, as it slowly registered what he had done, and how he'd been planning this all along. I was stunned. I knew he was vengeful, but I couldn't believe the last month had all been an act. 'How could you do that?' I said, 'he's your friend.'

'No he isn't. It was easily done, you helped by getting me the asbestos.'

I suddenly remembered I'd swapped meals with Dylan. I was the one who was going to get stomach cancer, not Dylan. I nearly said something, but stopped myself. If I told my father I'd eaten the meal, I was certain of another beating and I was getting enough of those, I didn't want to give him another reason.

Chapter 24

My father was due to fly to Malekula and went into the wardrobe in our bedroom to get some cash. I was packing for him, when suddenly he sat on the bed in a state of shock. 'The cash box has gone.'

As well as cash and personal documents my father kept the naked photos in there, including the one he'd taken of us. I felt sick. Someone, somewhere, had those photos. He asked the housegirl if she'd moved it. 'No, Masta, I thought you moved it.'

My father sat on the bed, 'What do I do now?' he kept asking himself.

The housegirl suggested we go to her uncle, who was a cleva, who could tell us who took it. She offered to show us the way and we drove out to his house, a tiny thatched hut. As we got out of the car, he came over to us. 'Hello,' he said as he shook hands, 'I was going to my gardens when I saw you coming. I wasn't sure when you would arrive so I stayed and waited for you.' I looked at the thick jungle surrounding the house. There was no way he'd physically seen us coming.

Our housegirl explained why we were there, but he seemed to already know. 'I need to come to your house. There are no thoughts here from the person who took your box.' He went inside to get his 'leaf medicine' and came back with a small, tightly woven native basket decorated with tiny shells and trading beads.

Back in our bedroom he opened his basket and unwrapped an assortment of what appeared to be dried leaves and twigs.

He scattered these over the wardrobe shelf and shut the doors. 'I will come here tonight, in my dreams, then I will be able to see the person. It is important that you both sleep in another room. Otherwise I might pick up your thoughts.' My father looked rather uncomfortable.

When we drove him home he said, 'I will come to your house tomorrow at nine and tell you who has the box.' He seemed very certain.

The next morning at nine, he was at our door. 'I know,' he said simply. 'I saw a box, a locked metal box painted green. There are many photos and things made from gold.'

I could see my father was sceptical. 'What sort of gold things?' The old man smiled, he knew he wasn't convinced.

'I saw a gold fish with green and blue colours, on a thin chain. It is a very beautiful fish, and belongs to your daughter.' My father bought that fish years ago and kept it sellotaped inside pink tissue paper. He continued, 'And I saw a ring with clear stones. It has something to do with a woman who has passed on, something to do with marriage.' He described the contents of the box with uncanny accuracy.

'So, did you see the man who took it?'

'It was a woman. A white woman, I saw her hand as she

reached for the box and read her thoughts. She took the silver coins on top of the box and put them to one side, she thought; those don't belong to me. Then she carried the box out of the room. She has a black dog, and a son; she still carries him on her hip. She has long hair, a funny colour, like the inside of a pumpkin.'

'Moira!' my father exclaimed. 'Can you see the box, do you know where it is?'

'No, she gave it to a younger man, because she couldn't open it without the key. He has buried it.'

'Do you know where?'

'No, it is in the bush, and when he finished he covered it with leaves.'

My father was convinced Dylan had the box and arranged to meet him at the Intercontinental Hotel. Dylan was already there when we arrived. 'What's this all about? You sounded mysterious on the phone.'

'I have a problem,' my father began. 'My cash box has been stolen, along with a small amount of cash and some private documents.'

'Have you contacted the police?' Dylan asked, not seeming that interested.

'No, it's awkward.' My father looked around him. 'There are also photos of black girls in there. It wouldn't look very good, people might get the wrong idea. I'm offering a reward for its recovery. I think Moira stole it. You could watch her, see if she has it. It wouldn't be difficult for you to find an excuse to visit, after all you're in the same block of flats.'

Two days later Dylan rang and my father arranged to meet him again. There was a peculiar atmosphere in Dylan's house. He had another visitor, a Chinese man. Nothing was said about the box and I left the lounge to go to the toilet. When I returned, my father and Dylan were about to leave. Dylan had the box somewhere else, and I was being left as a hostage with the Chinese man, in case something happened to Dylan. I wasn't happy, but I didn't have any say in the matter. When they returned they had the box, but the photos, cash and all the documents were missing. They were arguing as they came in through the front door. 'I still don't understand why you had to do that, there were letters from my mother.'

'I told you, Moira wanted the box back once I'd opened it, and I didn't think you'd want her to see the photos. They were pretty incriminating, and the letters were in Dutch, I didn't know what was in them, the fact you'd locked them up made me think they were incriminating too.'

'If you still have the photos please give them back, if it's money you want, I'll pay you.' He was pleading now.

'I don't want your money. I burnt them! I was trying to do you a favour, and I think under the circumstances, you should be grateful. I got your damn box back didn't I?'

'How do I know you burnt them?

'I burnt them in the toilet.'

My father went to see for himself, he ran his fingers under the lip of the toilet bowl, and they were black, from the greasy soot lodged there. 'So, you're telling the truth. I'm sorry, you're a good friend to me.'

We left a few moments later, Dylan walking us downstairs to the main entrance. Just as we reached the door, Moira came in. 'You fucking bitch,' my father screamed. 'You thieving bitch!'

Moira went as white as a sheet. 'What the hell are you talking about?'

'Stealing my cash box!' he yelled.

'I never stole your cash box!' Then she saw Dylan. 'I suppose you're in cahoots with him, you both make me sick!' she screamed as she slammed her door.

I didn't know what to believe any more. Especially as my father said goodbye to Dylan as if they were bosom buddies, and drove straight to the police station to lay a complaint about the burglary.

The next morning Dylan was arrested and taken in for questioning. At two in the afternoon the police came for me. My father was beside himself; he rang to warn me. 'Don't tell them anything about the photos or us, or we'll both end up in prison for a very long time.'

I was shocked. I didn't like what he did to me, I hated what he did to me, and it was frightening to learn I could go to jail for it as well. It seemed so unfair, but then there were times when I didn't understand anything.

Chapter 25

A police officer picked me up, shortly after two, and told me Detective Inspector Bradley would be interviewing me. I was shown into an office where Detective Inspector Bradley sat reading a manila file; he briefly looked up, then ignored me. I scratched my leg and counted the ceiling panels. 'Sit down, very good of you to come in to speak with us,' he finally said.

I studied his face while he arranged papers in the folder. 'Dylan said there were photos in the box.' He began abruptly, not looking at me, as though he wasn't really interested. 'Tell me about them.'

'They were Polaroid photos.'

'I want to know what they showed.'

'There were some photos of me.'

He stared hard at me, pursing his lips. I kept my eyes level with his, unable to drop them. 'So tell me about the burglary.'

I told him nearly everything, but I didn't tell him about my father wanting the photos back. He didn't interrupt, just leaned back, twiddling his pen. Finally, I came to the end.

'Dylan tells a different story.'

That surprised me. I sat in silence, not knowing what to say, I'd told the truth, not all of it, but most of it.

'He says your father paid him to steal the box, for insurance.'

It was plausible, he'd done that sort of thing before; but I'd seen his reaction when he found the box missing, and he'd have removed the photos first.

I shook my head. 'He doesn't have insurance, there wouldn't be any point.'

'Why would Dylan lie?'

'I don't know.'

He stood up and walked out of the room. I sat with the manila folder centimetres from my hand. Did he think I'd sneak a look? Was that why he'd left me? I didn't know, and I didn't care. I got up and pushed the blind aside so I could see outside, feeling very alone as I watched people in the street.

When he came back with a mug of coffee he told me to sit down. He seemed disappointed to find the folder exactly as he'd left it. 'Dylan tells me the photos were dirty ones.' I kept looking at the table as he stirred his coffee, scraping the bottom of his cup until it was annoying.

I looked up, 'Could I have a coffee?'

'No, you can't have a coffee, you don't seem to realise where you are, you're in a police station!'

I looked down resentfully, I knew where I was, but I hadn't done anything wrong. But then again, I had done something wrong, hadn't I? I suddenly felt afraid, perhaps the photos were in the file. Was that why he kept asking about them? Did he want me to incriminate myself?

I looked at him. 'They weren't dirty photos, they were just normal photos.'

'Dylan tells me you were naked. I don't think naked photos are normal.'

I didn't know what to say. Suddenly he slammed his palm down, making me jump. 'I'm running out of patience, young lady! I know they were dirty photos, I know your father took them. I want you to describe them.'

I still said nothing.

'Are you trying to tell me naked photos of yourself are perfectly normal?'

'Yes,' I nodded, 'these ones were. I was on the beach, I'd been swimming.'

'Naked?'

'Yes, I'd been swimming naked, lots of people do.'

'So these photos were taken at the beach? Who else was there?' He went on about the photos, occasionally scribbling something in the folder. In my mind, prison was only a false word away. From time to time, he changed the subject, talking about Moira and Dylan and my father, every time I thought he was finished he'd come back to the photos.

The interview lasted nearly eight hours. He left the room once more, this time for more than half an hour. At about nine, there was a hesitant knock. 'Come in!' Bradley snapped. A police officer told him my father wanted to see me. 'Tell him he'll have to wait.'

It was another hour before Detective Inspector Bradley went to the door. 'Send Mr van der Plaat in.' Then my father was standing there, I was happy to see him; hopefully I could go home now.

'I've finished questioning your daughter. You can take her home.' He paused in front of my father, his face inches away.

'You have a clever daughter, Mr van der Plaat. You're a very lucky man. I wonder if you will always be so lucky?' Then he swept out of the room, pushing past my father.

On the way home my father questioned me closely, then, finally satisfied I'd let nothing untoward slip, dropped the subject. Dylan was charged with receiving stolen property and the day after his court appearance, slipped out of the country on his South African passport. My father talked about extradition and raged that Dylan had escaped. I felt Dylan had suffered enough, after all he'd been forced into hiding. Needless to say, I kept my opinion to myself.

Frustrated, my father turned his anger onto Moira, talking of pressing charges against her. 'That'll show the world what a bad mother she is, she's nothing but a common criminal. No court in the world would allow her custody of James.'

I felt uneasy. Was this what it had all been about? Had my father arranged this all to get Moira out of the way? Had his plans gone awry when Dylan opened the box? I knew he'd been scheming to take James overseas without Moira's permission, planning to leave him with his sister in Holland. The problem was he didn't have James' vaccination certificates. Moira did.

Using James' name, he went to the clinic and received the necessary vaccinations himself. It wasn't difficult. He offered to fill out the forms for the nurse, as she seemed so busy. This false certificate was one of the papers Dylan had burnt.

The subject of charges against Moira was dropped after a short meeting with Moira's father. I don't know what was discussed, but whatever it was, it worked. Nothing more was said.

My life slipped back into its monotony of long school days, feeding animals and performing duties. I was followed by a black mood, which threatened to smother me. Sometimes I felt as though I could hardly breathe under its weight. It became part of my life. There were times when I was so down the thought of making a cup of tea or ironing my blouse was utterly exhausting. It was a mammoth effort to summon enough energy to get through the day. I struggled with my schoolwork and turned in the barest minimum for homework.

I still woke at daybreak. I'd lie in as long as I dared, listening to him sleeping, waiting for subtle changes in his breathing that would alert me to him waking. Then I'd be out of bed in a flash, before he could clasp a hand on my thigh and pull me over to his waiting penis. Most mornings I'd escape in time, but even so, I had to make up for it at night and over the weekends.

It was a Friday and we were coming back with the shopping. 'Do you love me?' my father asked.

He always asked me that. And I always replied, 'Yes, I love you.' And I did. He was my protector, my father and my only friend. It was his penis I hated, and his foul moods. I especially loved him when he was kind, when his voice was soft and gentle. 'Yes, I love you.'

'Did you know that in ancient Egypt the Pharaohs married their daughters?'

'No, I thought it was against the law.'

'It wasn't then, now people are really stupid and have made laws against it. One day the law will change, and fathers will be able to marry their daughters.'

'But I thought they changed the law because if there's a baby, it's deformed.'

'Who told you that rubbish?'

'Ian did, he showed me a picture of a cow with six legs, he said that came from inbreeding.'

I didn't tell him Ian had added I'd have a baby like that, or that Moira had told his family about what she'd seen.

'What would he know? He's just a stupid kid.' We turned into our house and my father parked the car. 'Do you truly love me?'

'Yes I do,' I said, failing to see the carefully laid trap.

'So would you marry me?'

'I can't,' I laughed, 'it's against the law.'

'But if it wasn't against the law, would you marry me?'

And there it was, I was trapped, mind trapped. If I said no, he'd say I didn't love him, then he'd be hurt and upset and angry. And I knew what happened when he was angry. If I said yes, what would God think? I took a gamble, I said yes. After all, how could he marry me? The next morning, Saturday, he told me to take my ring off, the one Tisha had given me years before, he said it needed cleaning.

Later that day we drove round the island. As he parked the car, he told me to wait, then he crossed the road and picked some dusty wildflowers. He came round and with a flourish opened the door and presented me with the bouquet. Then he asked me to get out of the car. We walked a few metres further up the gravel road, then he stopped. 'Here is the perfect place.'

I looked around; sometimes I could be really stupid. 'For what?'

'For us to marry.'

I felt sick. 'We can't! It's against the law and people have to be married by a priest.'

He explained that wasn't necessary. If we exchanged the marriage vows and I had a ring put on my finger, we'd be legally married, especially if the marriage was consummated afterwards. He continued, 'I want you to repeat the wedding vows after me. You, Tanjas van der Plaat, hereby take Ronald van der Plaat, to have and to hold, to love and obey ... '

I hesitated and he stared at me accusingly. 'I thought you loved me?'

'I do,' I replied automatically, wishing the ground would open and swallow me, but it didn't. It remained firm.

'Then.'

'I, Tanjas van der Plaat, hereby take Ronald van der Plaat to have and to hold...' I paused; I'd forgotten what came next.

'To love and obey,' he prompted.

'To love and obey,' I repeated.

I stared high above, at a vine curling up the tree we stood beneath. A cascade of blossoms spilled down from the thick twists of green. I guess that's why he chose it, to be beneath such glorious flowers as we married. I scarcely heard him recite his part of the wedding vows, and I barely noticed when he slipped Tisha's ring on my finger. He said it was a symbol of his love, and our becoming united as one. I was lost in the blueness of the sky somewhere, not thinking at all.

He told me we were married and kissed my mouth. I only just stopped myself from pushing him away, instead I squeezed my eyes shut and hoped God had been busy somewhere else. We drove home to consummate the marriage. I was now my father's wife. The trap had sprung shut.

We often drove past that place, where the blossoms had grown, and over time, they gradually formed a huge seedpod, woody in appearance and bigger than a boomerang. I read somewhere that Muslim people don't have to stay married, all they have to do to get divorced is state three times, 'I divorce thee,' and they're divorced. Every time we drove past that tree, I chanted those words in my mind, but it didn't make any difference. Not even when the pod finally dropped onto the dusty track and we drove over it, until it was indistinguishable from the other debris scattered around.

Chapter 26

On 4 October 1976 I turned sweet sixteen. My father positioned me on the bed, watching the clock. He wanted to have sex with a fifteen-year-old and a sixteen-year-old rolled into one. 'Sixteen is the age of consent,' he laughed as he thrust inside me, 'now you're legally old enough.'

I remained silent; my face squashed against his sweaty chest hairs. Legally old enough, but this wasn't legal. I'd never have a lover; he'd never allow it. Before my father married me, I clung to the slim hope that one day I'd have a boyfriend and escape. Now he told me I was a married woman, and he'd never allow me to commit adultery.

Eventually he rolled off and wiped his penis with his underpants. It was twenty past midnight. I'd been sixteen for twenty minutes. I showered, pushing the showerhead between my legs, the hot water nearly scalding me in my determination to kill every last sperm.

I dried myself and wiped the mirror. My face, sallow and unsmiling, stared back. My life stretched before me in frightening monotony. I had no illusions, no dreams. This was going to be my life. Other people would marry and have babies and live happily ever after, but not me. I prayed silently for a miracle. Maybe next year it would be different.

On 4 October 1977 I turned seventeen. My father positioned me on the bed, watching the clock. A year had gone by. How many times had I flushed myself out? I lost count ages ago.

Oh, things happened in that year. My father took me to Europe, stopping over in Indonesia. I remember the beauty, the kindness of the people, the five-star hotel where we stayed, and the shame of being beaten so savagely the people in the next room banged on the adjoining door. When he kept on kicking me, they must have called reception, because someone knocked on our door. My father opened it a crack, putting his foot behind it so they couldn't push in. I lay curled up in pain between the beds.

'Do you need clean towels?' several voices inquired.

'No, we already have clean towels.'

'Perhaps we can turn down your beds?'

'No, I want to rest, go away.' He shut the door and slid on the safety catch.

'Get off the floor, you fucking bitch, you're always so bloody dramatic. I'm going out, you can fucking well get your diary up to date.'

That's what the beating had been about. My diary hadn't been up to date, my tiny protest. It started because I couldn't remember how many times we'd had sex since we left Port Vila. He'd been trying to remember and demanded to see my diary, where I was supposed to code sex as a glass of milk.

He came back in a good humour, my diary was up to date and we went down to dinner. The staff were cold to me, friendly to my father. A few days later my father went to fetch his camera and while he was gone, one of the receptionists took me aside. 'You should be nicer to your husband. He loves you, it is not good of you to see other men.'

'But I didn't see anyone,' I exclaimed, wondering who they were confusing me with.

'Shh, we are only trying to help, your poor husband was so unhappy, he told us about your friend, he must love you very much to still keep you for his wife.'

In Bali we searched the rice paddies for snakes for a friend who owned a private zoo. We flew to Holland; my handbag filled with snakes, each wrapped in a pillowcase. My father insisted I be the one to carry them. Two of them were refused by the zoo – they were too poisonous. I felt sick; I'd flown halfway round the world with deadly snakes in my bag.

We went to England over the New Year and I met my brother Richard, now eleven years old. He was sweet, we played on his skateboard, but I kept falling off. We returned to Holland earlier than planned because his mother and my father quarrelled.

The problem of the snakes had been solved. My grandfather said they fought and bit each other, dying almost immediately. My aunt confided that the day we left he put the terrarium in the snow and they froze to death.

I mostly enjoyed the month with my aunt. My father didn't beat me and even allowed me to go shopping. She bought me a beautiful white knit dress, and afterwards we drank coffee in an elegant café. However, that was the only time; he was annoyed, he wanted to know why we'd taken so long.

He continued to have sex with me. We shared a room and early one morning, while my father was on the verge of coming, my aunt tried the door. 'Why is this door locked?' My father motioned me to remain silent. She banged again. 'Open this door, I don't like locked doors.'

My father came, hurriedly wiped himself with his underpants. 'Open the door,' he whispered.

I pulled on a pair of pants and a T-shirt and walked to the door, feeling wet stickiness between my legs. I pulled it open, feigning sleepiness. 'Sorry, I didn't know it was locked.' She looked over my shoulder; my father had pulled the covers over his head. 'Daddy's still asleep,' I whispered and pushed past into the bathroom.

I tried to clean myself with my fingers. As I carefully rinsed the drain of tell-tale curdled sperm, I thought about all the places with my father's sperm clinging to the inside of drainpipes and felt ill.

We returned to Port Vila, and my life revolved once more around school, feeding the animals and sex.

A tourist ship, the *Lindblad Explorer*, came to our island, filled with wealthy people wanting to catch a glimpse of the past before the future wiped it out, seeking primitive tribes and a world untouched by tourism. An Austrian customer of ours was on board and my father received a telex from the captain, inviting us to join them for the week they'd be travelling through the New Hebrides. In exchange, he asked that my father bring photos of the bush and tribal life, and give a lecture.

During our visit to Erromango, my father heard about a traditional ceremony in progress on the island of Tanna and arranged for permission to witness it. Tanna was home to Yasur, one of the world's most accessible live volcanoes, and the Toka festival, which celebrated the exchange of women from one village to another.

After being delivered to the beach, we began a long drive to the ash plains of Yasur, our jeep convoy winding along dirt roads, arriving at dusk to a grey, surreal landscape. It was barren save for a few pandanus trees, with an encircling wall of jungle in the distance. Steam rose over the hot water lake and the volcano stood sheer and dark, rumbling and emitting steam and poisonous gases to mingle with the low-hanging clouds.

The plain was filled with a thousand chanting warriors, their faces painted red, yellow and blue. They wore penis wrappers and woven headbands decorated with feathers and leaves and carried spears.

We were shown to an ash bank and I sat at the base, with a front row view. The ship's stewards bustled around, covering a long table with a spotless white tablecloth and laying out a gourmet banquet with bone china, crystal glasses, silver utensils and table napkins, behaving as though they laid out dinner near hordes of wild natives every night.

The Toka dancing began. A tiny group of women and girls to be exchanged huddled in the middle, their faces painted in intricate patterns, accentuating the beauty of their dark eyes. They were dressed in brightly coloured grass skirts, pareo material, feathers and bunches of leaves. The men began a slow dance towards them, chanting. The plain reverberated with the sounds of the volcano rumbling and a thousand men stamping, shaking the dance rattles around their knees. They paused about twenty metres from the women, then charged, thrusting with their spears and howling wildly. The women squealed and huddled closer. At the last second the men stopped. There was a momentary silence, then they moved away chanting softly and stamping rhythmically.

They danced through the night as the clouds drifted away and the moon became a tight white ball. The dancers became wilder and more frenzied, working themselves into a feverish pitch, their charges becoming more feral as they leapt amongst clouds of ash, the atmosphere electric.

I stood up to get a drink, when suddenly the men whirled round, standing silently a hundred metres away. They started moving towards me. I knew what was coming. They paused twenty metres away then charged. It was a terrifying sight, a thousand half-naked, wild painted men, waving spears and howling. It took every bit of control I had to stop myself leaping up the bank. I didn't want to lose face, so I stood my ground. The warriors stopped centimetres away. I caught the heavy musk smell of sweat and coconut oil; they were so close I could see their bloodshot eyes. There was a momentary silence as we stared at each other, the ash slowly settling, glowing eerily in the moonlight. Then they began to laugh. I laughed too, as the adrenaline subsided and behind me the wealthy people looking for adventure also laughed, a crescendo of relief as they began to breathe again.

They charged me three more times, then tired of me and charged an attractive blonde girl to my left. It was too much for her, and with a squeal of terror she rolled over backwards as the dancers encircled her.

As the sun rose, they brought out the Toka poles, tall posts decorated with feathers. We were shown the pigs laid out for the ceremony to follow. There were more than two hundred, trussed by their feet, lying side by side. When the pig killing began, I wandered off. I couldn't bear this part, the dreadful squealing, the smell of blood and thousands of flies. It was too much for the passengers as well and we returned to the ship. We stayed on board for another day, leaving early the following morning to fly back to Port Vila.

Chapter 27

During my school holidays, my father came up with another idea. I was to be his private prostitute. He told me to write out a list of sexual favours and the fee for each. I kept it simple, knowing I'd have to do whatever I wrote. It wasn't enough and he added to the list, then I had to rewrite it, with more than twenty options, ranging from straight sex, blow jobs and beating with a cane to tying up and anal intercourse.

He set up the flat downstairs with a double bed, red light bulbs and a table near the door for the list. When the mood took him, he'd send me to dress in clothes he'd laid out, and put on black eyeliner and bright red lipstick, insisting I also put lipstick on my nipples. I did as I was told. The sooner it started the sooner it would be over, was all I allowed myself to think.

He'd knock on the door, pretending to be a stranger, look over the list and make his choice, putting money in a saucer. He'd open a bottle of wine, drinking very little himself but plying me until I was well and truly drunk.

He played his part well, his face cruel and detached, and was always rougher than usual. I'd cry out in pain when he had anal intercourse and try to pull away, but he'd hold me tight and thrust even harder. He knew no one would be able to hear. 'Stop being such a sookie, think about the money I'm paying,' he'd rasp.

He was insatiable, coming as often as three times in one evening. When he was finally spent and left to go upstairs, he'd take the money back and put it in his pocket. The next day I'd be bleeding and hung over. One day the list disappeared, as well as the fibreglass fishing rod he used to beat me. We looked for them everywhere but never found them.

James was three and a half and spent less time with us, and there was very little contact between my father and Moira. One time while James was staying with us, I upset my father when I accidentally burnt the bacon. James wandered out into the garden and I went to fetch him, returning to find my father snatching the smoking pan off the stove. 'Why can't you be more fucking careful?'

He hurled the frying pan at the window, shards of glass showering across the sink. 'Why did you have to do that?' I said.

'Don't you fucking talk to me like that,' he snapped and snatched up the broom. With the first blow the head fell off and skidded into a corner. I curled up, begging him to stop. He flung the broomstick to the ground and began kicking me, screaming abuse.

James ran into the kitchen, crying. My father ignored him and I tried to crawl between the sink and the table, not noticing the broken glass in my panic. His shoe made violent contact with my hip, and I thought the pain would kill me, screaming in agony. It was too much for James; he leapt forward and clung to my father's leg, trying to stop him kicking me. I think my father was shocked, he suddenly seemed to regain his senses. He pulled James off his leg and walked out as James crawled onto my lap. 'Don't cry Tanjas, I'll look after you.'

I swept up the glass and washed the blood from my hands. I had raised areas on my legs and arms and a fist-sized bruise on my hip. As I went into the living room my father smiled at me as though nothing had happened. 'Would you like to go fishing?'

We drove to a small river and dropped our lines in the water. I noticed my father walked with a limp. 'I think I kicked you too hard,' he laughed, 'I've broken my toe.' I kept my thoughts to myself.

On 4 October 1978 I turned eighteen. Amongst my presents was a beautiful white cat with blue eyes, called Bijoux. When she was nine months old I discovered she was pregnant. She became even more affectionate, not letting me out of her sight and licking my hands for hours. When she had her kittens I made up a box and lined it with an old jumper, but she kept carrying her kittens to wherever I was sitting. Eventually my father lost his temper. 'Lock her up in the laundry,' he snapped.

On the weekend I hopped in the bath to wash my hair. My father climbed in with me. He had an erection; I hastily rinsed the soap from my hair, but I wasn't quick enough. While he was doing it I could hear yowling from downstairs. 'Stop, there's something wrong, I can hear Bijoux.'

'You and your bloody cat, sometimes I think you love her more than me.'

As I tried to pull free, the meowing becoming more desperate. I tried arguing, but he was getting irritated. 'Stop going on about it,' he snapped, 'she's stopped meowing.' And she had, but I couldn't shake the feeling that something was wrong.

All the while the hot water was running, gurgling as it trickled into the overflow pipe. He seemed to take forever, and when he finally came I leapt out, wrapped a towel around me and rushed downstairs.

As soon as I opened the door I knew what had happened. The gas heater had been working the whole time and used up all the oxygen – all the doors and windows were closed. I found Bijoux dead on the floor, suffocated. I couldn't stop screaming, hunting everywhere for the kittens. I found them in the bottom of the laundry basket, under the dirty washing, where Bijoux had hidden them. They were still alive.

My father found me lying her on the concrete of the carport. Her beautiful blue eyes were wide, staring into space and her mouth was open. My father was beside himself; he knelt down, trying to find a heartbeat. Then he poked his fingers down her throat, tilted her head back and started breathing into her lungs. I stood watching, tears streaming down my face, knowing the kittens didn't have a chance, still too young to survive on their own.

Bijoux didn't respond. My father flicked her on the nose, then flicked her eyes, still nothing, so he continued breathing into her. Suddenly she sneezed and began breathing. I carried her upstairs and my father followed with the kittens. It wasn't a happy ending. Bijoux was seriously brain-damaged. She couldn't see, she couldn't walk, her pupils were different sizes. I had to hand-feed her and carry her into the garden to help her go to the toilet. In spite of everything she continued producing milk for her babies. She couldn't clean them, so I took over, wiping them down twice a day.

After a month she seemed to be able to see a little and could feed herself. She was learning to walk again but had trouble stopping, crashing into walls. It was terrible to watch, but each day I saw improvements. The kittens were nearly old enough to be weaned and I started trying to get them to drink from a saucer.

I came home from school one day to find my father had built a small wire enclosure in the garden. We had a terrible row, but he was adamant, they were staying outside, he couldn't stand anything that was crippled or mental, and watching Bijoux was too much for him. I pleaded with him to add a roof. 'She's a bloody cat, she doesn't need a roof.' In the end, I covered half the cage with flattened out cardboard boxes, frustrated it was all I could do.

It rained heavily that night; I wanted to go out to check but my father wouldn't let me out of bed. In the morning she was dead, her beautiful white fur sodden and streaked with dirt as she lay stretched out in the mud. Her blue eyes were open, her kittens clustered against her, shivering and wet, meowing plaintively when they saw me. I carried them inside, dried and fed them.

Her death was a terrible tragedy, but I couldn't help but feel she was in a better place. Heaven was getting crowded, I remember thinking.

In 1979 my father began giving me methaqualone, a hypnotic drug heralded as one of the safest sleeping tablets on the market. In his mind it was the ideal alternative to alcohol, though sometimes he made me drink it with a glass of wine.

I hated the pills. They tasted bitter and it'd be more than forty-eight hours before I regained my balance. I felt nauseous, throwing up and sometimes fainting. At first he only gave me one, but soon increased it to three or four. Twenty minutes after taking them my limbs would go completely numb. I'd be unable to move, unable to push him away. He'd lean close and question me. Did I have a boyfriend? Had I told anyone? I wasn't going to tell anyone, was I? I used to pretend I was more out of it than I was; terrified I'd answer something incorrectly, unable to defend myself. When blackness finally took over it was a relief. I'd wake up sore in the morning, sometimes bleeding; frequently going to the doctor because of cystitis.

Sometimes I think it's best I don't know what he did during those absent hours. I know he took photos, his obsession with photographing me never dwindled. He started a series of photos, taken each year on the same day, in the same position. I hated that bloody camera and his constant wheedling to get me to pose.

On 4 October 1979 I turned nineteen. While I'd travelled extensively through the islands with my father, nothing had really changed. I found homes for three of the kittens and my father insisted on keeping the white one. I named him Polarbear Cat. My mother came down from Santo where she was now living, to have a screaming session with me – someone had told her I was working as a prostitute. I welcomed in my nineteenth year with the usual sex.

I finally decided I wanted to be a doctor. I'd seen so much suffering, children with broken arms, tuberculosis, malaria, malnutrition and I wanted to make a difference. I wanted to take the pain out of their eyes. It gave me the motivation to fight my depression and put my energy into study.

My father seemed all for it, flying me to Fiji at the end of 1979 to attend an interview at the Medical School. My chemistry results had been dismal, but even so, they said that if I improved them slightly, I'd have a place. I was ecstatic. I was going to be a doctor. I returned to school for one more year, repeating my classes. At the end of 1979 I was delighted to discover I'd boosted my grades enough for a place in Fiji. I'd be starting Pre Med in February 1980.

The day I left school, my father told me he wanted me to take a one-year break; I'd been working too hard. I was in no position to argue, but he promised to book me in for February 1981.

At the end of 1980, he told me he wasn't allowing me to go to Fiji. It would be too expensive and he didn't see why he should live alone. What could I do? I didn't have any money and I didn't know anyone.

1981 was one of the loneliest years of my life, the year I turned twenty-one. My diary makes sad reading. During the week I sat alone day after day with my cats, forbidden to leave the house. I cleaned and when there was nothing left to clean, I read. I'd sit on the balcony with a pot of tea, listening to classical music, and read my way through my father's library.

My only outings were when my father took me to buy groceries. During the weekend he worked in his workroom making fake artefacts. An old man had shown him how to make the 'dough' most New Hebridean art was made from, using a thick woody vine. The vine was grated, making a sticky, pithy mass that was easy to shape and set hard as wood. Once shaped onto spider-web matting, he added pig's tusks and painted them. Then he aged them with a special patina spray and gently smoked them in the smokehouse.

He had trouble keeping up with the demand from dealers around the world.

Moira had married a man with two children, the son a year older than James, and shortly after the wedding they moved to Sydney. I missed James terribly, but I was happy he had a normal family life.

Chapter 28

In May 1982, our harbour was crowded with yachts taking part in the Tauranga to Port Vila race. When they departed for Tauranga, not all of them made it. The *Golden Eagle* took a detour in Ouvea in New Caledonia, one of the French territory's outlying islands, striking the only uncharted rock in the bay and sinking within minutes. Undaunted, the crew swam the couple of hundred metres to shore.

The French cook from Ouvea's only hotel had seen the yacht sink and was there to greet them, with a silver tray, laden with champagne flutes and a bottle of champagne. They sat dripping wet on one of the world's most glorious beaches, in tropical sunshine, drinking French champagne!

My father received a telephone call from Lloyds and we flew to Ouvea. Apparently the yacht had sunk in a main shipping area and was a potential hazard.

Sasha, the resort owner, collected us from the airstrip wearing a long, elegant dress, and carrying a tiny poodle. 'It was so terrible, these poor men all wet from the sea, of course I put them up for free.'

I'd never seen anyone like him; he spoke and moved just like a woman. From time to time, he touched his hair, rearranging the flower behind his ear. He was so friendly, it would have been impossible not to like him.

We spent the next couple of days working out ways of raising and moving the *Golden Eagle*. The local gendarmes were very helpful, and at night we'd all crowd into the tiny restaurant, where the food was exquisite and Sasha would pile our plates high. My father, who couldn't speak French, had forbidden me to let on that I could. He wanted me to find out what they were talking about together, in case it related to something he should know about the *Golden Eagle*. So we spoke English, the gendarmes spoke French and we all laughed a lot. Often they would insult my father at great length in French, but I didn't translate.

After a couple of days we flew back to Port Vila and waited for Lloyds to decide the best course of action. Word came back from New Zealand we were to salvage the yacht.

We hired a yacht in Port Vila to bring all the necessary equipment, diving gear and metal drums we'd use for refloating the yacht. It was an exhausting week, working in the water all day, but eventually we lifted the yacht and towed it ashore. The gendarmes went out of their way to help us and in exchange, my father let them borrow the diving tanks.

On our second-to-last night, we went to the gendarmerie for cocktails. What a Mad Hatter's tea party that was! A long table in the garden was covered with a faded red-and-white checked cloth. It sheltered beneath a permanent thatched roof, from which several hurricane lanterns hung, attracting insects. We were offered a drink from an astounding array of dusty bottles and I soon forgot I wasn't supposed to be speaking French. Robert, the gendarme we had become friendly with on the previous trip, stared at me in horror. 'Mais, tu parles français!'

'Oui,' I admitted, laughing at his mortified expression.

'But you should have told me, what must you think? You heard all our insults.'

I leaned over and whispered, 'But don't worry, I didn't tell my father.' I sensed my father glaring at me, not understanding what we were talking about and angry I had disobeyed him.

At the end of the evening Robert invited us to come swimming the next morning. He wanted to show us a pool with sharks, and said to meet him at six.

I woke my father at five, and Sasha, in a long crimson dress, served us breakfast. My father was in one of his moods. 'I'm not bloody going.'

I tried to talk him round, careful not to anger him; I didn't want a scene, not with Sasha hovering. In the end I said, 'OK, you don't have to, but I'm not afraid of a few sharks.'

'Don't be so fucking arrogant,' he hissed, and would have said more, but Robert walked in with Jean Marc, another young gendarme. During the long drive my father tried to get out of it, suggesting we wait on the beach and watch. I refused to translate and he sat in the back, throwing me foul looks.

When we arrived at the diving spot the sea was calm, the sun still hadn't come up and the water looked grey and cold. I began to wonder if I hadn't let my enthusiasm get carried away. Robert pointed out the pool, about a half a kilometre away at the edge of the reef. Determined not to be a coward, I tugged off my dress and walked down to the water in my tiny bikini. I pulled on my flippers and rinsed my mask before putting it on, then waded into the water, gasping at the cold.

My father and Robert pulled on their wet suits and Jean Marc took off his jeans and T-shirt, diving in next to me. The water was shallow, only about two metres. I was beginning to get used to the cold, and convinced myself there'd be no sharks, then I noticed one casually swimming beside me. It wasn't that big, only one-and-half metres. I figured sharks were probably like dogs and could sense fear. I am not afraid, I kept repeating in my mind as I kept a careful eye on him. He was wonderfully sleek, grey, with a white belly, his dorsal fin only just breaking the water. Then he was gone.

When we reached the pool the current was incredibly strong and I had to cling to the coral to prevent myself being dragged in. A large school of unicorn fish swam by, accompanied by an enormous red parrotfish. And then I saw them. There seemed to be about twenty white tip sharks, all longer than me. They cruised slowly along the bottom, weaving in and out of each other. Robert swam over to me. 'You get a better view in the middle.'

'It's OK, I can see them from here,' I assured him, but he pried my hands off the coral, dragging me out into the open. I decided this Frenchman was nice, but quite crazy. Jean Marc and my father stayed at the edge, they obviously had more sense.

Robert kept a firm grip on my hand and pointed out the sharks cruising below. 'Aren't they magnificent?' he asked as we dog paddled on the surface for a moment. I poked my head back underwater; they were still there. I was beginning to feel more confident, the sharks hadn't ripped me apart the moment they set eyes on me. I felt laughter rising, after all, I thought, they're nothing but overgrown fish.

Suddenly Robert chased off after a shark that swam past, catching it by the tail, it flicked free and darted into one of the caves. I began to suspect Robert had been in the tropics too long.

As I watched, one of the larger ones rolled half on its back; I had the impression it was looking at me. Then it swam lazily in my direction. I was beyond fear, thinking my bikini wasn't going to be any protection against those teeth. It came within centimetres of my belly then turned, knocking my leg with its tail as it darted off.

When we swam back I was no longer afraid of the sharks, I was more concerned that the elastic of my pants had snapped. It was awkward swimming and trying to keep them up. I reached the shore elated, I had swum amongst sharks and not made a fool of myself.

Robert and Jean Marc thought I was brave, but my father said I was stupid.

While we dried ourselves, Jean Marc asked if I might stay longer on the island, spend some time with him. I felt sad, even though I really wanted to, I knew it was out of the question. My father would never allow it.

He asked me for my address, and I said I'd give it to him later, but I never did. He was a nice person; there was no future in writing to a girl like me.

Chapter 29

I went back to sitting on the balcony at home. Cystitis seemed to overtake my life, every two or three days I'd be overwhelmed by pain, excruciating burning agony. I was forever at the doctors' but they couldn't find a cause. I'd sit on the terrace and cry because it hurt so much.

I felt unbelievably lonely, I'd read all the books, some of them several times. I started writing to amuse myself. Not the diaries, though I still had to keep them. My father checked them to make sure I hadn't included something he didn't want and they were up to date. I began writing short stories and poetry. Sometimes, at my father's request, I'd write him a story. For Christmas he wanted a story called *The Sex Maniac*.

In 1983 we received a letter from the Vanuatu Government. I was standing outside the Post Office with him when he opened it. I remember the sea, sparkling under the midday sun, the dark green of the bush across the road, and dried leaves swirling around our feet as he read it to me. We were being deported. We had thirty days to tidy up our affairs and leave. Just like that. My father collapsed onto the steps, clutching the letter in his hands and I went away in my head. Vanuatu was my country, it was part of my soul. Why was this happening? Where we would go? What was going to happen to the animals?

My father went to see one of the ministers. They had heard rumours my father and I were living as man and wife. Life was unjust. The only parts of my life that brought me joy were my cats and the tropics outside my balcony, and I was going to lose them because of his penis. I wished it would drop off.

My father wanted to fight the deportation order. He'd prove he wasn't having sex with me. 'You'll have to prove you're a virgin.' He was losing it. 'No one will be able to tell for certain, I've made an appointment for you to see Dr Rosselinni.' Dr Rosselinni had been a good friend of my parents years before in Australia. He'd bounced me on his knee as a toddler.

The next day he drove me there and parked outside. 'Make sure you come back with that certificate. Our future depends on it.

'Do you understand the importance of this?' He grabbed hold of my chin and turned my face to look at him. 'I'll hold you responsible if you don't get it.'

I knew it was more than my life was worth to come back empty-handed. Dr Rosselinni greeted me enthusiastically and told me to sit down. 'And what can I do for you?'

I told him the cover story my father had coached me through the night before. My girlfriends were teasing me that I wasn't a virgin, and the gossip was getting out of hand.

'This blasted town, nothing but gossip,' he muttered as he

scribbled something on my file. Then he looked up. 'Are you a virgin?'

'Yes,' I lied, hating myself.

'Then it's no problem, I'll just do a quick examination. Pop your panties off behind the screen and lie down on the couch.'

I stared at him in horror. I hadn't realised he was going to look down there. I did as he instructed, squeezing my eyes shut as I lay back and he lifted my legs and pushed my heels against my bottom. He pulled my knees apart and began poking down there with a spatula and a light.

'What's happened to you,' he exclaimed, sounding horrified. 'You have a deep tear down one side, how did that happen?'

'I ... I don't know,' I mumbled uncomfortably. I could have died from embarrassment.

He examined me for a few more minutes and then switched off the light, and pulled off his gloves. 'You can put your panties on.'

He stared thoughtfully at me. 'I believe you, when you tell me you're a virgin, because I believe you're a good girl, but I can't give you a certificate of virginity.'

I began crying. Dr Rosselinni handed me a tissue and I told him about our deportation order and the 'rumours'. He agreed to write me a certificate. 'I'm sorry, but I can't state you are intact. I will, however, word it to appear as though you are a virgin.'

I handed the paper to my father, who wasn't pleased, but it was the best he was getting. He dropped me off at home and went into town to see the Minister. I showered, trying to scrub away the dirty feeling. Dirty, because of my lies and dirty because now someone knew what sort of girl I was.

The Minister wasn't fooled and we received another letter reminding us of our departure date. In desperation, my father flew me to New Caledonia, and I went through the same procedure, this time coming away with a correctly worded certificate, backdated by one year. The Minister sent it back to my father, telling him there were enough witnesses. They knew the truth.

Time was running out. We had nowhere to go, but my father remembered a school friend living in Auckland. He rang and arranged for us to stay with him until we were on our feet.

My father bought a container and we packed our belongings. He carefully secreted the packets of methaqualone inside empty Polaroid film containers, worried about being caught smuggling the drug into New Zealand. He hid the naked photographs of me inside several artefacts, wrapping them in plastic. Finally we had everything packed. A truck came and took it to the wharf and the house was empty.

We sent most of the animals to Holland, to my father's friend who owned the zoo. The hardest moment was parting from Mousecat. I caught a last glimpse as they wheeled him out to the plane. He was staring at me through the wire of his cage, yowling loudly. I was heartbroken. I'd put my favourite orange jumper in the cage for him to sit on, hoping the familiar smell would give him some comfort. I stared into his green eyes until they finally wheeled him out of sight.

Two weeks later we left Port Vila. The last night I had a strange dream. I was hovering in the air with an old cleva. We swooped over the sea as dusk fell and I asked him if I'd ever come back.

'You will come when you no longer want to, not before,' he said.

I asked him if I would ever be free and he flew me low

over the hills and across the coast. Below us rode two men on horses, they rode a little distance apart and I knew they didn't know each other. I flew down and landed on the sand. The first rider reached me and I looked up at him. He had dark hair and his brown laughing eyes reminded me of a carving of Buddha. He slowed as he neared me, I wanted to talk to him but I couldn't find the words. He walked the horse round me in a wide circle waiting, but when I still stood in silence, he kicked his heels against the horse's flanks and galloped into the distance.

The second man smiled, his blue eyes strangely bright. I finally found the words and started talking to him, after a few moments he leaned down and helped me onto his horse. We rode off together and I could feel his arms around me, warming me from the chill night air. Then I was back in the air with the cleva. When I asked him what it meant he told me the meaning would come clear, in time.

We found our seats in the aircraft, mine next to a Japanese man. I sat on something and awkwardly stood up again. There was an orange fountain pen, with a gold clip. I picked it up and asked him if it was his. 'No, not mine,' he replied.

I sat down and he leaned over. 'Maybe it a sign from God, maybe sign you should write.' He laughed at his little joke and I tried to smile through my gathering tears.

We began to taxi down the runway and I remembered the day I arrived in Port Vila. I couldn't hold the tears any longer and started to cry. 'Goodbye,' I whispered.

Then we were in the air flying over the coconut trees and into the clouds.

Chapter 30

We arrived in New Zealand on 14 August 1983, and my father's friend was there to meet us. We stayed for three months in a caravan in his garden and he and his wife were very kind. When their tenants moved from the house next door, they offered it to us for a very reasonable rent.

Life was grey and depressing. We lived in the bedroom, curtains drawn, warming ourselves by the solitary bar of an electric heater. I was forbidden to open the windows, someone might see in through a lifted curtain. The bedroom stank of cooking, sweat, rancid sperm and unwashed bedding. I wasn't allowed to change the sheets and my father's pillow had a grey sheen; he rarely washed.

He talked incessantly about a suicide pact, that is when he wasn't talking about the day we were going back, obsessed with his land and the house he'd build. The house he never built when he had the money and the opportunity. I realised he lived in a fantasy world, a world of dreams, without the ability to turn his dreams into reality.

He believed everything he could have been or could

have done had been stolen when we were kicked out of Vanuatu. When we first arrived he was offered a good position in New Guinea, but they found out we were persona non grata in Vanuatu and the job fell through. Because I'd been born in New Zealand I was eligible for benefit, and I went on the dole.

During those first months I was never allowed out of his sight. Neighbours tried to be friendly, including a young blond man who came to the door to introduce himself and offered to show me around, take me to the beach. Oh, how I would have loved that, to have pulled on my coat like any other young woman, follow him up the drive to his car and escape from the sordidness. But my father pushed the door shut in his face and accused me of being a slut.

He turned all his energies into sex, spending hours planning sexual marathons. While I was in the shower he'd prepare the bedroom, putting a red cloth over the lamp, laying out the ropes, the oil and the 'toys'. I'd stand under the hot water, willing myself to get out and face whatever was coming. Usually the water ran cold, forcing me out. I'd open the door and the red glow would be emanating from the bedroom. He'd tie me spread-eagled to the bed. 'I don't want to,' I'd say, but I might as well have said nothing.

I remember so much, in such detail, but I can't remember the tying up. I remember the ropes on the bed, the smell, his expression, then blankness. I remember everything that took place afterwards, the gags, the blindfolds and the wax for my ears. His grunting and the pain of the bulldog clips he applied to my nipples, belly and pubic area. The pain of the ten lashes with a bamboo stick, or eight or twelve, depending on how the dice lay. But I can't remember the tying up.

He beat me for nothing at all, once knocking me out. I

remember finding myself face-down on the floor with him standing over me, screaming, 'You fucking whore, I barely touched you.' I was so giddy I couldn't stand, and when I finally got to my feet, I threw up, barely making it to the bathroom. Another time he was lying on his back, I was on top of him, when he started to swear at me, 'You filthy cunt, I hate you, hate you.' He spat the words out, ranting and raving. I stopped moving, wanting to get away, feeling humiliated. 'I didn't tell you to stop fucking,' he snarled and began slapping me across the face.

I climbed off him and stood by the bed, my face smarting. 'Who do you think I am?' I asked bitterly.

'You're nothing but a whore,' he retorted as I ran into the bathroom and balanced on the edge of the bath, my head in my hands. His words went round in my mind as I rocked there, naked, unaware of the cold. If I was a whore, he'd made me one. Eventually I had to come out. I went into the bedroom to find some clothes and he told me to make him a cup of tea, he was thirsty.

During the week, we'd drive to the post office at Queen Elizabeth Square, hoping for mail that never came. The letter he was expecting was one from Vanuatu, saying we could come home. One particular day the sun was out, so we explored the square and found a gallery selling Oceanic art. We went in and introduced ourselves. My father was well known for his art collection and Keith, the owner, recognised our names immediately. He invited us for coffee and a friendship began. After a couple of weeks he asked if I'd take care of his shop while he was overseas. I jumped at the opportunity and my father took it to include himself. Keith showed me the ins and outs and took me to Webb's Auction Rooms to show me items he wanted me to bid on while he was away. He introduced me to a man arranging antique mirrors. 'If you have any problems, just ask Graeme.'

Graeme was in his thirties and exceedingly handsome. He was part Maori, with jet-black hair and smiling eyes. I felt at ease in his company and grew to like him very much. After that we met frequently, my father always present, and I was content to sit outside their conversation, sipping coffee. Sometimes I wondered if he liked me, or was attracted to me, but I'd quickly push this thought out of my mind. Who could like me? I was certain he was only being polite.

One afternoon my father and I had been visiting Keith and I'd been sent to run an errand, when I bumped into Graeme. He took me by the arm. 'I heard something that upset me,' he said.

'What, what did you hear?' I asked, not expecting it to have anything to do with me.

'It was something Alastair told me.' It's a small world, isn't it? Alastair, the artist who had painted me in Vanuatu, was flat sharing with Graeme and another friend. 'I just want to know if it's true, it won't make any difference to how I feel about you. He told me your father has sex with you.'

With a great effort, I laughed. 'Don't be ridiculous, of course he doesn't.'

What else could I say? Yes, he has sex with me, several times a week. Graeme looked relieved. 'You're not angry?'

'No of course not, people like to gossip.'

'But you know you can always talk to me if you need to.'

Yeah right, I thought, and then what? I liked Graeme, but he had no idea the kind of man my father was. No one could protect me from my father.

I never relayed this conversation, I knew it'd be enough to put Graeme on the list of enemies in my father's mind.

However, I gradually began to think about telling him the truth. Perhaps he could help me. I stewed on it for weeks. Finally, I decided I'd speak to him. The spur came one Friday night when I refused to take the methaqualone. 'If you think it's so wonderful, why don't you take it yourself?' I yelled.

'Because it's sexier if you take it,' he simpered, trying to be charming.

I had trouble hiding my anger, but I managed. 'I'm sick of feeling ill the next day.'

In the end, telling me it was perfectly safe, he agreed to take it if I seduced him. 'But only one tablet, because I have a delicate constitution.'

He swallowed the bitter pill after much performance. Then he told me to undress him, wanting me to fulfil my side of the bargain. I took as long as I dared, waiting for him to pass out, but he just lay there rambling abuse at me. I refused to touch him. Dirty old man lying in a filthy bed, I remember thinking. I wished he were dead. I was shocked at myself. It was the first time I'd allowed such a thought to cross my mind.

It would be the solution to all my problems if he simply dropped dead. It would have been so easy for me to pick up a pillow and smother him. I thought about it. I sat in the armchair in the corner of the room, watching him lie there asleep on his back, snoring. He could use me, he could beat me and abuse me, and do whatever he wanted to my body, but that night I swore he'd never get my mind.

My father snorted, and rolled to his feet. I tried to catch his arm, but he jerked away from me. 'Fuck off bitch,' he slurred, staggering into the kitchen. 'I gotta piss.'

'Let me help you to the toilet,' I said, trying to steady him.

He punched out at me, then took hold of his penis and began spraying the kitchen wall. As urine streamed down the flaking wallpaper and pooled on the floor, I tried to stop him. He stamped his feet like a little child and punched me again, moving further down the kitchen, urinating all the while. He was completely insane, the methaqualone had taken away the veneer he normally hid behind. Finally he staggered back into the bedroom and left me with the stench.

That was one of the low moments of my life. I knelt on my knees in the kitchen with rags and a bucket of hot soapy water, trying to remove every trace. It stained the wallpaper and had run behind the skirting board and under the broken linoleum. I had to get out of this situation, either get out or go mad. As I savagely scrubbed his stench from my hands, I decided to talk to Graeme.

The next time we went to the auction we arrived late and stood at the back. Graeme waved between lot numbers, but seemed distracted, his attention on the front row. I stood on tiptoe, trying to see over the crowd. Then I saw her, a tall attractive woman, seated in the front row. I was devastated. If Graeme had a girlfriend he wouldn't have room in his life to help me. Now what? In the end I decided to wait until the auction was over, perhaps it was his sister. When the auction came to an end and he hopped down, there was no room for doubt. The woman slid an arm through his and introduced him to the elderly couple sitting with her. For once I was grateful when my father tugged at my sleeve. 'Come on,' he said, 'I don't feel like talking to any of these idiots.'

I thought long and hard that night, as I lay in bed next to my sleeping father. I couldn't take much more of this. I needed a job; at least that'd get me out of the house during the day. It wasn't going to be easy, my father was against me working – he wanted to keep me where he could control me. I tried to work out the best way to broach the subject without angering him. Eventually I fell asleep without reaching a solution.

Providence came to the rescue. I received a letter from the Labour Department; I'd been on the benefit long enough and they were sending me to several job interviews. I walked a tightrope. My father would drive me to the interviews, giving me strict instructions on how to avoid being employed. I knew that if I got the job he'd get really angry, but if I didn't I'd be stuck in the house all day with him. I decided to go all out to be employed. However, I'd never been to a job interview, and I'd never worked. Eventually one of the supervisors at the Labour Department lost her temper. 'You're deliberately trying to avoid work,' she snapped as I sat down at her desk.

'I'm not,' I explained earnestly. She had a job for me, working as a seamstress in a South Auckland factory. I could have kissed her feet in gratitude; even though the job was miles away from where I was living. She dismissed me with a disapproving smile, happy she'd dealt with another dole scrounger.

My father went berserk when I told him. 'You're not working in a bloody factory!'

'I don't have a choice, they'll cut our money off if I don't go.'

As fate would have it, the supervisor rang back that afternoon, she'd found a more suitable position, two streets away from where I lived. I was to start work at Royal Road Primary School as the school librarian, on some sort of back-to-work scheme.

The headmaster was one of the kindest men I'd ever met, a gentleman of the old school with courteous manners who quickly put me at my ease. Another woman, Rachel, was also there on the work scheme, doing blow-up books. This involved copying pictures out of a book onto large sheets of paper, making a giant copy of the original, which was easier for the teacher to read and show a classroom of children. She confided that she couldn't draw to save herself.

My job was to organise the books, keep the library tidy and read to the children during lunch break. If they'd been flying foxes, snakes or even tiger cubs I'd have no problem, but these were children. If the truth be known, I was afraid of them. Rachel, on the other hand, adored children. We decided to swap jobs. The headmaster couldn't see any reason why we shouldn't, and so began some of the most delightful days of my life up to that point. I was given a back room, where I painted to my heart's content.

With my first pay packet, my father allowed me to buy a tiny radio and I sat in artistic solitude, listening to popular music, singing along as I worked. I was as happy as humanly possible during working hours. Coming home was horrible. As the hands of my watch slid towards five my heart would sink and while I rinsed out the paintbrushes I'd wonder what was waiting for me at home. In a way, my temporary freedom made it harder to bear and I began to refuse him more often. Not that it made any difference.

One day we went to collect the mail, it was raining so my father waited outside in the car. I dashed in and hurried over to our box. I had to step round a man sitting close by. He stared at me as I unlocked it, making me nervous. I started pulling out the letters and locked the box. Suddenly he stood up, startling me, and I dropped the mail. He stood in my way, preventing me from picking it up.

'You're nothing but a cock tease,' he hissed then turned away leaving me stunned. What was all that about? I picked up the mail and hurried out to the car where I told my father what had happened. 'Probably a nutter,' he explained. 'Auckland's full of them.'

A couple of days later we drove to Grey Lynn, a suburb of Auckland; my father wanted to get some of his photos of me developed. I waited in the car. After he'd been gone for more than half an hour, I opened the glove box. There were some letters stuffed in the map book, addressed to me and already opened. I turned the envelopes over; I didn't recognise the sender. I slid out the folded sheet of paper from the top one and began to read. My blood turned cold. It was dated two weeks previously, apparently replying to a letter written in my name.

It began ... So, when you arrive, the front door will be ajar, and talked about bondage, chains, whips and dripping candle wax. It ended ... don't be late, I'll have to punish you if you are.

I spotted my father coming out of the building and stuffed the paper back in the envelope, shoving them all back into the glove box. With monumental effort I smiled as he got in the car; I didn't dare let him know I'd seen the letter. All the while I was thinking ... Oh God, that was the man at the post office!

Later I found my father was advertising in the personal column of the *New Zealand Herald*, pretending to be a woman. After that, I was too afraid to collect the mail. What if that man was there again? What if he wasn't the only man my father was writing to?

It got worse. My father met a man with a passion for little girls. They used to meet while I was at work, to look at photos and magazines depicting children having sex with adults and being tied up and tortured. My father used to talk ad nauseam about the things he'd seen. When I told him it sickened me and asked why he looked at them, he told me I didn't understand. 'He's the one who's sick, I only look because I'm curious to see what sort of a man he really is. I personally find it disgusting.' I didn't want to hear any more and walked out of the room, but he followed me. 'He showed me a book on bondage techniques. Some of the ideas were sexy. I'm going to try them out. One of them was a woman suspended upside down from the ceiling.'

I sat on the couch in silence. My nightmare closing around me, smothering me, a lamb to the slaughter. I interrupted his description. 'It wouldn't be possible, it would be too painful.' I was hoping to dissuade him, but it backfired, instead it motivated him to prove it could be done.

The following night when he picked me up from work he told me he'd been thinking about this new sexy idea. When we got home he showed me a drawing he'd done, of a woman suspended upside down. By the weekend he'd devised a method of suspending me from the ceiling. He'd purchased pulleys and more ropes, drilled holes in the ceiling and on the floor, and screwed the pulleys in place, arranged so I'd be suspended over the bed.

I came out of the shower to the glow of the red lamp and went away in my head. The pain of the ropes on my ankles was unbearable. I was blindfolded, but I could feel him wrapping ropes round my breasts, criss-crossing the rope over and under them tightly, until they hurt almost as unbearably as my ankles. Finally, he was satisfied.

Then came the problem. He couldn't enter me; he tried frantically, standing on tiptoes on the soft mattress, constantly losing his balance before he could get it in. He was getting more and more frustrated, eventually giving up on that idea and wriggling under my suspended head, trying to poke it into my mouth, but he couldn't manage that either.

It would have been funny if it hadn't been so humiliating.

He swore under his breath, he was losing his erection. In the end, he stood there masturbating. He came against me and I could feel his slime trickling on my skin. Then there was silence and I saw the flash of the Polaroid camera, and heard the sound it makes when the photo comes out. Afterwards he told me he hadn't really enjoyed it. I asked him about the photo, but he denied taking any. He must have thought me a real idiot. The sad thing is that he was right.

I found the photo, hidden at the back of the cupboard, amongst the bulldog clips and ropes and other 'toys' while he was in the garden. I stared at the picture in horror. It was easier to handle what was happening to me in reality than to see it in a photo. I could go away in my head. Being confronted with the photo of myself, bound and blindfolded, hanging upside down, my hair tangled over my face and streaming down over the bed, was too much. I felt as though my head was going to explode. I knew he'd taken photos of me tied up, I knew he kept them in a plastic bag in the safe, but I never looked at them.

Thinking about that photo nearly cost me my life the next time he suspended me from the ceiling. This time he thrashed me soundly with the bamboo cane, telling me he found the red streaks sexy. Then he brought a candle into the room. He wanted to drip hot candle wax on me. That was too much, I begged and pleaded for him not to. His only response was to tape my mouth shut, with heavy black tape, retying my blindfold so tightly it dug into the bridge of my nose.

Suspended upside down I felt him pushing the candle into me, then I heard him strike a match. I squirmed, causing more pain. I could feel the wax dripping, burning and then I went away in my head. I went away in my head but saw the photo and how I must look.

I felt so alone, humiliation and degradation swept over me and I began to cry silently, tears soaking into the blackness of my blindfold. But the big problem with crying when you're tied upside down is that your nose blocks. I suddenly couldn't breathe. The tape was stuck over my mouth and my nose was blocked.

I was terrified, I was suffocating. I screamed in the back of my throat trying to attract my father's attention, but he did nothing. In blind terror I swung myself back and forth, straining at the ropes, trying to free myself, desperately trying to breathe, tearing the skin on my wrists.

I knew I was going to die if I didn't free myself. My lungs were on fire and I could feel myself blacking out. Then suddenly my hand was free, I'd yanked the pulley free from the floor, and I tore at the tape gagging my mouth, scratching my face. Finally I ripped it loose and sucked in precious air, still hanging upside down, hot wax spilling onto me. I tore the blindfold from my eyes. My father was just standing there. 'Why didn't you help me?' I gasped.

He shrugged, 'I didn't realise you had a problem.'

Afterwards I went into the bathroom and carefully wiped the superficial scratches on my face with Dettol. My wrists and ankles were another story. They were bruised and rubbed raw, but my right wrist was the worst. It was agonising and seeping blood where the rope had flayed the skin in my desperate attempt to free myself. Why? I kept asking myself, why did he just stand there? I didn't believe his explanation. I hated him.

Chapter 31

I was perpetually tired. It wasn't that my new job was strenuous – perhaps I wasn't eating properly. My father would pick me up from work and we'd go shopping. He was obsessive about what we ate, reading the labels to see what additives had been used. We always went to the same store, always walked down the aisles in the same order, if I forgot something, I wasn't allowed to go back. It would have to wait until next time, and I shouldn't have been so stupid as to forget it. Once he decided on our purchases, we'd make our way to the checkout, he'd hand me the money so I could pay, then I'd give him the change.

At home, I'd clean the mess created during the day, which generally took about an hour and when the house was in order, I'd get the laundry and fill the concrete tub in the tiny wash house. I hated washing by hand. His underpants were always so filthy, stained and stuck together with dried sperm. Sometimes they were so bad I'd throw them in the rubbish bin, hiding them underneath the household waste. On rare occasions, I'd manage to persuade him to let me change the sheets. They were so dirty I'd have to scrub them a second time, as the soap powder wouldn't foam first time round. When the washing was hung on the line I could prepare dinner. My father meanwhile would be watching television. I'd bring the plates into the bedroom. 'Why did you take so long? You're obsessive, always bloody cleaning. I don't know how it gets so dirty, I don't make a mess.'

I'd remain silent at this point. I didn't make the mess. Perhaps I was an obsessive cleaner. I couldn't stand filthy surroundings, somehow it made everything even more unbearable.

I hated my life. All around me at work were women my age and I felt awkward, like a silly teenager, not twenty-three at all. I wished I could be free like them, but it wasn't possible. I was carrying the weight of what was happening at home and I couldn't see a way out. I was earning, but I had to hand the money over to my father.

Even so, I was changing, becoming aggressive, fighting back, arguing with him. I didn't care that he beat me; I was used to it. I counted hours. It didn't matter how bad it got at home; it was only so many hours until I had to be at work. Sex was something to be done as quickly as possible, then put behind me, forgotten about. I'd shut it completely out of my mind. I'd say no when he touched me; it didn't make any difference, he still did whatever he wanted.

One Saturday we drove into town to check the mail. My father was in a terrible mood. I'd knocked the rear-view mirror when I was getting in the car. He fiddled round for ages, twisting the mirror back and forth as he tried to reposition it. 'Fuck!' he screamed and lashed out at me, smashing me across the ribs with his fist. Then he reversed full speed out of the garage into the middle of the road. 'If we have an accident now, it'll be your bloody fault.'

He raced down the road, slewing round the corner on the wrong side, grinding gears in his anger. Halfway down the motorway he changed lanes in front of a car without indicating, forcing the driver to slam on the brakes. The driver tooted angrily, and chased after us, flashing his lights. My father gave him the finger in the rear vision mirror and kept weaving in and out of the traffic, his mouth set in a tight line. The car gave chase and then cut in front of us, forcing my father to brake. 'Fucking bastard, what's he doing, trying to kill someone driving like that?'

We overtook the car again, just before reaching the end of the motorway. We drew to a stop, the other car directly behind. He tooted angrily at us the whole time the light was red and my father lost his temper. He drove forward a few metres then backed straight into the car behind. There was the sound of breaking glass and bending metal and then the lights turned green. My father raced off, tyres screeching. I looked over my shoulder, catching a glimpse of the man getting out of his car, his front bumper lying twisted half off, orange and white glass scattered across the road.

My father raced through downtown Auckland, constantly checking his rear-view mirror to see if we were being followed. 'If the police stop us, he smashed into us when we stopped at the lights, understood?' I nodded; I wasn't going to contradict him when he was in that mood.

He turned into the Britomart car park and we parked at the top. After checking the mail, we walked up to Albert Street and my father placed an advertisement in the newspaper. I waited outside, then we walked up to the

Auckland Art Gallery for a coffee. He didn't want to go home yet, in case the police were looking for him.

A couple of hours later we returned to the car, rowing about what he'd done, and he punched me hard in front of passers-by. I was so embarrassed I ran ahead of him, all the way back to the car. He was still furious when he arrived at the top of the stairwell. 'Who the fuck do you think you are, running away from me like that?' he yelled as he caught sight of me.

'I've had enough of you,' I said, quietly as he came over. 'I don't see why I should take any more of this treatment.'

'So what are you saying? You're leaving me? Why?'

'Because it's not right.'

'What's not right?'

There it was, the opportunity to tell him. I couldn't find the right words. 'It's against the law,' I ended up saying lamely.

He stared at me with such fury I backed away. 'What the hell are you saying?' he screamed. I lost my courage; the words refused to come out of my throat. He stepped towards me, his face red and contorted. 'You're just as fucking guilty,' he spat. 'You little bastard, what is this? You're suddenly the goody-goody now. You should become a missionary, then you can go to Africa and teach the fucking blacks.' Spittle clung to his beard.

I said nothing; we were standing by the railing running round the top of the building. Suddenly he leapt onto the railings and swung his feet over, balancing precariously on the edge. 'I'm going to jump, you fucking bastard, is that what you want?'

'Don't jump,' I begged, terrified he would, aware that people in the building across the way must be witnessing this humiliating spectacle.

'Then tell me you're not going to leave me!'

I was crying now, pleading with him to get down off

the rails. Promising him anything he wanted. Eventually he climbed down.

'Let that be a lesson to you,' he said, as we finally got into the car. What a fool I was, I should have told him to jump.

My job came to an end, it had only been for six months and the time had come to leave. The headmaster came to see me that last day, as I washed the paintbrushes for the last time. He told me he would have liked me to stay another six months, but the funding request to keep me had been turned down. I was sorry to hear it. I stopped briefly in the staff room on my way out, and said my last goodbyes, then I walked out to where my father waited to take me home.

I was back, trapped day after day, night after night in my father's constant company. He never let me out of his sight, not even to go to the toilet – I had to leave the door open. This had become his latest phobia. Closed doors. He'd become enraged if any door was shut, with the exception of the front door.

I missed my job, the teachers and even the children. I had to find another job. It wouldn't be so difficult I decided, not now that I had a wonderful reference. I went back to the Labour Department, where someone suggested I do a course, and I discovered they would pay for the courses. And so began my road to self-improvement. My father wasn't happy, but couldn't argue about the cost, nor could he argue about the merits of education.

I did a short computer course, learning how to turn a computer on and off and not really understanding anything else. But that was OK, because there was no examination, only a certificate stating I'd attended the course. I tried to find work again, but when that failed I returned to the list of available courses.

There was a secretarial course that sounded interesting, but first I had to learn to type. So I attended a two-week intensive typing course and learnt where all the keys were on the typewriter. I came away unbelievably proud. I could type twenty-eight words a minute, without looking at my fingers. I was then enrolled in a three-month Pitman's secretarial course. The class was socially divided between the 'dole bludgers' and the 'rich kids'. The rich kids made our lives miserable with their catty remarks, stuck up noses and beautiful clothes. We'd ignore them as best we could, and we worked harder, understanding the importance of the paper we'd walk away with. We knew what it was like to be cold, hungry and poor. The rich kids still had that lesson to learn. I still couldn't get work, and there were no more courses I was eligible to attend. I went back on the dole.

I began to have nightmares. I was always escaping, terrified for my life, I'd run down dimly lit roads, through gardens and deserted parking buildings. I always ended up in a small room listening to footsteps running down the hall, the footsteps of someone who wanted to kill me. I'd tear at the window, trying to open it. Sometimes there'd be bars over the windows, then the door would slowly open and as the killer slipped into the room I'd wake up.

I'd lie back, drenched in sweat, my heart pounding and wonder which was the worse place. Back in my dreams with the unseen killer, or here next to the man who was killing me slowly.

My father's latest sex game was writing out small cards of instructions telling me what I had to do to him, or what he was going to do to me. He had dozens of them, neatly written on small white pieces of cardboard. He'd turn them face down and I'd have to pick one. How I wished he'd become impotent.

Chapter 32

Finally I had a job, in a medical insurance company. I paid the bills and my father used the rest.

I celebrated my twenty-seventh birthday in Bora Bora. My father and I were staying with Barry, an American art collector we met while we were living in Seaside Village in Vanuatu.

On my birthday, I woke before dawn. I crept out of the room and walked across the damp ground to the wharf. The sea front was deserted and I sat on the wooden beams at the end of a jetty and stared into the still, dark depths.

I remembered turning seventeen. Ten years had gone by, just like that, and nothing had changed. More than ten years of waiting, but there had been no miracle. Ten years!

A lump of fear lodged like a coconut in my stomach. I was no closer to escaping, or being rescued. My life hadn't improved, just continued deteriorating, slowly but surely. Any dreams I had of being rescued, of falling in love and having a family, were fading. No one would fall in love with me. How could they? I was sallow, unsmiling and stupid. My father said no one would want me, they'd only want my body, they'd fuck me for a week and throw me in the street where I belonged. I'd reached the stage where I believed him. That was all I was good for.

The sun slowly slid over the horizon, catching at a patch of oil, creating shimmering rainbows on the surface of a sea so clear it seemed as though the moored boats hovered in the air. It matched my mind, a surreal world where I tried to cling to reality. It was so frustrating, so many secrets. Eighteen years had passed since my father crossed the sacred line separating right from wrong, stealing my innocence. He was still doing it. I knew some people saw me as a difficult daughter and felt sorry for my father, having to raise a girl like me. A perfect example was my birthday cake. Last night my father had revealed my forthcoming birthday. When Barry asked how old I was going to be, I said I would be twenty-seven tomorrow. I could see they were surprised; they thought I was much younger.

My father coughed, 'She's pretending to be older than she really is. She will be twenty-three tomorrow.'

My face burned with embarrassment as everyone laughed. I knew my passport would prove I was telling the truth. But where would that get me? A momentary victory that would be laughed off by my father, then when we were alone, I'd be beaten for embarrassing him.

I stopped waiting for the miracle, what was the point? I'd come to understand I would never escape; I would never be free. It was too late. The hard truth was he had finally broken my spirit. I was twenty-seven, and I was completely friendless, so unbearably lonely. I wrapped my arms over my head as I sobbed. I couldn't pick up the telephone, as they did in the movies, and ring someone. I couldn't even ring Lifeline. It would be just my luck to have my father answer the telephone, he was now one of their counsellors.

Sometimes my anguish was so great I screamed or banged my head with my fists. I knew I was tottering on the edge of insanity. I couldn't live like this any more. I didn't want to live like this any more. There was the simple truth, the simple answer. I'd heard that people who commit suicide go to hell, well so what? I was already in hell.

Suddenly I thought of Lorry, from Port Vila days. He'd been at our school for a year; his domineering father was an alcoholic. Lorry was a loner, like me, and the butt of everyone's jokes. I guess he'd been waiting for the miracle to come along as well.

He hanged himself in his father's workshop. Lorry had wanted to escape from his father; he'd asked people for money to buy a ticket so he could go to Australia. If only he'd waited, people would say, if only he'd waited for something to come along. Things would have improved for him. Perhaps they were right.

I thought about my life, it hadn't all been hell. I'd travelled the world, I'd stood beneath a full moon with a thousand native warriors on the ash planes of Yasur. I'd swum amongst sharks and walked across a beach in paradise. I still had the pebbles I'd collected so long ago. I'd earned the name Walk Far Woman. But where was Walk Far Woman now? Her spirit was broken.

Sometimes I felt as though I was just a shell, and my soul was still playing with the spirits on Colardo's plantation, not realising my body had gone to another country. Yes, there had been wonderful times, but they were long gone.

My subjugation was complete, I was my father's slave; I

did nothing without his permission. He didn't need to work, my money belonged to him. It allowed him to stay home, making fakes for the art world.

Over the years he'd become more cruel and perverse with his sex games. If he thought about something, he did it, if he heard about something, he did it and if he read about something, he did it. He did it all to me. I was the perfect sex toy. I had no privacy at all. He hated me getting up at night, even to go to the toilet. Sometimes I'd lie in bed, busting to go, too terrified to disobey him. There was a long list of things I wasn't allowed to do. I wasn't allowed to shave my legs, or cut my hair, although once a week he'd shave my pubic hair. He'd stand in the hall outside the bathroom, listening to me brush my hair. 'I can hear you breaking your hair,' he'd scream.

He'd gather the hairs from my brush and dump them in front of me, telling me to comb them out and plait them together so I could see how much hair I was destroying.

In the morning, he'd tell me what I was to wear. It wasn't worth arguing, my clothes would be thrown out or burnt as punishment. He chose my make-up, the colour of my lipstick, the shade of my nail polish.

He'd buy me expensive gifts and then check them for damage, beating me for not being careful enough. He'd even check my high heels for scratches. It didn't matter how careful I was, he was always angry with me. I wasn't allowed to buy anything without his permission. I had a bank account; I had a chequebook. I could sign a cheque, but I never did without his prior approval. He'd even told me how to write my signature. It was very similar to his.

He drove me to work in the morning, driving aggressively and if I foolishly defended the other drivers, he'd start yelling at me. More often than not I'd arrive at work in tears. Even then, I wasn't free. He'd ring me several times to ensure I was at work and then turn up at lunchtime. He'd ring again in the afternoon. It was the same every single working day.

No, the miracle had never come, and I knew in my heart it never would. I had no way out of this hell, except through suicide. I decided to wait, just a little longer. I found a piece of paper, wrote a date, one year from then, and drew a crucifix. If nothing had changed by that date I'd kill myself. I put the piece of paper in my handbag, and every so often, as the months went by, I would take it out and smile. I had a release date from hell.

Chapter 33

I was now working for a Finance Company, as private secretary to the manager, and I owed it all to the wonderful lady at the employment agency. I'd been trying for months to get another job, then one day she sat me down in her office. 'You'll never get a job looking like that. What you need is a dressy jacket and a short skirt, and you need to get your hair out of the way.'

I went shopping with my father. We found a white jacket on sale, tucked at the waist and very elegant. I already had a suitable skirt. The day before the next batch of interviews I bleached the hair on my legs. If I wasn't allowed to shave I'd make them as inconspicuous as possible.

I spent ages in front of the mirror, struggling to achieve a tidy look. Finally I brushed it back and twisted it up into a tight bun, holding it in place with a chopstick. I looked at my reflection with some satisfaction – the picture of efficiency. My father thought I looked like a lesbian.

I went to seven job interviews, armed with certificates and

glowing references; I was cheerful and bubbly, asking all the right questions and exaggerating my abilities. At the end of the week I'd been offered four positions, the other three said I was over-qualified. That was kind of them.

Henry, my new boss, was nearing retirement. There was only one other person in our branch, Charles. On the first day Henry showed me the computer. I skilfully turned it on, to show I knew computers. I'd been a little over-enthusiastic about my skills, but was certain I could learn quickly. 'You'll have to go over it with me, I'm used to a different system,' I explained when I couldn't make head nor tail of what he was showing me.

'Don't worry, Dale is coming up from Wellington to show you how it all works.'

Dale arrived a few days later. We'd been in front of the computer for about half an hour when she turned to me. 'You haven't touched a computer in your life, have you?' she asked quietly.

I could feel my face flush and decided truth was the best option. 'No, not really, but I need the job,' I whispered.

'I won't let on, I'll start at the beginning and by the end of the week you'll know what you're doing.' Before she returned to Wellington she gave me her direct line. 'If you run into any problems, just call and I'll talk you through.'

I could have hugged her. I loved my new job. I'd been clever this time and told my father I wasn't allowed personal calls. He could no longer ring me, but he was still there, every lunchtime, without fail.

The date on my piece of paper crept closer. It was Friday, four days before I planned to go to heaven. I'd worked everything out. Providence was on my side. On Tuesday my father would be at Lifeline, on night duty. After he left I'd ring a taxi and go out to Huia. From there I'd walk into the bush and find a place where I'd never be found. I didn't want my father taking photos of my dead body.

I'd thought of a hundred ways to kill myself, deciding in the end to cut my wrists. Bleeding to death seemed the easiest way to leave this world. I was very philosophical, waiting for Tuesday with anticipation. Only four more days and I'd be free. I'd go to heaven and see my Opa, Louis Armstrong, Garbageguts, Bijoux and so many others.

At five o'clock I went downstairs to wait for my father. I didn't know it then, but the miracle had come and the wheels of change had started to turn.

He was in a wonderful mood. 'I still haven't discovered how to polish the mother of pearl, so I went to Grafton Traders this afternoon. The owner wasn't able to help but a customer came in and he told me that if anyone could help he'd be able to.' I only half listened, I was thinking about Tuesday, only one more weekend to get through. 'He said the customer, Bill, was a stonecutter and knew everything there was to know about stones. His workshop is just down the road from where you work, and he's invited us there tomorrow.'

It was the last thing in the world I wanted to do. A man whose life revolved around rocks – I couldn't imagine anything worse, but that night I remembered the pebbles I'd collected when I was Walk Far Woman. Perhaps Bill could tell me what they were.

In the morning I asked my father to get the stones out of the safe but he refused, worried they were valuable and Bill might swap them. He told me I could describe them, if he was any good at his job Bill would know what they were. This time I was determined, I was the one who collected the stones, I was the one who carried them halfway round the island. I managed to persuade him but he was now in a filthy mood. He couldn't stand it when I argued with him.

Windsor House was shabby and the graffiti-decorated lift rattled slowly to the fifth floor. As we stood in front of the glass door of Auckland Gemcutters, I looked through the dusty windows as my father rang the bell. A dark-haired woman peered round the door of an inner office and then disappeared. A moment later she returned, followed by a man in jeans and an unbelievably grubby sweatshirt.

As my father introduced me, Bill took my hand in his firm grip, looking directly into my eyes with his startling blue ones and I suddenly found it hard to breathe. It was the most peculiar feeling. I could have sworn I'd known him all my life. 'Give the poor man back his hand,' my father suddenly commented. I flushed, realising we were still holding hands. Bill laughed and I shook hands with his wife, Hilda.

It was the most wonderful day. My father was soon deep in conversation with Hilda and left me to talk to Bill. He pointed to a chair near his workbench and I sat down as he began telling me about his job. He was a gemcutter, not a stonecutter, and showed me a stone he'd just finished faceting. He tipped the gem into the palm of my hand, telling me it was morganite, a pink beryl. It sparkled under the light as I tilted it back and forth.

We talked for hours. He told me about cutting diamonds and emeralds in Africa, mining amethysts and sapphires in Australia and collecting trips through Asia. He made me laugh and once I'd overcome my shyness, I told him about the islands and my trip round Malekula and the beach, showing him the clear stones I'd collected. He told me they were topazes.

While we were talking I remember thinking, 'If my life

had been different, this is a man I would have liked to marry.' When he showed us his faceting machine I was fascinated, leaning over him as he polished the facets of a ruby. He talked all the while, explaining what he was doing. 'It's important to cut by feel, not to look at the dials. That's faceting by numbers. A lot of amateurs cut like that, but it slows you down.' He looked up at me, 'That's what I'd tell you, if I was teaching you to cut.'

Someone suggested we go out for a meal. I looked at the clock in amazement; it was already past six. We went to the Metropole in Parnell and I spent most of the evening talking to Hilda. Afterwards we walked to the car park, where our cars were parked next to each other. Bill and I stood talking between the cars. Hilda wound down her window and called out, 'Are you two going to stand in the rain all night?'

I hadn't even noticed it was raining. We laughed, then hurried round to our separate car doors and hopped in, then my father followed them out of the car park. Bill and Hilda turned left and drove up the hill. We turned right. I had the peculiar feeling I was in the wrong car.

That night I couldn't sleep. I lay motionless next to my father, reliving the afternoon, playing back the conversation in my mind. Did he mean he wanted to teach me? Was he offering to teach me? Wouldn't it be amazing to take a rough dirty piece and create a sparkling gem like the morganite? Or cut one of my topazes. I couldn't get the thought out of my mind and in the morning I asked my father about it. 'Why don't you ask him?' he said. 'We could make a lot of money if you learnt to facet.' I hadn't even thought about that.

I decided I'd ask Bill on Monday, on my way back from the post office. If he'd teach me I'd throw away the piece of paper, if not I'd go to Huia. On Monday I got as far as the lift before my courage failed me. I returned to the office. Tomorrow I'd ask. Tomorrow I'd be more determined. I lost courage each time. On the fourth occasion, I was hesitating in front of the open lift when a man pushed past. 'Hurry up, I can't hold the door open all day.'

It was now or never. My hands were perspiring and my heart beat furiously as I rang the doorbell. Bill opened the door, breaking into a huge smile when he saw me. 'I was wondering if you'd come by,' he said. I was overcome with shyness and my voice squeaked when I explained I couldn't stay long. 'Long enough for a cup of tea?'

I nodded. We went into his workshop and he introduced me to Peter, a Burmese man, who was working with him. I watched the clock nervously; I was running out of time. When I gathered up the courage to ask if he would teach me, my words came out all tangled together, 'Wouldyouteachmetocut?'

'What did you say?'

When I repeated myself slowly, he said yes. I was stunned into silence. He said he'd ring me at work when he had time to teach me. I danced all the way down in the lift. He was going to teach me to cut. I was going to facet. Out on the footpath I tossed the scrap of paper into the gutter. Heaven would have to wait!

I told my father on the way home about my visit to Bill's workshop. 'He won't ring. He was only being polite.'

I didn't believe him, I was sure Bill would ring. Nevertheless, the days went by and he still hadn't called. By Friday, I was convinced my father was right. Bill had better things to do than teach a stupid, uninteresting person like me. At five to five Henry was standing next to my desk while I typed an urgent letter. The telephone rang and he picked up the receiver. 'It's for you,' he exclaimed, looking surprised. No one ever rang me.

It was Bill! 'I've put the kettle on,' he said and then hung up.

'Who was that?' Henry asked.

'A friend,' I said proudly.

'Thank goodness for that, I was beginning to think you didn't have any.'

I finished the letter and Henry said I could go. 'Have a nice weekend,' he called as I raced out of the door, still pulling my coat on. I walked amongst the clouds as I went to meet my father. I was going to facet a stone, and I had a friend.

Together we went up to Bill's workshop, and once the tea was made he sat me down at his faceting machine and my first lesson began. He had pre-formed a piece of smoky quartz for my first stone. I finished the crown that evening and Bill invited me to come back the next day to finish it. I was excited, I could hardly sleep.

I slept in, waking up with my father's erect penis pressing against my tailbone, as he pulled me closer trying to enter me. I could smell the baby oil. I hated waking up with his penis poking me. I loathed the feeling of the oil and the pain and stickiness of sex. I especially disliked it in the mornings. I felt so utterly trapped.

Late in the afternoon I polished my last facet. The stone was ready. Bill cleaned away the shellac, not letting me see it until it was perfectly clean. Then he made me close my eyes and put out my hand. I squeezed them shut while he tilted the stone onto my hands. 'You can open your eyes now.' I looked at the jewel in my hand and I was speechless. It twinkled as I rolled it round in my palm. 'Now you've gone and put fingerprints all over it,' he laughed, 'let me show you how to hold it.' He cleaned it with the hem of his shirt and then lay it on the back of my hand between my closed fingers. 'There, now you can look at it, what do you think?'

'I can't believe it, it's so beautiful.'

Bill put it in a tiny plastic bag and held it out to me. 'It's yours now, to look at whenever you want. A gemcutter has to keep his first stone, it's a tradition.'

I ate, slept and drank gemcutting. Everywhere I went I saw angles and patterns. I stared at cracks in pavements and studied the windows lining the high buildings all around Quay Towers, where I worked. Colours became the hue of stones. The whole world had changed its perspective.

Bill rang on Monday. If I liked I could come in every Saturday and cut. I was ecstatic. Hilda was there most Saturdays organising the accounts, though we never talked very much; I was too involved with what I was doing. My father also came; sometimes he'd sit in the outer office and talk with Hilda, though mostly he sat at the diamond machine, watching over me and occasionally talking with Bill.

One day Henry called me into his office and told me to close the door. 'I'm very concerned about the errors you're making. We can't afford mistakes, not when we're dealing with millions of dollars.'

I bit my lip nervously. I had been making mistakes, and Charles had been covering for me, checking my work before it went to Henry.

'Have you got a problem at home? It's not like you to make mistakes.'

'No, everything is fine.' I told him I thought it was the medicine I was taking, it made me feel woozy.

'Then I suggest you go back to your doctor. I'll give you a second chance. But if the mistakes continue I'll have no choice but to dismiss you.'

I promised him I'd pull myself together and went back to my desk. My father had continued giving me methaqualone, I don't know how many tablets he was giving me now, he crushed them, but it was enough to make a heaped teaspoon. I never really knew if he did that so I couldn't count the tablets or whether it was to ensure I took it all. It was worse, taking them powdered, and I'd gag as I tried to swallow. I don't know what he did while I was unconscious. I know he liked to poke things into me, anything that would fit. Once he'd used a hand cream tube, it hurt and I begged him to stop. When he finally pulled it out it was smeared with blood and there were shreds of skin caught under the cap. One morning I went to the toilet after a methaqualone bout, feeling really uncomfortable. I passed a ping pong ball and a clothes peg. After that, every time I got a pain in my stomach I became paranoid about what else might be lodged in my lower intestines.

When he picked me up from work I told him what Henry had said and we ended up fighting. I tried to make him agree to stop giving me methaqualone. He decided he'd still give it to me but only on long weekends, so I'd have time to get over the side effects.

I stopped making mistakes and there was no more talk of dismissal. Charles started teaching me how to put a loan proposal together. I loved it; it was interesting, researching people's financial backgrounds, seeing how we could make a deal work. After a time he gave me some of the easier applications and let me do the proposals on my own, before he checked and signed them.

It also became my job to chase overdue accounts and I discovered I enjoyed dealing with people. I knew what it was like to be broke, I was a sympathetic listener, and did my best to help them, working out ways for them to make part payments. When they realised I genuinely wanted to help, they stopped avoiding my telephone calls. I was losing my shyness, becoming more confident.

My thirtieth birthday came and went. I continued going to Bill's workshop with my father. One Saturday, after he'd been there an hour, he suddenly stood up. 'This is boring.' I looked at him; worried that this would be the end of my lessons. Instead he told me he was going out for a while; he'd be back at six to pick me up. Then he left.

I was alone with Bill. I was terrified – I had no idea how to behave or what to expect. Bill was cutting opals for a customer in Germany and I needed help with my stone but was too nervous to ask. Eventually he heard I'd switched my machine off and asked if I'd finished. I felt tongue-tied, but eventually managed to pull myself together. 'I've started polishing the facets, but it seems as though the lap is scratching.'

Bill came over and looked at the stone. 'It's not the polishing lap, you'll have to go back over your facets again with the pre-polishing lap. Some of the scratches from the grinding lap are much deeper, so when you start polishing they become more obvious.'

Once he'd fixed the problem, he asked if I'd like a cup of tea. By this stage I was such a nervous wreck I refused. He made himself a cup and sat down next to me. He tried to engage me in conversation but I was abrupt and eventually he gave up and went back to his opals. I felt worse now; what must he think of me?

My father returned at six, and the three of us went to eat in a Chinese restaurant. Only then did I relax.

Chapter 34

In November 1990 my father and I flew to the Solomon Islands for a holiday. It was a nightmare. I'd insisted that we go somewhere I chose, pointing out that I was the one earning the money, it was only fair that sometimes, just sometimes, I did what I wanted. He argued that he'd raised me, paid for my education and trips around the world. He'd had no help from my mother so it was only right I gave him my earnings now. I owed him for my upbringing. But in the end he agreed, providing it was somewhere he could buy turtle shell for his artefacts.

I chose to go to the Reef Islands in the Solomons, to a resort on Pigeon Island, a tiny island in the middle of nowhere. I was missing the tropics, I wanted to swim amongst coral, smell frangipani and drink green coconuts.

We flew to Honiara, from there to the island of Makira, then on to Lata, on Ndende Island, where we were met by the resort owners' son. Ben was the strong, silent type, carrying both our suitcases and refusing my help.

I took my shoes off and paddled in the sea, feeling the

tropics seeping into my bones. I could have danced with joy, except that my father was in a filthy mood. He wasn't amused when he realised we were going to travel across open sea in a small boat. I couldn't see the problem. 'I'm not getting into that death trap,' he snapped, as Ben loaded the suitcases into the boat. 'It could bloody sink.'

So what? I thought. This was a beautiful place to die. Apart from cutting, I had nothing to live for. I said, 'You don't have to go if you don't want to. I'm going with or without you.' I hadn't come this far to have him spoil everything. Eventually he followed me into the boat, cursing because he got his shoes wet.

Ben smiled; he'd heard the conversation, but remained silent. I smiled back, deciding I liked him. We chugged out to the open ocean and eventually left Ndende behind. The ocean was unbelievably calm and the deepest blue, like an Australian sapphire. After a couple of hours we passed Tinakula, an active volcano. Ben told me people had lived on its slopes, but the continuous eruptions eventually destroyed their gardens and now they lived on the mainland. It was a spectacular sight, rising abruptly out of the depths, topped by tiny wisps that could have been clouds, but weren't.

I enjoyed myself immensely, as my father fumed and made a point of ignoring me. Two could play that game, so I sat next to Ben, who told me about the region and the folklore. We talked at great length about sea spirits.

Just before sunset the sky and the sea turned pink. A thousand boobies descended and settled around us, bobbing up and down on the slight swell, preening their feathers and preparing for the night. It was breathtaking. When it grew dark Ben had no problem navigating by the stars and I suddenly saw the lights of a tiny thatch built out over the water – Pigeon Island.

The lights were from our bungalow. Later in our room, after a pleasant dinner with Ben's parents, my father started raging at me, how irresponsible I was. I ignored him and went to bed, taking the side closest to the bathroom.

The next morning we met the two other guests, both nurses. Over morning coffee we sat and talked as my father sat sullenly in the corner. Eventually he made it clear he wanted to return to our room. His bad mood was beginning to get to me. Here we were in paradise, and because he didn't want to be here, he was determined to spoil it for me. Finally I lost my temper and we ended up having a terrible row that could have gone on for hours except that Ben turned up and invited us on a boat trip amongst the tiny atolls. I agreed at once.

It was a wonderful day; we passed islands so tiny there was only room for five or six coconut trees clustered together. My father cheered up when he managed to buy some feather money rolls. The long rolls were made from the red breast feathers of a nearly extinct finch, and used to buy brides. He also bought some turtle shell. While he was making his purchases, Ben and I stood in the shade and drank cool, refreshing green coconuts.

Later as the day began to cool, we stopped at an atoll across from Pigeon Island and I saw a frigate bird in a tiny metal cage. I stared at it, horrified. Frigate birds are born to fly over the ocean, only coming to land to breed and avoid storms. But this one had been trapped in this wretched cage all its life, it had never known what it was to fly. Ben came and stood next to me. 'It's terrible to think about, isn't it?' I nodded. In a lot of respects we were similar, we were practically the same age, we'd both grown up in a tropical culture and been allowed to run wild. We both knew there was no point in suggesting the owners set it free. They'd never understand.

That night my father insisted on sex. He wanted to put a pin in the map. A couple of months earlier he'd bought a world map and several boxes of coloured pins. A green pin was for sex, a pink one for where he'd come inside me and a red pin for when he got me pregnant. He was talking about starting a family. I didn't want to think about it.

The next day he refused our hosts' lunch invitation. His good mood hadn't lasted. There I was in paradise, thirty years old and not allowed to leave the room. I sat looking out at the water, watching the colourful fish that swam and darted in the rock pools, ignoring his constant torrent of abuse. I'd heard it all before, I already knew I was frigid, stupid and arrogant. I was changing. I planned to move out the day we returned to New Zealand. The frigate bird had made me think – for the first time in my life I realised that all I had to do was open the cage door and fly out. Then I could soar as high as I liked, and if I burnt my wings, it was my choice to do so.

The following day there was a knock on our door. The two nurses wanted to talk with me. I went and stood behind the hut with them, in the shade of a breadfruit tree. 'Is everything all right?' one asked.

I didn't know what to say.

'We were worried about you, something doesn't seem right,' said the other.

I was going to tell them, I was going to tell them everything wasn't all right but I suddenly realised my father was standing in the bathroom listening.

'Everything is fine,' I smiled, 'it's just that the heat is too much for us.'

They didn't believe me, but what could they do? I left them shortly afterwards, returning to my father's renewed anger. 'What the hell did they want?'

'They wanted to know if I'd like to go for a walk.'

'Why would they want to go for a walk with a stupid bitch like you?'

It was too much. Something snapped in my head and I lost my temper. I started screaming at him, calling him names and told him that as soon as we got back to New Zealand I was leaving. That was a really dumb thing to do. He was so enraged he punched me.

'That's why I'm leaving you!' I hissed.

'You want to leave, fine, but you'll be back, you won't manage without me. A week working on K Road and you'll be back.'

K Road is a notorious red-light haunt in Auckland.

'Unlike you, I have a job, I don't need to work on K Road!'

'You fucking arrogant bitch,' he screamed. 'If I don't have you, nobody will.'

'See if I care,' I replied quietly, his words hitting home. If no one would have me, I'd be better off living alone.

He continued with his verbal lashing, but I'd had enough. I walked out of the room, went into the bathroom and had a shower. I was determined. I was going to leave. Nothing would stop me.

When I came out, he'd made me a cup of tea. He was very kind, gentle and apologetic for his treatment over the last couple of days. The isolation had got to him, he explained.

I should have been suspicious, but I was so grateful for his change of mood it didn't occur to me to look for a motive. In the afternoon he let me go out by myself for a swim. I snorkelled amongst the coral and the brightly coloured fish, it was lovely to feel the warm caress of limpid sea against my skin after all these years. I came out of the water feeling revitalised, refreshed, and more resolute than ever to try to escape from the nightmare of my life.

As I walked up the track, rubbing my hair with a towel, I met Ben. He invited me to come back with him for a drink. As part of my new determination I accepted, without asking my father's permission. We sat together, out in the open, drinking tea. 'Isn't it romantic here?' he said.

I looked at the beauty of my surroundings, the air filled with the strong peppermint smell of the spirit tree. I thought about my life. 'No, there's nothing romantic about this,' I said quietly.

He laughed, a hard cynical laugh. 'No, you're right, it isn't romantic at all. You're not like a tourist; you're an island girl. Tourists always think this is such a romantic spot. But we both know the truth of our lives.'

We fell silent again, each lost in our own thoughts. After a while he asked if I like Tahitian salad. I nodded. 'If you like, I'll make it for you and your father tonight.'

I accepted and that night I helped Ben prepare the fresh fish, while my father sat at the kitchen table watching. He refused to eat the salad and Ben obligingly made him an omelette.

We finished the meal with Baileys, discussing our return trip to Lata the next morning. Ben was a little concerned because the weather was deteriorating. The wind had picked up, but I hoped it wouldn't stop us from leaving. I wanted to get back to New Zealand as soon as possible.

Back in the bungalow, my father apologised again. I had another shower and when I came out of the bathroom, he'd ground up a whole lot of methaqualone. I refused. 'I don't want to have sex,' I said firmly, my heart sinking.

'No, it's not for sex, I'm worried about you, you're so stressed.' He kept going on and on.

'It's too much,' I insisted. He'd ground up a heaped tablespoon this time.

'It's no more than usual,' he said, trying to persuade me. It was easier to give in. If I knew then what I know now, I would have fought like a wild cat, but unfortunately, I didn't. I put the spoon in my mouth, swallowing half. 'More water,' I choked, and he turned to fill the glass from the tap. In one fluid movement I tipped the rest into the pocket of my cardigan and put the spoon back into my mouth, before he turned back. That split second of quick thinking saved my life.

The effects of the methaqualone hit me very quickly. I went over to the bed, dropping my clothes on the floor as I got under the covers. My father read a book and I fell asleep.

I dreamt I was drowning. I struggled through the waters of my dream, knowing I had to wake up. I fought hard and woke to find I couldn't breathe and the room was full of flying sea spirits with huge teeth, tearing at people running across the ceiling. Severed arms and legs lay on the floor and as one of the monsters tore at a woman's belly, intestines trailed across the bed. Blood was everywhere. It was so real, so terrifyingly real, I could see them, I could feel them, but I knew I was hallucinating. I couldn't move. I tried to scream, but it was the scream of nightmares, the scream that makes no sound. I desperately tried to suck air into my lungs, struggling to push myself into a sitting position, but my right side didn't work. I kicked out with my left leg, pulling the covers off my father and waking him. As he turned on the light I kept kicking at the bed, trying to push myself up against the bed head. I finally managed to suck in a mouthful of air and gasped, 'I can't breathe!'

He pulled me into a sitting position, and I found with great effort, I could pull air into my lungs. My right arm and leg were a dead weight, I tried to concentrate on moving them but it wasn't the normal feeling of a limb that's gone to sleep, this was different, there was no pain as blood rushed back. I was so dizzy, so nauseous. I kept blacking out, and each time I slipped into the blackness I stopped breathing and would be drowning again. I'd fight my way back to consciousness but I was so tired, it was so hard to stay awake. I sucked in another lungful of air, 'Get the nurses,' I gasped, fighting to remain conscious.

My father leaned over me, his eyes cold, frightening me. 'No.'

I didn't understand why he said no. I lay for a few seconds, trying to force my lungs to work, then managed another gasp of air. 'I'm dying, get nurses.' It was so hard to get the words out.

He just leaned back on his pillow. I was so frightened, in my mind I saw the miles of black ocean separating us from Lata, and the vast distance to the nearest hospital. I had never been so alone.

'Help me... going to be sick,' I gasped.

But he did nothing. I felt vomit rising, and with great difficulty rolled myself over the edge of the bed and fell heavily onto the floor. I tried to crawl with my one good arm and leg to the bathroom, passing out halfway. I don't know how long I lay there. I came to, the cold of the floor feeling strange because only half of my naked body could feel it.

The monsters faded and were replaced by occasional lightning in my head. I turned towards my father, expecting him to help me, but he was lying on the bed, staring at me, masturbating. I thought I would go insane. I needed a doctor,

I needed help and he was masturbating. Perhaps it was my state of mind, but it seemed to me he had the biggest erection he'd ever had.

Waves of nausea flooded over me, and I struggled to the bathroom. My recollection after this is hazy. I remember reaching the bathroom, I remember vomiting on the floor near the toilet, then passing out again, waking with my father pulling me violently by my hair, rough concrete scraping my body. Then he was lying on top of me, forcing his huge erection into me. I screamed in pain, then I was on my back, and I couldn't breathe. He was thrusting roughly into me, screaming abuse and I could smell vomit on my face and in my hair.

The memories are like someone turning the light on and off. In the blackness there was nothing, then the lights would come on, and there was the pain of him raping me, concrete cold and rough against my skin. The harshness of his voice as he swore at me, his hands savagely pulling at my hair. Then the lights would go out again. On, off, on, off. And all the while I desperately struggled to suck air into my lungs. It was the most important thing, the pain didn't matter, what my father was doing didn't matter, every second was spent concentrating on getting enough air to survive the next few seconds. Lightning kept flashing in my head, then I spiralled down into blackness, unable to save myself.

I dreamt I was in bed with Bill, in a sunny room. 'It's all right,' he said, gently stroking my cheek, 'you're safe now. I'm here.'

'What are you doing here? You're married to Hilda. We shouldn't be here.'

He laughed softly, 'We're married, Hilda was a long time ago, don't you remember?'

It was so peaceful lying there, feeling Bill caressing my cheek, so peaceful after all the pain. Then someone knocked on the door.

I woke up with a shock. I could breathe again. It was pitch-black, and for a moment I was terrified I'd gone blind. I was on the daybed, propped up against the wall and dressed in my pareo. My hair was damp and fresh smelling as though it'd just been washed. I could hear my father snoring. The knocking came again. I struggled to my feet, and found I had the use of my arm and leg. I felt for the light switch, glancing around the room. I was amazed to see the room completely tidy, our suitcases packed and standing neatly against the wall, a change of clothes for my father folded on top.

I pulled open the door and Ben stood in the pre-gloom. 'Are you all right? I had bad dreams about you.'

'I'm better now.' And I was, except for the lightning that kept striking in my head. My father woke up and demanded to know whom I was talking to.

'Ben,' I said. Hating him beyond hate. 'I'm going to check the weather,' I added and stepped out. As I shut the door, I heard him telling me to wait for him to get dressed. I pulled at Ben's arm, making him follow me up the path. 'What's the weather doing?' I asked as we walked across the island. 'I can't stay here another night, please take us back today.'

'I don't know, it'll be rough, your father won't like it. He might not want to leave.'

'Can't you lie to him, tell him it's normal, tell him anything, it's really important I get back to Lata.' I knew there was a doctor in Lata and if the worst came to the worst I could get away from my father. What happened to me last night wasn't an accident. I had no doubt in my mind that if I hadn't tipped the rest of the methaqualone into my pocket I'd be dead. The fact that my father had refused to get help confirmed it. My hatred and loathing of him had been replaced with fear. I remembered his words of the day before. 'If I don't have you no one will.' They took on a new meaning.

I heard a branch breaking behind us and turned. Speak of the devil, I thought, as my father came into view. 'Here you are,' he smiled, 'I've been looking for you.' Then he turned to Ben, 'Looks a bit rough, doesn't it?'

I looked anxiously at Ben, hoping he'd stick to his word. 'No, that's normal for here, we always have breakers first thing in the morning.'

I was unable to eat a thing at breakfast, I was still nauseous. I was worried about the lightning in my head and wondered if I'd had a stroke. Was that why I'd been paralysed down one side? My father asked me how I was feeling, his voice full of concern. I politely said I felt much better, thank you.

'I think Ben tried to poison you last night, I reckon he gave you a poisonous fish.'

'Why would he do that?' I'd prepared the fish last night, and it had been tuna, not a reef fish.

'You're so naive, you think Ben is a nice guy, but he's mad, really insane, his father was telling me he should be locked up. He's killed people before.'

There was a time when I would have believed him. But I'd changed, I didn't believe him any more. What he was suggesting was laughable.

The trip back to Lata was hellish; we were drenched with sea spray and thoroughly battered about. That afternoon my father insisted we walk to the airport, to make a telephone call. I stood in the doorway, entranced by the smell of frangipani blossoms. Well, I'd drunk my green coconuts, swum in the tropical ocean and now I was smelling frangipanis. Dreams can come true, I thought, but only if you work at them.

My father whistled to me, waving at me to come over to the phone. I hated it when he whistled, I wasn't a dog. 'What do you want?'

In response, he handed me the phone receiver, 'Speak,' he said.

I was shocked and pleasantly surprised to find Bill on the other end. He seemed as surprised as I was. Apparently, my father hadn't said a word, just handed me the telephone as soon as the collect call had gone through.

We talked for about twenty minutes then my father took the phone and asked Bill to find out if it was still legal to bring turtle shell into New Zealand. He arranged to ring back the next day at the same time and hung up. My father always had an ulterior motive for everything he did.

We checked into the one and only local guesthouse. There was an intriguing collection of guests. Pierre, a Frenchman, was desperately grateful I could speak French. He was a postal worker seeking adventure, and now that he'd found it wasn't sure he liked it. There were two Australian men, always whispering to each other and Harry, a large Solomon Islander, black as polished ebony. He told me he was an undercover police officer, working on a case. 'Don't tell anyone else, I just let you know, so if something happens in the night you don't get worried.'

We were due to fly out the next day, and looking forward to eating in a restaurant as soon as we got back to Honiara. There were no restaurants on Ndende, and scarcely anything you could call a shop. We were all slowly running out of supplies. Harry walked with my father and I to a nearby village where he knew someone who sold food. The 'shop' was nearly bare, with a meagre selection, black tea, sugar, milk powder, white rice and tinned mackerel in tomato sauce. But wonder of wonders, he had several dozen tins of orangeade. I bought a dozen, several tins of mackerel and a loaf of bread.

Back at the guesthouse I explored the kitchen and found a deep freeze. The fridge had died a long time ago, and was empty aside from a bag of native string beans, each pod nearly a metre long. They'd been there a while judging by the brown spots. I put the orangeade in the deep freeze and when they were frozen solid we sat outside cooling ourselves with the tins and drinking the juice as it slowly melted.

The next morning we learned our plane had broken down in Makira and we had to wait until a mechanic was found who could fix the problem. That evening as the unbearable heat gradually diminished all the guests gathered in the sitting room. We had a problem, now that our plane had been delayed we didn't have enough food. In the end, someone suggested that as the only woman, I should sort out a meal. How was I meant to produce a meal for six with nothing?

I demanded everyone bring me anything edible they had. My father and I had the tins of mackerel, Pierre had a bunch of tiny wild bananas, Harry had two cups of rice and the Australians had an onion. We had a bit of a fight over the onion. I was in the kitchen wondering how I was going to achieve the impossible when they came in and took it back. I'm ashamed to admit I lost my temper. I tried to snatch it back, and in the struggle some of the skin flaked off and fell to the floor.

'For Christ's sake,' the younger one snapped, 'it's only an onion!'

'Well if it's only an onion then give it back,' I demanded unreasonably. After all, it was their onion.

Finally I managed to wrestle it from him and snatched up a knife and began peeling it. They stared at me in disgust. 'Well, if you want it so much, you can have it.' They stalked out of the kitchen. I decided I needed lemons and went out into the living room and told the men to find me some. They wandered outside without a murmur of protest. I guess they didn't want to upset me any further.

Back in the kitchen I found a bottle of peanut oil and half a bag of damp sugar at the back of a cupboard. After about twenty minutes, Harry came back with two lemons, which I fried gently with the onions then added the mackerel.

I eventually served fish casserole with fluffy rice and fried beans, followed by a dessert of caramelised bananas, covered in flaming rum. I felt quite proud of all the compliments. Mind you, we were so hungry I don't suppose it would have mattered what it tasted like. The Australians forgave me for stealing their onion.

That night the guesthouse was raided. There was a loud banging on our door and when I got up to answer it several police officers crowded into our room. One of them asked me which room the Australians were in. 'Next door, I think,' I said and climbed back into bed as they apologised for waking me. I tried to go back to sleep as they kicked open the door of the neighbouring room. There was a lot of banging and shouting and then silence as the jeeps drove away.

In the morning the Australians were gone, and Harry told me his job was done. The Australians had been planning to smuggle artefacts out of the country, their suitcases had been full of ancient treasures. I thought about all the artefacts in my father's suitcase and said nothing.

Later that morning we received a message that our plane had arrived and would be taking off in half an hour.

Chapter 35

B ack in Honiara my father rang Bill, going out of the room to make the call. When he returned he told me Bill said there was no problem importing turtle shell. Later he insisted on packing the turtle shell pieces in my suitcase, and we had another fight. 'I'm sure there won't be a problem, but just in case there is, it is better if it's in your suitcase, because you're only a child, you won't get into trouble for smuggling it in.'

'I'm not a child,' I yelled, 'I'm thirty years old!'

'Age has nothing to do with it, just because you're thirty doesn't mean you're an adult.'

Sometimes it was impossible to reason with him. I was stopped going through customs, as I knew I would be. It was normal, ever since I'd gone to visit my mother in Noumea several years before. My father was furious and rang Customs, telling them I was a drug courier. He'd hoped to stop me leaving the country; they missed me on the way out but stopped me on my return, when I was thoroughly searched. The customs officer was most apologetic when he accidentally squirted foundation all over a white dress. We got chatting and he told me he was leaving at the end of the week and invited me to lunch. I regretfully declined but he told me about the telephone call they'd received. It was easy to work out who it was, only the ticketing officer and my father knew I was travelling.

Coming back from Honiara my father said we should go through customs separately. I was pulled to one side and my suitcase searched. When they found the turtle shell, I told them it belonged to my father, pointing him out in the queue. It was confiscated. My father screamed at me all the way home. I had no right to say it was his, he was going to sort Bill out for lying to him.

I rang Bill the next morning; he couldn't understand how my father had misunderstood him. 'I rang Customs, and was told that under no circumstances could it be imported.'

Bill had become the enemy. Over the years I'd discovered a pattern in my father's friendships. He'd meet someone and his life would revolve around them, then after about six months he'd discover a flaw and lose respect. Over time he'd start criticising them, finding fault, sneering behind their backs. The next phase would be open hostility, as they became the enemy. The final stage was when he had to get even with the enemy, for some slight, imaginary or otherwise.

He'd reached the stage where Bill had become the enemy and I wasn't allowed to consort with the enemy. I was shattered, but came up with a new plan. I told him I no longer had a regular lunch hour, and wouldn't know when I could meet him. That left my lunch hours free, and I'd spend them with Bill and Peter, an hour of sanity and laughter to look forward to.

This went on for several months. One day, as Bill was on

the phone, I came to a shattering realisation. I was in love
with him. I lay my knife and fork down on my untouched
plate, picked up my handbag and walked out of the
workshop. Being in love was a powerful, all-consuming
feeling. Being in love with a happily married man was
devastating. I knew that if I stayed someone would get hurt.
I didn't trust myself to keep my feelings to myself. Bill rang
me shortly after I returned to work. 'What's the matter? You
just left, without saying goodbye.'

'Nothing's the matter,' I said. I was short with him, telling
him I wouldn't be coming round any more then I hung up,
raced to the toilets and cried my eyes out. The next few
months were horrible; I couldn't get Bill out of my mind.

My home life hadn't improved, with my father becoming
increasingly demanding. I'd changed, and we fought more
often, fights that raged late into the night, exhausting me,
driving me to the point of banging my head with my fists.
Afterwards, when my father finally went to bed, I'd sit
somewhere, rocking back and forth sucking my thumb,
thinking I had to leave, unable to move. Hours would go by, as
I was locked in my head. I'd talk to myself. 'Come on Tanjas,
it's easy to leave, just get up and walk towards the door.'

'I can't,' I'd reply, feeling numb.

'You can, you're Walk Far Woman, get up, come on, walk
to the door.'

But it was impossible. I couldn't do it. I'd try to picture
what it would be like if I opened the door. My mind would
go blank, I'd stop thinking. Freedom was such an
unachievable goal I couldn't even picture it. I think my mind
simply closed down. I knew I was slipping over the edge,
finally going crazy. My father often told me I'd end my days
in a nut house. I was beginning to think he was right.

Henry broke the terrible news to Charles and I that he had inoperable cancer. We were distraught, but he was very positive, saying he had to have radiotherapy and he would be right as rain. Time passed and he grew thinner and his hair started coming out in clumps, but he still played golf and was unbelievably cheerful.

Our company was sold to National Australia Bank. Charles was transferred to Papatoetoe and Henry and I were sent to head office, in Grafton Road, where I was going to be trained as a teller and Henry was going to be a Head Office branch manager.

I hadn't seen Bill for months, but I was still hopelessly in love with him. At night, to stop myself becoming crazy, I started writing. I was writing an adventure story, set in the Reef Islands, losing myself completely in the tropics and the intrigue. I decided to buy a computer. It was unbelievably expensive, but I got a loan from my bank and became the proud owner of a laptop. Finally, I'd bought something for me. It was a wonderful feeling, being able to pour my heart out into the computer, and know my father would be unable to access any of it.

One day, out of the blue, Bill rang, inviting me to the workshop for lunch. Peter had cooked something especially for me. My head told me to say no, but my heart had other ideas and I agreed. Ten minutes later, I was back in the workshop. How I'd missed that place, how I'd missed Peter. God, how I loved Bill. He went to make a cup of tea and Peter smiled at me. 'We missed you.'

'I missed you too.'

'You missed Bill most of all,' he said.

I nodded, suddenly unable to talk.

'Bill lives in Grafton now, he and Hilda have split up.'

I stared at him, a tangle of thoughts running through my mind. Bill had been very happy with Hilda, telling me often how he loved her. It didn't occur to me then that this meant Bill was free. I wasn't a great thinker.

The next day Bill rang me at work. 'Are you in love with anyone?' he asked.

'No,' I lied. 'I don't have time to love anyone.'

'Well,' he persisted, 'if you did love anyone, who would it be? What sort of a man could you love?'

I fell silent, thinking. 'Um, I don't know, let's see. He'd have to be older than me, I have no time for silly boys. He'd have to have his own business, not be trapped by someone else's timetable and he'd have to be a nonsmoker.'

'That cuts me out then.'

We both laughed. We talked for more than an hour, no one seemed to mind.

On Friday afternoon Henry came and sat on the edge of my desk. He was so thin, it hurt to look at him. 'I think I've finally kicked this cancer. The treatments are finished and I'm feeling on top of the world.'

I stood up and hugged him, something I'd never done before and we both got a little emotional. That was the last time I saw him.

On Monday morning Charles rang and told me Henry had passed away peacefully in his sleep. I sat in Henry's office, crying my eyes out. Despite my father, I wore black to the funeral. He was furious; he hated me wearing black. There were hundreds of people; Henry had been a good man, well-liked and respected. I missed him a lot, and as we prayed, I wondered why it was that good people seem to die young. Perhaps it's because they've learned the lessons of this life, and are rewarded with heaven.

Chapter 36

My father wanted me to go to Holland with him, but I said I couldn't get time off work. I'd done my last travelling alone with him. I didn't trust him not to try to harm me again. In the end he went for ten days, leaving me with strict instructions. He'd checked the bus timetable, and had calculated how long it would take me to walk from the bus stop to the house. He told me he'd ring every day at twenty to six. I wasn't allowed to go shopping and I wasn't allowed to leave the house at the weekend. He'd ring me first thing in the morning and sometime during the night to make sure I was there.

On Friday Bill rang and asked if I wanted to see snow. 'I was thinking of taking you to Mount Ruapehu for the day.'

I threw caution to the wind and said I'd love to see snow. That day truly was a gift from God. When he picked me up it was still dark. I locked the house, trembling with excitement and the knowledge of the trouble I would be in if my father found out. In the car we talked and talked, I loved the sound of his voice, I could listen to it forever.

When we stopped in Matamata for breakfast I called my father from a telephone box, apologising for not getting to the telephone in time. I had no idea whether he'd rung or not, but figured he could only assume someone else had rung. I told him I'd been in the bath. I knew he'd be furious, because I wasn't allowed to have a bath unless he was at home. As I'd anticipated he was angry with me for disobeying him, and didn't notice the background noises. As an extra precaution I'd left the phone off the hook at home. I planned to ring him as soon as I got home and apologise for not putting the receiver down correctly, telling him I'd only just noticed.

As we rounded a bend Bill said I'd catch sight of Mt Ruapehu over the next hill. I'll never forget that moment. The first rays of the sun caught the dewdrops in the ti trees along the side of the road, turning them into sparkling diamonds. The timing was perfect, the night mist just lifting and the colours of the sky turning the snow-capped mountain pink. I squealed with delight, I couldn't help myself. I hadn't realised New Zealand could be beautiful. I'd been judging it with the melancholy eyes of one who aches for the tropics.

When we got to Mt Ruapehu I was in fairyland. It was just like a postcard, the ground covered with knee-deep snow. All the trees were white, with icicles sparkling in the sunshine. I'd seen snow before, a thin dusting on the pavements in Holland and I'd played with Richard in the English sludge, but this was different. We played for hours. Later Bill suggested we go higher, in a ski lift. I was all for it, until I saw what a ski lift was. 'I'm absolutely not going up in that,' I said. 'I hate heights.'

The next chair caught me from behind and before I knew what was happening, I was high in the air, clutching onto the safety bar for dear life. Bill followed in the next one. 'You should see your face,' he called out as we swept over huge drops.

I survived. I always do. Bill had brought some large black rubbish bags with him, and we spent a delightful hour sliding down gentle slopes, annoying the skiers with our childish behaviour. My jeans were getting damp so we went indoors to the coffee shop and warmed ourselves over bowls of soup.

On the drive back up to Auckland we stopped near Mangakino at a small coffee shop and ordered meat pies, chips and a pot of tea. After we'd eaten, Bill leaned back in his chair and read the paper, offering me the front pages.

I watched him and discovered I'd never felt so wonderfully at ease, so relaxed, so unbelievably happy. Bill hadn't screamed at me, hit me, or even got angry with me. To the outside world we seemed like an ordinary couple. That was a good feeling.

I rang my father as soon as I got home. He was furious because he'd been trying to ring me, but there was nothing he could do to me from Holland. Afterwards I had a long soak in the bath to spite him.

Bill came round on Sunday afternoon. I couldn't stop smiling and offered him a cup of tea. While I filled the kettle I asked him to get some cups from the cupboard, completely forgetting the list my father kept there, the one with my periods. I turned to see him staring at it with a thoughtful expression, then without a word he walked out of the kitchen.

In horror my stomach tightened, and my skin turned to ice. Oh God, he'd worked out what it was! What was I going to do now, what was I going to say? I had to try to remain normal, as though nothing had happened, perhaps he'd think he'd misunderstood. 'What's the matter,' I asked as I stepped out on the terrace.

'Nothing, I just needed some fresh air.'

I suggested we walk to the beach. Seagulls circled and soared overhead as I searched for something to say. 'I wonder what it would be like to fly?' I finally said.

Bill turned and stared at me. 'Would you like to fly?' he asked quietly.

I stared back, trying to understand his look. 'Yes, I would, to soar as high as I liked, up amongst the clouds.'

He looked down, and I had the impression his thoughts were a long way away. We walked to the sandy spit and along the water's edge in companionable silence, and he taught me to skip stones across the water. Later we returned to the house and he sat in the living room while I made a pot of tea.

My father returned from Holland with gifts and naked photographs of a teenage girl he'd met. While we were talking he noticed the parting in my hair was sunburned. 'How the hell did you get sunburned?' he demanded, his good humour evaporating. 'I told you not to go out.'

I decided to tell him the truth; maybe I should have lied.

'How can you be so fucking selfish?' he raged. 'You could have been killed, and then who would have looked after me? Or you could have been raped.'

This was too much. 'The only one who rapes me is you!'

Next thing he was dragging me across the room by my hair. He banged my head against the wall, and I fought back, punching him hard. I'd had enough of being beaten. 'I'm thirty-one,' I screamed, 'you haven't got the right to hit me.'

'I have every right, you don't have the right to disobey me, you fucking bitch.'

'No, you don't,' I screamed and punched him again.

'You're so fucking arrogant, you deserve it,' he screamed as he smashed me against the wall. Later I sat in the bathroom, wondering what was so wrong about such a wonderful day.

On Friday night my father went to Lifeline and, taking a terrible risk, I went with Bill to an Italian restaurant. It was a lovely evening, relaxed and full of laughter. Sometimes I caught Bill looking at me, and the way he looked made me wonder if he might be falling in love with me. I told myself it was wishful thinking. He drove me home, dropping me off out of sight of the house. Before I got out, he took my hand. He seemed awkward. 'Tanjas, one day you'll be ready to talk, and when you are I'll be ready to listen.'

I looked down, at a loss for words. I quickly squeezed his hand and got out. We both knew what he was talking about, but I didn't know if I'd be able to talk. I'd kept a secret for twenty-two years, I didn't know if I'd be able to let it out now.

Over Christmas my father took me to Solitaire Lodge. Such a beautiful place, a place to share with someone you love, not a place to have to have sex with your father. The telephone rang as we walked in the door on our return home. My father picked up the receiver. It was Bill, wishing us a Happy Christmas. 'Just a moment, I'll get her for you,' he said but instead he took the radio, turned it up to full volume and placed it right next to the telephone.

I shoved past him, pushed the radio away and picked up the receiver. 'Hi, Bill, sorry I took so... '

My father snatched the receiver and slammed it down. 'The arrogance of that bastard, I'm the one who decides if we have a happy Christmas or not! He's sniffing round you like a dog.'

I was beginning to get angry. 'So what if he is, I'm a single woman. There's nothing wrong with someone being interested in me.'

'You're not fucking single, you're married to me.'

He was back on that track again. I turned my back on him and picked up the receiver. 'I'm going to ring Bill,' I said firmly.

'Right, that's it, I'm going to that bastard's workshop and I'm going to kill him.'

At first, I didn't take him seriously, then I heard him sharpening the bush knife. I waited to see if he was bluffing, but when he walked towards the front door I raced after him. Catching him as he pulled open the door, I grabbed him by his shirt and yanked him backwards, slamming him against the wall, kicking the door shut. He shoved against me, the bush knife still in his hands. 'Get out of the fucking way, I'm going to kill that cunt!'

I was so enraged I grabbed him by his shirt and smashed him back against the wall, nearly lifting him off the ground. 'Don't you dare, don't you dare!' I screamed, shoving him against the wall.

He went white and for the first time in my life I saw fear in his eyes. 'You're mad!'

'Too bloody right I'm mad, you leave Bill out of this!'

I let go of him and went and sat in the living room. I decided that if he did drive off, I'd call and warn Bill, then I heard him go into his room, locking the door.

In the New Year I began working as a cashier at the Newmarket branch of the bank. I enjoyed it immensely, loving the contact with customers. My father started picking me up for lunch again, and ringing me. I didn't see so much of Bill; it was impossible to get away. A friend from head office unwittingly came to my rescue, telling me it was being talked about that I never attended Friday evening drinks.

I explained my father would never agree and between us, we contrived a meeting one lunchtime when my father was there. She brought up the topic and put my father in a position where he could only say, 'Of course, it is entirely up to Tanjas what she does.' After that I'd go upstairs and mingle with my colleagues, then sometimes I'd sneak out and meet Bill for a meal. I had to be home by ten-thirty, and would catch a taxi at ten, to ensure I was home on time.

One night I came home at quarter to eleven to find the front door ajar. I pushed it open and went inside, carefully closing it behind me. My father was sitting on the couch, wearing a striped shirt and tie. Over his lap and covering his lower body was a thick blanket. He was watching television and patted the couch next to him. 'Come and watch television with me.'

I didn't feel like it, but I was grateful he was in a good mood although I was a few minutes late. I sat next to him and he lifted the blanket and covered my legs with part of it. That's when I discovered he was naked from the waist down and had an erection, already oiled.

'I don't feel like it,' I said, but he ignored me as usual and pushed me down on the couch, pulling my panties to one side. He was very rough, and as he came, I saw his face. It was something I normally avoided doing, looking at him. It was distorted, his lips pulled back, obscenely red against the black of his beard. I shuddered, unable to get that split second out of my mind. Then he looked at me. 'Just wanted to know if you'd fucked someone else,' he said as he withdrew, leaving his stickiness between my legs. I went into the bathroom and turned on the shower, hating him, loathing him, soaping myself over and over and rinsing myself inside with scalding hot water. Why didn't he just drop dead?

I started studying again. I'd enjoyed doing the loan offers with Charles and I thought I'd like to move in that direction. I discovered there were banking papers I could do. It was wonderful; it took up entire weekends. In all I sat five papers. Mathematics had never been one of my strong points, but perhaps it was easier now because there was a reason behind the calculations. My father took the certificates from me, saying they were his.

One day when my father picked me up from work he told me he'd been reading about golden showers. I cringed. I didn't want to go through that again – black plastic on the floor and him urinating on me. But this time it was slightly different. This time he wanted me to tie him up and urinate in his mouth. The idea was repugnant; I stared at him in disgust, wondering where this was all going to end. He brought the topic up the next evening, and the next. It became his latest obsession. After two weeks I caved in. I tied him to the bed, on top of the black plastic, determined to pee in his mouth and get it over and done with. With a bit of luck, he'd be revolted and that would be the last of it.

Only problem was the idea disgusted me so much I couldn't urinate. I sat crouched over his blindfolded face desperately trying to relax my urethra. Eventually I went into the kitchen and drank a litre of water. Then I went back, crouching over him. Finally I did it. I urinated in his mouth. I expected him to gag, or show some signs of revulsion but he swallowed it down and kept telling me how sexy it was.

I was nearly sick. God, he disgusted me. I untied him and although I'd avoided sex, I went into the bathroom and scrubbed myself all over. I felt unbelievably filthy and degraded, as though I'd never be clean again.

In September I missed a period. I stood in the kitchen staring at the list, frantically hoping I'd miscounted. I had period-like pains and for days I kept rushing to the toilet, hoping for telltale red spots. They didn't come.

When I told my father, I was stunned at his reaction. 'You fucking whore,' he screamed, 'who have you been screwing around with?'

We both knew he was the father. The father of both of us, I couldn't help thinking. Over the next week, I walked across the jagged edges of his moods and several times he screamed at me to get out of his sight because he couldn't bear to see me. Once I felt him staring at me from the doorway of his locked room. The hatred in his eyes was frightening.

Then one day he picked me up from work, cheerful and full of talk about our new family. Sitting me down on the couch he went and squeezed two glasses of orange juice. He'd been researching – it was important I drank lots of orange juice and I wasn't allowed to eat salt, no more tea or coffee. The list went on and on.

He'd been shopping, buying baby clothes. There was a tiny pink jacket with matching cap, and a pair of the tiniest shoes I'd ever seen, Italian leather, white with ribbons. He apologised for not believing he was the father, he'd checked the list, and laughed as he told me it wasn't surprising I was pregnant. He started talking about how he was looking forward to it and all I could think was, what if it's a girl?

He'd beat her, he'd touch her and one day he'd rape her. He'd steal her childhood and her life, just as he had done with me. The tragic part was that I believed there was nothing I could do about it. How many times had I stood in terror of what was going to come, my skin tight with fear? How many times had I gone to his bed, like a lamb to the slaughter, unable to do anything? My life stretched into the darkness, and now it would be even more terrible, because he'd never let her go, he'd hold her over me.

I sat and listened to him and all the time I wanted to scream so loud the windows would shatter. I wanted to hear the sound of breaking glass.

I desperately tried to keep my head together. I could feel myself shutting off from the world. My father became even more controlling, increasing his telephone calls to me at work and sending me flowers. Then he had to go away for a few days. I was left with a mountain of oranges and long lists of instructions.

Someone had told me a joke. It was the one about the woman who falls into a flooding river. A man throws a life jacket attached to a line, yelling at her to grab the jacket. She calls back, 'No, I'll wait for God to rescue me.'

Then she's swept further down a river and just as she's pulled under a low bridge a man reaches down and tries to catch her, calling out to her to grab hold of his hands, to which she replies, 'No, I'll wait for God to rescue me.'

Finally she's dragged out to sea and a helicopter hovers over her and a man winches down a rope, calling out to her to grab hold of it, to which she replies, 'No, I'm waiting for God to rescue me.'

Finally the helicopter flies off and the woman is surrounded by sharks. 'God, help me,' she cries. A loud voice booms down from the heavens, 'I've sent you three men and a helicopter, what more do you want?'

I rang Bill, telling him I was in terrible trouble. He picked me up from work and we drove back to his flat. Now that the moment had arrived, I struggled to find the words. I was afraid that although he'd said he was ready to listen, he might not be able to handle what I had to say. 'I'm pregnant,' I finally said.

He sat next to me on the couch and asked if it was my father. I nodded, and he took me in his arms and stroked my hair, rocking me back and forth.

I started talking. I told him everything and all the while he held on to me, comforting me. I couldn't stop, I had so much to say. At four in the morning I ran out of words, then without warning, I threw up. I cringed, expecting a blow, but none came. Bill fetched a facecloth and tenderly wiped my face, then he cleaned the floor. At seven, he left for work, looking exhausted. Neither of us had slept. He rang work for me, saying I was sick and came back at lunchtime to make me something to eat. I half expected him to tell me to leave his flat, but it didn't happen.

I slept the afternoon away, and was woken by Bill gently caressing my cheek. It was already dark. I stayed with Bill that night, and we talked as I sat hunched up on his bed, my back against the pillows. Bill brought me a cup of tea and after putting it down on the bedside table, sat on the edge of the bed. 'What do you want to do about the pregnancy?'

I shook my head slowly, 'I don't know.' I began to cry. 'I just keep hoping it'll go away, that this is all just a nightmare and I'll wake up and not be pregnant.'

'It isn't going to go away, you'll have to decide what you want to do. You have several options. You could have an abortion.'

I shook my head, 'I could never do that. It's not her fault we share a father.'

'You have to think about the child as well, what sort of a life would she have? One day she might find out.'

'I could have her adopted, then she'd never have to know,' I was thinking out loud.

'Tanjas, I know you, you'd never be able to give her away, and it would drive you crazy, not knowing where she is, or the kind of people she's with.'

Then he said something that touched me deeply and I began to realise he must care for me very much. 'You could tell people the baby is mine.' I stared at him, and burst into tears again. 'I'm serious, it could work if you move away from your father and we tell everyone the baby is mine.'

'You don't understand, my father would never let me go. He'd kill me first, he'd kill anyone who got in his way.'

'I'm not afraid of him, he's good at terrorising women and children, not grown men.'

In the end I accepted Bill's offer, and between us we came up with a plan that just might work. I slept that night curled up against him and I had never felt so safe in my entire life.

Chapter 37

My father returned from overseas and I told him I'd been thinking. 'I don't have a boyfriend and people are going to suspect you're the father. I think I should move out for three months, then when I come back we can say I got pregnant, and I don't know who the father is.'

He sat down suddenly. 'So you're leaving me?'

'No, of course not, only for three months.' As I spoke I thought, over my dead body, I'm never coming back.

'Who'll look after me, who'll cook and clean for me?'

'I can always come back to the house to do that, it won't be a problem.'

Eventually he agreed. I couldn't believe I was finally leaving this nightmare. A couple of days later I told my father I'd found a flat. After work we drove to Bill's now empty flat. As arranged, he'd moved into a tiny flat at his parents' home. As I showed my father where to park, he looked at me strangely. 'So you're really going through with this?'

'Of course, we can't afford to have people talking,' I

replied, terrified he'd change his mind. On the way home he surprised me, saying he'd let me have some of my things for the flat.

On 4 October 1992 I turned thirty-two and had sex with my father for the last time. I stood in the shower and lathered soap all over myself and for the very last time I washed his sperm down the drain. The next day we shuttled back and forth between the house and my new flat. As we drove back to the house he started crying.

He pulled the car over to the side of the road and leaned over the steering wheel sobbing. 'Please don't leave me, I can't live without you.'

'It'll be only be for three months,' I said, trying to comfort him.

'I can't pay the rent; I don't have any money. What am I going to do? If you leave me I'll end up on the street.'

My resolve nearly weakened. Despite everything, he was my father. Then I remembered the tiny life within me, and knew she deserved a chance of happiness. I remembered Bill asking me if I wanted to fly, and I remembered the name given to me a long time ago, Dancing Bird. The time had come for Dancing Bird to spread her wings and take flight.

'You'll have to be strong,' I said, 'and you'll have to find a job, I'll pay your bills until then.'

That night he held onto me all night, not sleeping. 'This might be the last night I ever have you in my arms,' he said. 'I want to remember all of it.'

The next morning, his face swollen with crying, he drove me to Grafton Road and dropped me off. After I let myself into the flat I walked to the window and looked out. He was still parked outside. Then, as I watched, he started up the car and drove up the hill. I stood there motionless. It had happened. Our plan had worked. The miracle had finally come and I was free.

I really believed then it was over. I was wrong. My father began to hound me. He'd turn up at all hours, I'd come back to abusive notes, asking where the fuck I was. Sometimes there'd be huge bouquets of flowers, with a note telling me how much he loved me. He'd turn up at work, wanting to take me to lunch. He'd be friendly, but his mood could change very quickly and I was on edge all the time. As promised, I'd go back several times a week to cook and clean. He still controlled me; I had to ring him every day at set hours. And I did – I didn't know how not to.

When the three months were up I was going to have to tell him I wasn't coming back. I was terrified of his reaction – either he'd become so enraged he'd kill me, or he'd kill himself. I wasn't sure I could handle being responsible for his death. He appeared to be suffering from depression. He stopped washing and sometimes stank when he picked me up, despite his clean shirts. The house was absolute chaos, the cupboards empty. I think the only time he ate was when I cooked a meal or we went out to a restaurant.

One day he showed me a note, written in red ink on the back of a business card. It began, 'When you find this, you will be in big trouble.' It went on to describe what he planned to do with me, once he'd tied me up in the garage. I stared at it in horror. Was he going to force me to have sex with him again? 'You'll find this one day,' he said as he put it in his pocket.

In November, while I was at my father's house, God in his wisdom chose to take my baby back to heaven. I started getting terrible cramps and began to bleed. My father came into the toilet and when he saw the blood in the bowl he went crazy and started punching me as I stood there with my panties round my knees.

'You fucking bitch, you've murdered our child, you've had an abortion.'

'No, I haven't,' I screamed as I rolled up a huge wad of toilet paper and pulled my panties up.

He grabbed me by my hair, 'Then what the fuck is that?' he roared, as he shoved my face towards the bowl. I started crying and between my sobs, I promised I hadn't had an abortion, I was miscarrying. His mood changed. He suddenly became loving and caring, helping me into his bed. As I lay there, he rang the Emergency Clinic in Remuera. 'My wife is miscarrying,' he said, as soon as they answered.

Oh God, now he'd want me to come back, he'd force me to stay. I was so terrified I started hyperventilating. The cramps were terrible, coming in waves. When he finally hung up, he started putting pillows under my feet. 'They say the only thing you can do now is rest and keep your legs up.'

I struggled to sit up. 'I can't rest, I have an appointment,' I lied, desperately trying to come up with an excuse to leave.

'You're not fucking going anywhere, do I have to tie you up?'

If he tied me up, he could do anything. I stopped arguing. At six o'clock I was still his prisoner. I pleaded with him to let me go back to my flat, but he wouldn't hear of it. Finally, I went crazy. I leapt out of bed and snatched up the phone. 'If you don't let me go, I'm going to ring the police.' I was screaming at the top of my voice.

He snatched the phone and I ran into the hall. I could feel blood between my legs, but I didn't care, I pulled the front door open and ran outside. Halfway down the road I doubled up with pain and sat down, waiting for the wave to subside.

My father came after me in the car. 'Get in, I'll take you back to your flat,' he said simply.

He dropped me back at the flat, telling me to ring him later and let him know how I was. As soon as I was indoors I rang Bill and told him I was miscarrying. I was in the shower when he arrived. 'You need to go to hospital,' he said.

'No, I can't, they'll find out.'

'They won't, and even if they do, it doesn't matter, you should see a doctor.'

But I refused, I wasn't going to take the risk. On Monday I returned to work; my father came and wanted me to go and have a coffee. I explained I couldn't, there was no other cashier to relieve me. He lost his temper and started screaming at me, calling me names. Finally he left, but he was waiting for me at lunchtime. To avoid a scene I had lunch with him and told him I was never coming back. He assured me I would, eventually Bill would tire of fucking me and throw me into the street. Then I'd have no option than to crawl back to him.

That night, when I returned to my flat, it was empty. My father had taken everything, including my clothes. He'd overlooked two dresses hanging on the washing line and an old metal bread bin that had belonged to my grandmother. Fortunately I'd left my laptop at Bill's parents' house, I'd been using it there the night before. I was furious, how dare he break into my flat? I rang him. 'Why did you take all my stuff?'

'Your stuff, that's a laugh, nothing belongs to you, everything belongs to me.'

'How can you say that? How can you say all my things belong to you?'

'Oh, they belong to you, but only if you live with me.'

I fell silent, astounded at his logic. I eventually hung up;

he refused to give me my passport, certificates and driver's licence. He was adamant they all belonged to him.

I sat on the carpet in the living room, looking at the clouds. Gradually the sun set and the room filled with shadows. I remembered so many other times I'd sat alone, waiting for darkness. It suddenly struck me. I didn't only have three dresses, one pair of panties, an old bread bin and a laptop computer. I had something much more valuable, something more precious. I had myself. I was thirty-two years old and had somehow survived the twenty-three year nightmare. Finally, I belonged to me. Life stretched before me. A life filled with days and nights, in which I could choose to do whatever I wanted. I held the world in my hands. I was finally free.

I gave notice on the flat. I didn't want to live there any more, not after my father had managed to get in. I moved in with Bill, sharing the tiny flat at his parents' house. I felt much safer, I was never on my own as there was always at least one member of his family around. It was a lovely feeling, being part of a family.

I had to buy some clothes but I had no money, my father had cleaned out my account. I asked Bill if I could borrow some and he handed me his wallet, telling me to take what I needed. I asked him to come with me, because I'd never bought clothes on my own. His sister recommended a dress shop on the North Shore and we went there. I couldn't decide, asking Bill which dress I should buy. 'Don't ask me,' he laughed, 'you're the one who'll be wearing it.'

'But I don't know what suits me.'

'Well, what colour do you like?'

'Blue,' I said, without stopping to think. 'No, blue is my father's favourite colour.' I stood there, and it suddenly dawned on me that I didn't know what my favourite colour was. Eventually I bought a black dress. I stood for ages before the mirror, not sure if I liked what I saw because I liked black or because my father hated black. In the end I decided my father hating black was a good enough reason to buy it. When I went to pay, Bill stopped me. 'One isn't enough, go and find some others.' I went back to the racks, feeling ridiculously happy. I came away, my shopping bags filled with all the colours of the rainbow. We stopped at Bill's bank on the way home and he made me a signatory to his accounts and gave me his chequebook.

At home I tried them on for Bill's mother. Later, she took me to one side and asked me if I didn't think I should wear a bra under my new dresses. I agreed. I rather liked the idea. The next day I went into Newmarket, where I stared in dismay at the huge selection, wondering how one chose a bra. Eventually, with the help of a sympathetic saleswoman, I came away with several bras and a selection of panties. I smiled proudly as I put them away in the drawer. I'd chosen them myself; my father was never going to see or touch them.

Very slowly, through the kindness and understanding of my new family, I began to heal. The years of conditioning and controlled responses slowly peeled away. It was a very long stony road, but my direction was clear. It was a time of painful self-examination, and as time passed, the full enormity of the horror my life had been became apparent.

I fell over many times, but there was always someone to help me back onto my feet when I needed it. Most importantly, I was given the space to walk alone and gained my independence. I grew to know myself, and as my contact with normal, everyday people increased, I discovered I quite liked the real me.

However the problems with my father did not simply fade away, and on 14 August 1996 Bill and I said goodbye to all our friends and my new family, telling everyone we were going to Australia. Instead we flew to Germany. We were going into hiding, trying to begin a new life away from my father.

Chapter 38

On 13 September 1998 my heart stopped. I'd been sick for two days, with a lousy cold but when I woke that morning I felt better than I had for a long time. I stretched lazily back into the pillows. Bill was fast asleep. I carefully untangled our legs and pushed my sleeping Boston terrier down the bed. I slipped out of bed, leaving the sleeping beauties. Quietly shutting the door, I wandered into the kitchen. I needed a drink and a cigarette. I took a container of orange juice out of the fridge and sat at the breakfast table, watching spirals of cigarette smoke catch the sunlight and thinking about the job packets piling up at work. I decided to make Bill a cup of tea and got up to put the kettle on. Suddenly I felt really bad – something was very wrong. I struggled towards the bedroom but didn't make it. I remember reaching out to open the door then plunging into darkness.

When I opened my eyes I was lying on the floor, a man giving me mouth to mouth resuscitation. 'Oh, thank God,' he breathed. His face was white and it took me a few seconds to realise it was Bill. He told me Pukey had woken him, yelping and tugging at his arm. He didn't know how long I'd been lying there. I wasn't breathing and he couldn't find a heartbeat. It took him nearly two minutes of CPR before my heart started again.

The next half an hour was a bit of a blur. I later learned that Bill rang Elisa, our boss' wife, who rang my doctor and between them they got the ambulance to me in less than twelve minutes. The ambulance officers carried me down from our flat on a stretcher.

One of them sat in the back of the ambulance holding my hand as we raced through the village streets to the hospital in Augsburg.

My heart stopped a further five times that day. Throughout the next twenty hours five doctors and two professors fought to save my life, three of them working without break until four the next morning. Each time my heart stopped, they started it again. I had countless blood tests, X-rays, CT scans, ECGs, you name it, I had it, the tests finally finishing at two in the morning. Meanwhile Bill sat alone in the corridor, listening to my heart monitor, dying a thousand deaths every time he heard my heart stop, waiting until a doctor came out and told him, 'It's OK, we got it started again.'

Each time I passed out the doctors would slap my face and yell 'Hello' until I opened my eyes. I felt so bad, I really didn't mind dying. The blackness was a wonderful peaceful place. I kept throwing up and passing out and the doctors kept slapping my face, asking me silly questions. What was my name? How old was I? I was getting fed up with being slapped. One doctor had the idea I'd been taking drugs and had overdosed. 'What drugs have you taken?' he demanded. I kept denying I'd taken any, but he wouldn't give up.

Finally frustrated he said, 'You're going to die, I need to know if you've taken drugs.'

'I don't take drugs,' I hissed at him. He went quiet, I think he realised I was telling the truth. At three in the afternoon they told Bill my blood pressure had dropped to a dangerous level and they were unable to stop it falling further. They explained there was no hope, unless he was able to think of something in my history that could give them a clue as to what was happening.

By now, it had become difficult to talk. I could barely whisper. Much later a priest came and performed the last rites, his fingers as he made the sign of the cross on my forehead were cool and comforting. He spoke German, but it didn't matter. I knew he was absolving me of my sins and for this, I was very grateful.

Then the three doctors were back; they were going to put in a temporary pacemaker. It would hurt, they told me. They were right. Each time they tried, they failed. My blood vessels had collapsed, making it virtually impossible to run the wire through my neck into my heart.

They decided to try one more time, this time through my leg. The pain was unbearable, I could feel the wire every centimetre of the way, but there was an audible sigh of relief as they finally got the tiny electrode in place. They brought Bill in and told him they'd managed to stabilise me. They added he should go home and sleep, promising I'd still be there in the morning. I was pleased to hear it, although I didn't believe them.

Bill took my hand. 'I have to go home.' He looked so tired. 'I'll be back in the morning.' But his eyes told me what he was really thinking. I knew he thought he was seeing me for the last time. He kissed me, such a sad kiss and left. It was

4 a.m. The doctors disappeared and I lay in the dimly lit room, agonising over the thought of Bill having to face life on his own. Then I slept.

A male nurse woke me. He washed me gently, wiping the vomit from my face with a damp flannel. Carefully he drew off my gown and sponged my body, removing the sweat and the dry blood from my throat and the tube running into my left leg. Then he dressed me in a fresh gown.

'Would you like a drink of water?' he asked quietly. I nodded, sipping the water a little at a time as he suggested. As I finished, he gently smoothed the hair out of my eyes. He wheeled me into an intensive care ward and handed me over to the night staff. They hooked me to another heart monitor, put in a catheter, placed me on a drip and inserted two contraptions into my veins with taps for easy removal of blood.

It was several days before I had the strength to properly open my eyes. Bill seemed to be there all the time, almost living at the hospital. His presence was wonderfully reassuring. The nurses were very understanding and used to sneak him in outside visiting hours.

The tests continued, but still no one knew what was wrong with me. Every morning at 4 a.m. one of the doctors would gently wake me. After taking blood for testing, he'd pull a chair next to the bed and talk softly, asking me if I knew anything about my past that might help them understand what was happening. One night Bill told me I should tell him about the methaqualone, but I couldn't see that it was relevant.

After Bill left I remembered the night on Pigeon Island and wondered if there might be a link. I didn't know how I was going to tell the doctor; I didn't want to shock him, but when I did I saw compassion in his eyes. He left me and came back a couple of hours later. He'd been to the hospital pharmacist and found that methaqualone had been taken off the market in Germany in the early eighties because of serious side effects. He believed they'd finally found the cause of my problem.

I lay there, trying not to get angry. Lying in hospital attached to a heart monitor, struggling to stay alive, was not a time to get angry. Would I never be free of my father's abuse? If I died, he would have killed me as surely as if he'd knifed me. Now I had another reason to stay alive. I wasn't going to let him get away with it, not any more. If I died, he'd get away with all those years of abuse. I would have taken it to my grave with me.

My chances of surviving were slim, my condition deteriorating. There's a fine line between being ill enough to require a pacemaker, and strong enough to survive the operation to implant it. I felt I'd reached the bottom of my reserves, I was utterly exhausted and it was becoming difficult to stay focused. They hoped to operate the next morning, but as things stood there was no room in the schedule. One of the nurses confided I had a chance if someone died. I liked her honesty, but it was hard thinking that my life depended on someone else dying.

I wrote to Bill that night, telling him how much I loved him, how grateful I was for the seven years of happiness we'd shared, telling him he was my hero. I finished the letter with seven xs, a kiss for every year. I folded it inside a piece of paper, wrote his name on it and put it in my bag. Then I lay back, hoping I'd still be alive in the morning.

I was, and I was rushed to surgery and became the proud owner of a pacemaker. It was another three weeks before they let me go home. Another four months before I was allowed to return to work. Another eight months before I could find my way home by myself. It was to be expected, my brain had been starved of oxygen. I lost all memory of the three or four months prior to my heart stopping. I had difficulty reading and it was impossible to remember names. I was very lucky. It could have been much worse. I told Bill I was finally ready to take my father to court. It had taken me a long time to gather the strength, but now I was strong enough.

Seven months before, I'd written to the New Zealand Police, describing some of the things my father had done to me. I tried to keep it short, but it's difficult to write a brief synopsis of twenty-three years of abuse. I also asked if it was possible to lay charges against my father from overseas. It took some time before I received a polite letter, asking if I could furnish witnesses. I sat down and tried to remember anyone who might hold a piece of the jigsaw puzzle.

Detective Rob Hanna wrote back, telling me he'd been given my file and would be contacting the witnesses to verify my story. I rang him a couple of weeks later. He sounded very nice; I'd been expecting someone hard and officious. He was also very open, telling me that they'd put my letter to one side, certain it was another piece of crank mail. However, when he received my list of more than twenty witnesses, he started making calls. He realised I was telling the truth after speaking to our first landlords in New Zealand, especially after they showed him the repaired holes in the bedroom ceiling. He told me it was going to take time, at least two years before it reached court. I told him my life with my father had taught me patience, if nothing else.

The police did their utmost to help find witnesses, but often I only had a first name, an occupation and a vague idea of where they might be. After all, more than twenty-five years had passed in some cases. I began searching as well, determined the truth would finally come out, spending hours searching the Internet. My phone bills were scary. Every time I found a witness, it felt as though I'd won a small victory. It took me more than eighteen months to find a particular doctor. 'I've waited thirty years for you to ring me,' were his first words, when I gave my name. It was the same with so many people. They'd tell me they'd known what was going on, but they hadn't known what to do, of the guilt they'd felt over the years. I began to realise there were so many people I could have turned to. If only I'd known.

Not all the witnesses wanted to help. Moira became quite hostile. 'You need to grow up,' she said, 'get a life and leave your father to start a new life.'

My brother James said, 'You must have enjoyed it, otherwise you wouldn't have stayed.' His words hurt so badly. How could anyone believe that?

Slowly the police put their case together. They even found Diana, now married and living in Auckland. She remembered the photos my father had taken at Eton all those years ago. Claire and her family remembered the bruises.

Meanwhile the doctors who'd saved my life researched the side-effects of methaqualone, slowly putting together a picture of what had happened.

I was exhausted and run down. I couldn't sleep, worrying constantly that I wouldn't be able to get enough evidence. I was afraid that if I didn't, my father would walk free. I knew he'd never admit his guilt. I also knew I'd never be safe until he was behind bars. Since coming to Germany we'd moved five times, and each time he'd tracked me down, continuing his reign of terror on my mind, contacting anyone I knew in the past, telling them I was a criminal and a drug addict.

When I learned my old school was having a reunion, Bill suggested I fly to Port Vila. At first I wasn't sure I could face the memories, but decided I'd try one last time to repair the years of trouble between my mother and myself. I rang her and arranged to stay with her in New Caledonia, where she was now living, before flying on to Port Vila for the reunion. I made her promise she wouldn't tell my father I was coming.

The first days were amazing. We talked, laughed and enjoyed each other's company, agreeing not to talk about my father. It felt as though the past was finally where it belonged. She told me she'd booked a ticket to come with me to Port Vila. I was rather surprised, I'd looked forward to being on my own. The morning we were to fly to Port Vila, I received a phone call from the New Zealand police. My father had boarded a flight for Port Vila and would there in a couple of hours. They advised me not to continue on to Vanuatu.

My mother saw my face when I hung up, and I realised the time had come to tell her I was taking my father to court. That he was on the plane to Port Vila. She didn't say much, but after her husband left for work she became quite cold to me. I couldn't understand her attitude. I told her I wasn't going to Port Vila and she went a little crazy. I turned to walk out of the room when she attacked, thumping me on my back and shoving me out of the room. In the ensuing argument, I learnt my mother had arranged for my father to join us.

In the end, we flew to Port Vila after my father's return to Auckland. Another nightmare holiday. My mother lost it completely after she received a phone call from my father's pregnant girlfriend. My father had been arrested and locked up overnight.

I already knew this, I'd been in regular contact with the police. They told me they'd interviewed him and he'd protested his innocence. They'd also searched his house, finding a box of naked photos of me hidden in the ceiling and his 'toys'. My mother raged at me to drop the case. I asked her not to take sides, but she said she still loved my father, she loved him more than me – I'd never been a proper daughter.

Rob Hanna rang again, this time asking me to come to New Zealand to go through the exhibits and date the photos. They were concerned I'd have trouble coping with seeing the photos of myself.

Rob and his boss, Detective Sergeant John Brunton (J.B.), met me at Auckland Airport and drove me to a hotel where they checked me in under a false name and arranged for all visits and phone calls to be monitored. I warmed to them both immediately, they were so different from what I'd been expecting. The next day I was introduced to several other officers and promptly forgot everyone's names. I had no idea so many people were working on the case. I was put into an interview room and shown a four-hour video of their interview with my father. He hadn't changed. I had to tell myself it was only a video, he didn't know I was in Auckland. They wanted me to write down any lies I picked up. I gave up after a while, there were too many.

Then we started going through the photos, so many photos. I looked through them and I felt like crying for the little girl, the teenager and the woman who had been me. It was hard, but as Rob said, I could do it, if I could survive those years and having them taken, then I could manage to leaf through them now. 'It must be nice to finally see me with my clothes on,' I joked, trying to make light of them. He laughed, happy, I think, that the ice had been broken. I was relieved as well. I'd been worried about the knowing looks I was going to get, but they never happened. Not once did they make me feel uncomfortable, awkward or embarrassed.

Later we looked through the other exhibits they'd taken from my father's house. That was more difficult. We went through the boxes of handcuffs, bulldog clips, candles, ropes, clamps, blindfolds, gags ... on and on. There was even a bottle of baby oil. I wanted to throw up when I caught a whiff of it. Then they showed me the note he had in his top pocket at Auckland airport on his return from Port Vila.

'He hasn't changed much,' I commented, trying to keep a level voice. It was the note he'd written in red ink. The one where he said that when I found this note I'd be in big trouble. Why did he have that note with him? What had he been planning to do? What had my parents been planning?

Then they showed me more naked photos – Moira, Lidia, Susanna, Ama, Diana and other women and children, whose faces I knew, but whose names I couldn't remember, and more women and children I didn't know. They had dozens of bondage photos of his latest girlfriend, tied up exactly as I'd described. There were differences though. Now instead of ropes tied tightly round the breasts he used steel clamps. My stomach tightened with rage. He hadn't changed, he'd found another victim. I looked at her swollen belly, carrying my father's child and I looked at her eyes, another controlled person. She was my age, had long hair and was Asian. An Asian immigrant, who couldn't speak English very well; the perfect woman for my father.

It was two years after my heart failure before I finally understood what had happened. The doctors spent hours researching on the Internet, tracking down every piece of information on methaqualone. Armed with the results from all my tests they worked their way through the centimetres of paperwork in my file. Finally I received a call; they had a finding. I hadn't been able to understand how the methaqualone caused my heart to stop after so many years. I should have paid more attention in biology.

One of the doctors painstakingly explained what had gone wrong and why. The heart has two natural pacemakers. When the primary pacemaker gives up, even for a short period, the secondary one takes over. It's not as efficient and can't work as fast as the primary one, but it can keep you alive. In my case, my primary pacemaker had been destroyed in the Solomon Islands. The symptoms I described were classic methaqualone overdose symptoms. They told me I was lucky to have survived, another milligram would have killed me.

The day my heart stopped was the day my secondary pacemaker began giving up. They weren't designed to work forever. When I heard this, I said I was lucky I hadn't died. She looked at me for a moment and said, 'You did die, you were clinically dead.' I came away pleased I finally understood what had happened and very, very angry I was still paying for his perverted sexual urges.

There was another kick from my father. Bill and I decided we were finally settled enough in our new life to begin the family I so badly wanted, but it became apparent we were going to need help and we were sent to a fertility clinic.

They advised me against having a baby, telling me that even if I survived the pregnancy there was a very real possibility, because of the methaqualone, that there could be serious complications with the child. They asked me if I was prepared for that, did I have the right to take that risk?

There really was only one answer. My father not only

stole my childhood, and so many years, he stole motherhood from me. He was still making babies, my youngest sibling thirty-nine years younger than me, but I couldn't have children. Sometimes I felt life really wasn't fair.

Chapter 39

We finally had a date for the court case – 9 October 2000. I flew to New Zealand on 29 September. As much as I would have loved Bill's support, this was something I had to do on my own. I wanted to stand in that court and face my father; make him understand I wasn't the timid creature he had successfully enslaved for twenty-three years. I wasn't going to turn into a cowed little girl on the stand, something he'd assured his lawyer would happen.

I now had short blonde hair, different make-up and had changed my style of dressing. At Auckland Airport I walked up to a uniformed policeman to introduce myself. I was embarrassed to find the man standing next to him was J.B., Detective Hanna's boss! We had a good laugh at my new look and it was a wonderful safe feeling, being unrecognisable.

He checked me into a hotel and I was given a couple of days to get over jet lag. I spent most of it in my room watching television and eating sitting cross-legged on the bed.

First I had an appointment with Margaret Honeyman, a

psychiatrist who'd be putting a report together on the effect of the years of abuse. Then I was introduced to the prosecution team, Philip Hamlin and Deb Bell.

My father had managed to have some of the evidence taken out. The photos of his girlfriend were no longer admissible. I could understand that. But I found it hard to take that the note he had in his pocket was also no longer admissible. He said he'd written it for his girlfriend.

We went over my statements, and it was decided that certain sections wouldn't be covered, in consideration of the jury. They didn't want to shock them. It was something that had bothered me from the start. I'd had twenty-three years to get used to what was happening to me, and it still affected my life and my behaviour. I couldn't get the pictures out of my head. How was it going to be for them?

Then finally it was 9 October. I was now 40 years old and going to face the demons of my past. I sat with Rob and J.B. in a small side room drinking tea and trying not to panic. Rob leaned forward. 'Hey, don't worry, after ten minutes you'll wonder why you were so nervous, and when you come out at morning tea time you'll feel a wonderful sense of relief.'

I smiled; somehow, he always knew exactly the right thing to say. J.B. tossed his polystyrene cup into the wastepaper basket. 'You'll be fine,' he said, 'you don't have to look around the room, just look at Philip Hamlin, he'll guide you through it. Remember, no matter how nervous you feel, your father will be feeling much worse.'

My name was called and I was led into the courtroom. I stepped into a room filled with faces – so many people, I remember thinking, as I was conducted to the witness box.

I was shaking as I sat down and nervously looked at the prosecution team. I didn't look at the jury. I didn't look at the judge. I knew where my father would be sitting, between two guards behind a screen. I heard him clear his throat.

The clerk of the court placed a Bible in my hands and I took courage from the feel of the worn leather binding against my fingers.

The time had finally come. Unbidden, the words of Lewis Carroll leapt into my mind. 'The time has come,' the walrus said, 'to talk of many things... '

I sat down as Philip Hamlin approached the witness stand. He began by asking my name. 'Tanjas... ' I croaked into the microphone, and began breathing heavily, the sound echoing round the court. I hated that; I hated that he could hear my breathing. The judge suggested I might like to move it, which I did. The breathing stopped.

I answered the next few questions without problem, then display boards were brought out, with the photos of the houses I'd lived in during the years in Vanuatu; to help the jury follow the sequence of events. Philip Hamlin had a time line of events and his questions lead me through the years, starting with Lelepa Landing. They'd told me to carefully consider each question and answer it slowly, allowing the typist to keep up with my words. I went back in my mind and looked at my memories, but I was afraid to get too close, to feel too much. I was frightened I'd break down, and I was determined I wasn't going to let him see me cry. I described the events, feeling disjointed, unmoved, but once I started it was difficult having to stop so the typist could keep up. Whenever that happened I'd sit, not allowing myself to think. From time to time the judge would ask me a question, once joking about the condition of the roads in Vanuatu. I think he was trying to put me at ease.

We came to the part where my mother left, and I was a

little girl again, standing in the corridor listening to her high heels clicking down the concrete steps, her words, 'You can rot in hell,' echoing through my mind. Hurting me after all this time. Then, while the typist was catching up, I felt anger smouldering beneath the surface. She left me behind and I rotted in hell. I was her only child and she abandoned me. The anger was good, it prevented me crying.

There were breaks for morning tea, lunch and afternoon tea. Times when I could smoke and talk to myself, tell myself I could do this. Each time I was led out of the courtroom by the court clerk, a lovely woman, motherly and full of words of encouragement. That first tea break, she was like an angry hen. I felt quite sorry for the men. 'Where are her support women? Why hasn't she got support people?' J.B. looked sheepish and Rob looked at me, 'Hey, it's not our fault, she doesn't want them.'

I leapt to their defence. 'It's OK, they offered, but I want to do this on my own.'

She looked from me to the two detectives as though she wasn't quite sure she believed us and then unruffled her feathers. 'Well if you change your mind, let me know.'

Back in the courtroom we worked our way through the years. We'd left Vanuatu and were now covering events in Auckland. Rob had been correct. It was as though the weight of the world was slowly lifting from my shoulders.

I was feeling proud of myself. I hadn't broken down once. Then I had to talk about when he tied me upside down. I was back there, struggling to breathe, so immersed in the past I tried to pull the tape off my mouth as I talked and then I couldn't talk any more. I'd been describing how my nose had blocked with my tears. 'I couldn't breathe,' I wailed. And my throat choked up and tears started streaming down my face. I tried to speak, but sobs wrapped themselves round my words. Deb was watching me closely, sending encouragement with her eyes. The court clerk brought me a box of tissues and the judge asked if I'd like a drink of water. I didn't but decided it might help. I blew my nose and tried hard to put my feelings back in the locked rooms of my mind.

As I sipped the water, I looked round the room and found I wasn't the only person crying. I was ashamed I'd broken down, and angry with myself for crying in front of him. During the lunch break Philip Hamlin reassured me. 'I was beginning to worry, it'd be much better if you were a basket case, dribbling and jerking.' He laughed, trying to cheer me up.

I could see his point but I didn't care if the jury thought my lack of emotion strange. I didn't know how I was supposed to react. I could only be me. I guess everyone reacts differently, copes the best they can, and this was my way.

At one point the jury was sent out. We'd decided to fight to get the note and some other drawings back into the case. Hamlin questioned me about the note, giving it to me to read. I didn't want to touch it, but I behaved myself, holding it between my fingertips. Why couldn't he just tell the truth? He was the one who'd said that morally there was nothing wrong with what he was doing. I realised with sudden clarity it was because he knew he'd abused me. All those years he'd lied to me and manipulated me, knowing he was wrong. And now he was hiding behind his lies, making me suffer all over again.

When Philip Hamlin had finished with his questions about the exhibits, my father's lawyer came to the stand. Allan Roberts had a deep booming voice and his manner and the fact he was defending my father rubbed me up the wrong way. I could feel the flash of anger in my eyes as he began questioning me. I could hear my replies, and knew I was sounding angry, antagonistic. I wanted to grab him by his silly tie and shake him for defending a man like that. I stopped talking, trying hard to calm down, to put an even tone back into my words. He was only doing a job I told myself, and his tie was perfectly normal.

Afterwards Rob read me the riot act; I wasn't allowed to use that tone the next time Allan Roberts spoke to me. It wouldn't help me to be antagonistic. I promised faithfully to Rob, and myself, that tomorrow I'd behave myself. I hoped I'd be able to.

Then it was back in court and the new evidence was shown to the jury. I watched them, as I waited for the questioning to begin. I could see the shock on their faces. I guess it's one thing to hear about the note, quite another to see the defendant's own handwriting and read the things he'd written.

We moved onto the photos. I'd been dreading this. The books of photos were passed around and then we went through every single one. I had to describe when they were taken, how old I was, and where they were taken. I had to keep thinking of the girl in the photos as someone else. Time was running out, and the defence requested we adjourn and continue the next morning. I nearly cried with frustration. 'Oh God, please no,' I inadvertently said aloud, rocking back and forth on my chair. I stopped, breathing deeply. The judge decided we would continue. I was shaking when I finally left the courtroom, and the court clerk gave me a huge hug. 'You're doing fine,' she whispered. 'You're a strong woman.'

The next day we covered more ground and then we came to the trip to Pigeon Island. When I reached the part about lying on the floor, begging for help while he masturbated, I broke down. I couldn't stop crying. The judge asked if I'd like to take a short recess, but I refused. I wanted to get this over and done with. I kept on talking, the words catching in my throat. I had to stop when I remembered lying in the vomit, feeling the concrete on my naked body, hearing his abusive words and the pain of him tearing between my legs. I was back there, struggling again to survive, to draw air into my lungs, wanting to push him away. I stopped to blow my nose and wipe my face, trying to keep it together. I looked around the room. Most of the jury was crying, or wiping their eyes. Philip Hamlin had the most peculiar expression on his face, Deb was dabbing her eyes and my father's lawyer became very busy arranging papers in a file, looking away from the jury. It looked to me as if he was struggling to keep his emotions in check as well. Behind him, in the gallery I saw Rob Hanna. I was stunned to see he was also crying.

Afterwards Rob took me outside so I could have a cigarette. 'You know, it was one thing to read the things that happened to you, you can be removed when it's written down in black and white. But it was shattering to hear you talking, hear you describing what happened. I don't think there was a dry eye in the courtroom.'

I bet my father's eyes were dry, I thought cynically as we returned. He was probably enjoying the memory. It was good the screen was there, I didn't trust myself not to take my new-found rage out on him.

They brought out more of the exhibits. This time it was a collection of my father's toys. Neatly pinned up on fibreboard were the ropes, handcuffs, bulldog clips, blindfolds, clamps, candles, even the baby oil. They balanced it against the side of the witness box, nearly touching me. I wanted to climb out of the box, I didn't want them near me and as I looked at the bottle of baby oil I struggled not to throw up. I had to identify the items and was very glad when they put them out of sight.

The questions continued. 'Did you love your father?' asked Philip Hamlin.

'Yes, I did, I loved my father very much. He was my father and my best friend.'

'Do you still love your father?'

'No, I despise him. I despise him for what he's done to me.'

Philip Hamlin had gone over the questions he would ask me but one of his last questions was a complete surprise. 'What did you want?' he asked quietly.

I was stunned. What did I want? What did he mean? 'I'm sorry, I don't understand.'

'What did you want, what did you wish for when you were with your father?'

I thought about it for a moment, and knew what I'd always wanted. 'I wanted to be normal, I wanted to be a normal teenager with normal parents. Just an ordinary person.' My words tailed off, as the desire to be those things hit me, the loneliness of wanting to be like anyone else. I wished none of this had happened, that I didn't need to be in this courtroom, that I'd had a life like Claire; my epitome of normality.

Then it was the defence's turn. I'd been steeling myself for Allan Roberts' questions. I'd been warned it could get dirty, though he had to be careful not to be seen to be badgering me. I was surprised, he was fairly considerate, but still annoyed the hell out of me. He had this infuriating manner of saying 'So you say,' after every statement. I realised he had to intimate that everything I said was alleged. I understood that, but it didn't make me feel any more kindly towards him. When he asked me if I might have exaggerated events, I was stunned. It was one of the few times I replied through my teeth, 'No, I didn't exaggerate any of it, there was no need.'

Later he returned to the pregnancy, to the baby clothes, wanting me to describe them. I remembered the feel of the soft pink wool, the smell as I carefully wrapped them up again. The memory of being pregnant. I began crying quietly. Tears for an unwanted child God took back, and tears for wanted children who could never be streamed down my cheeks, indistinguishable from each other.

There were surprises. 'Isn't it a fact that none of this is true, you're writing a book on incest and making all this up for your book?' he asked quietly.

I hated these double questions, but I was gradually beginning to understand the way he was thinking and appreciated he wasn't demanding yes and no answers. He seemed patient, almost kindly at times.

'Yes it's true I started to write a book, but I stopped. It was too hard dealing with the memories, and no it's not true that I made all this up.'

'So it's true you want to be a writer?'

'Yes, I think it would be wonderful to write a book and get it published.'

He brought out a thick stack of computer printout pages, wanting me to explain them. I flipped through and started trembling with rage when I recognised them. Some were love letters I'd written to Bill, others were pieces of the romance I'd been writing. I wasn't angry with Allan Roberts. I was furious with my father. These papers had gone missing from my flat well after I'd broken off all contact with him. This meant he'd been in my home, gone through my things, stolen my writing. Invaded my private space.

The judge called a recess, he didn't think it was fair that I hadn't had time to peruse the pages prior to questioning and they were later withdrawn.

Another time Allan Roberts suggested I had a wild sexual fantasy; I was obsessed with sex. He showed me a book and asked if I was familiar with it. I'd never seen it before and I can't remember the title now but it dealt with women's secret sexual fantasies. He told me my father said it was my book. I nearly laughed, my father was such a liar. 'I've never seen it before, but I've read similar books, I read all the books on my father's bookshelf.'

Slowly, we worked our way through his questions. From my obsession with my body and forcing my father to take naked photos of me, to my twisted sexual desires. I have to say Allan Roberts worded the questions very carefully so as not to upset me.

He brought out a book I'd done for my father, cartoon drawings about the life of a sheep. A sheep that discovers what really happens to sheep, escapes and eventually finds love on a tiny island safe from people. One of the drawings depicted two sheep making love. 'Is it not true that you wanted to publish this book, that you felt it perfectly acceptable for children to see copulating sheep?'

'No, it's not true. I drew the book for my father, I drew the sheep making love for my father, I knew it was something he wanted, he was the one who took it to a publisher to see if it could be published. I didn't think it was appropriate at all.'

He withdrew it from the exhibits. It's funny, I thought, how everyone missed the point. I'd done that book as a secret dig against my father. It was a story about escape, not sex, and it had a happy ending.

Amongst his last questions he asked if I was doing all this because I was angry with my father, because he'd refused to give me away when I married, and had refused to pay for the wedding. I nearly lost my temper. It had been a long two and half days on the stand and it was beginning to get to me. My father had threatened to kill Bill and I when we got married, we had to make special arrangements to block the road to prevent him turning up at the church. I calmed myself before I replied. 'I never asked my father to give me away, I didn't want him there, it would have been totally inappropriate and I certainly never asked him for money. I've never asked him for money. Not once. I wouldn't want his money.' Then I fell silent.

He stood reading through his notes and finally looked up at me. 'Thank you, I have no more questions.' He smiled as he spoke and I caught a glimpse of something in his eyes, was it compassion?

Then I was outside and I'd done it. I could have danced for joy. I'd actually done it! I felt light-headed with relief. I'd done my part, now it was up to the other twenty-two witnesses to testify, and then it would be up to the jury.

The night before the jury retired to consider their verdict I woke shortly after 2 a.m. The hour of black shadows and spirits knocking on windows and rattling doors, calling up our deepest fears and feasting on them. The loneliness of the hotel room wrapped itself around me. I turned up the television and made myself a Milo, tactics to avoid thinking. I sat in the bay window of my tenth-floor room, nestled amongst the heavy curtains, and stared out. Gentle rain was falling on the city centre, smudging the night lights, forming pools of liquid rubies and emeralds on the wet darkness of the roads as the traffic lights changed. Unwittingly, I slipped into the darkened corridors of my mind, opening a door into a room, my nostrils catching a whiff of baby oil. I stepped amongst the jumble of memories, glimpses of the past fluttering as I disturbed the dusty piles. His face, swollen with lust as he came, loomed up before me, before being replaced by another image of him, his face full of hatred, staring at me in the hallway, frightening me after all these years. I became aware of the humming of the fridge and my thoughts returned to the present.

The notion I'd been avoiding all this time insinuated itself into my consciousness. What if they found him not guilty? He'd walk free, free to continue tormenting me, to track me down, stronger than before. I'd be branded a liar. Would my mind survive? And supposing I stayed sane, would I have to go back into hiding? I'd have no choice, he'd hunt me down and eventually he'd find me.

I'd have to disappear again. I knew Bill would move again but there was only so much a person could take. In those early hours in the darkness I wondered if Bill would think I was worth it. I began to cry. Would the nightmare finally end with a guilty verdict or was another nightmare about to be unleashed? I knew I should stop crying, but I couldn't. I cried like I'd never cried before, hysterical sobbing that wouldn't slow down, the tears of so many years. The rain stopped and the skyline began to lighten before I finally managed to bring them under control. Then the phone rang. It was Bill, ringing from Germany. 'Oh Bill,' I wailed down the phone, 'what if he's found not guilty?'

Bill laughed. 'Not a chance,' he said. 'I don't think you have anything to worry about on that score.'

'But what if the jury thinks even her own mother says she's lying?'

'They've listened to all the witnesses and heard all the evidence and one thing you can be sure of is that they aren't stupid.'

As always Bill cheered me up. When the police came to pick me up I was outwardly calm. I'd cried enough for the moment, I knew I wouldn't break down. I watched the clock, willing the jury to hurry up as I sat in the Crown Prosecution Witness waiting room. J.B. made me countless cups of tea and tried to persuade me to read magazines. I tried, but I was too nervous, the print danced out of focus. The jury was out for five-and-a-half hours, but it seemed like forever. Then Rob came into the room. 'The jury's back. They've reached a verdict.'

The moment had arrived. I felt peculiarly calm. Before we went downstairs J.B. cautioned us not to react when the verdict was read out. We would go in, listen to the verdict and then leave in a dignified manner.

I followed them into the courtroom, my heart pounding so hard I wondered how my pacemaker could cope. We entered the hushed room. I caught sight of my sister-in-law seated in the row behind me, her presence was most comforting. J.B. sat on my right and Rob on my left. Another officer had been sent to sit next to my mother, blocking her exit. I'd expressed concern at her reaction should my father be found guilty. She'd gone on the stand against me, as she said she would. Hers was the ultimate betrayal and the pain it caused is beyond description. There were other people in the gallery, other witnesses, a reporter and members of the public. I sat looking in front of me; the tension was unbearable. A side door opened and in a moment I knew my father would be led in. Should I look away, or down? I decided I wouldn't look down. I'd keep my head high and look straight ahead.

My father was led in and then we were ready. The judge asked the foreman if the jury had reached their verdict. 'We have, Your Honour.' I began shaking, feeling a cold sweat bathe my entire body. I concentrated on breathing deeply, evenly. My heart was beating so hard I was afraid I'd have a heart attack before the verdict was read out.

Just as the foreman was about to begin, the judge stopped him. He apologised, he hadn't directed the jury to consider one of the charges. There ensued a lengthy discussion. I sat there, trying to remain calm.

Then the judge asked the foreman to read out the jury's verdict. He began by reading out the first charge. Then I heard the word I'd been waiting for, praying for.

Guilty.

Rob reached over and grabbed my hand and squeezed it. 'We've done it,' he whispered, emotion choking his voice. My sister-in-law couldn't contain herself and whooped, her voice tailing off as she remembered she wasn't meant to make a noise. Tears of relief flooded into my eyes and I blinked them back. It was finally over.

Afterwards, in the Prosecution Chambers, there were hugs all round. I was overwhelmed, these people had all done so much for me. But most of all they'd believed me and words would never be enough to thank them for that.

Later, I went outside. I sat on the steps of the High Court as the verdict began to sink in, and lit a cigarette. It was a glorious spring day. I looked around me, thinking about all the really good people there were in the world; the words of a song I first heard so long ago in Vanuatu came into my heart and I hummed it softly to myself. I stood up and crushed my cigarette out beneath my shoe. 'Yes,' I said as I went back indoors to join the others, 'It truly is a wonderful world.'

Chapter 40

On 2nd May 2001, Bill and I returned home to live in New Zealand. We felt it was finally safe to come back. Of course I should have seen it coming. My father, still insisting he was innocent, had appealed. Each time the date of the appeal neared, it would be deferred, and a new hearing date set. His new lawyer, the latest in a long line, claiming he needed more time to search through the court transcripts.

I kept up a brave front, but inside I felt shattered. The strain of continued deferrals started to take a terrible toll. My nightmares returned in full force. In the early hours of the morning, despite everyone's reassurances, the unspeakable prospect of a retrial terrified and haunted me.

The appeal was finally heard on 1 August 2001 at 10 a.m. in the Auckland High Court. Sitting on the bench were Chief Justice Sian Elias, Justice Thomas and Justice Anderson. Phil Hamlin represented the Crown and my father was represented by Kevin Ryan QC.

Surrounded by friends and family, I listened as the

hearing commenced; I was trembling uncontrollably. It began with Kevin Ryan explaining that my father had withdrawn his appeal against conviction. I was stunned when he said my father had conceded I was telling the truth and he was showing some remorse. He went on to say my father was a broken man in prison, and the sole basis of the appeal was that hope should spring eternal and the element of mercy was important; it is healing to forgive.

He appealed to the court on the grounds of my father's ill health, saying that for a man of his age, fourteen years was effectively a death sentence. While he realised my father was too old for reformation, redemption was important. He also said I had told the truth; it was my father who chose to live a lie.

He talked about the case against my father being absolutely abhorrent, with overtones of sadism and slavery, but that the sentencing needed to be balanced against the sheer revulsion of the crime. Although clearly a denunciatory sentence was required, the court should also recognise the subjective factors mitigating the sentence – my father's age meant that fourteen years was a harsher sentence than for a younger man.

Kevin Ryan asked that my father's current nine-year and five-year terms, presently being served cumulatively, be served concurrently. When he finished speaking, Phil Hamlin told the court he had nothing to add to his written submissions. The Justices then adjourned to consider their verdict, and the Chief Justice said they would reconvene at midday to deliver their decision.

At midday we sat in the courtroom again, and stood nervously as the Justices returned. In short, they dismissed the appeal. In her summary, Chief Justice Elias gave their reasons for denial, discussing the original judge's decisions, confirming that he was correct in making the sentences for the various offences cumulative, rather than concurrent, because of the seriousness and the nature of the offending. While there was minimal risk of my father re-offending, it had been demonstrated to the court that I had cause to fear him in the future because of his ongoing persecution of me, and that I was entitled to the protection of a lengthy prison sentence.

Then it was over. I didn't know whether to laugh or cry, and then there were hugs all round. Now to start my life, and put the past where it belongs. In the words of the court, which best sum up my feelings, 'The complainant was completely vindicated by the evidence, for she had been telling the truth.'

Postscript

Of course my father had to prove the court right. He continued his persecution of me. I expected no less of him. A few months after the appeal had been heard, Bill and I packed up everything, including Pukey, and moved to Roxburgh, in Central Otago. I had fallen in love with the South Island and we had bought the house of our dreams – a beautiful old run-down stone cottage with rambling rose gardens and large ponds filled with goldfish and water lilies.

Over the summer months we renovated the house and had time to watch the world go by, making new friends and enjoying life to the full. We still cut gemstones for the jewellery trade and picked fruit in the summer to supplement our income. Life was good. Then came the phone call. A fax had been sent to my lawyers in error. There was a warrant out for my arrest.

In a way it was very funny, but in another way it was not funny at all. It was deadly serious and no laughing matter. The harassment had begun again, in a new and even more vicious way. I immediately presented myself to the tiny local police station. Eventually the warrant was sent down to Roxburgh and I was duly arrested, charged, and released on bail. I was charged with fraud: 'The illegal use of a document for pecuniary gain'. It was not a Crown Prosecution; the police were carrying out the act of arresting and charging, merely as bailiffs. This was a private prosecution instigated by my father in prison. If found guilty I was looking at six years imprisonment maximum.

The charge related to a sworn affidavit I had made when I had decided to retrieve some of my possessions, some of which I had left behind, some he had removed from my flat, and some which had been used during the trial as evidence and had to be returned by the police to the rightful owner. Among the items were the photos used during the trial and thousands of negatives still in boxes, clothes of mine, shoes, ornaments, a valuable painting, personal documents and books. The idea that my father might be given back the photos was infuriating, yet he was demanding to have them. He countered my claim, insisting that everything belonged to him (even my panties and shoes). I was determined to fight to the bitter end. Then I was informed that my father had been given the right during the hearing to question me, in person, if he so desired.

Well, everyone has a limit, and this was mine. I was incredulous. He had abused me for all those years, was in prison for what he had done, and I was expected to sit in a courtroom where he possibly could question me. People have called me courageous, brave, strong. I was none of those things that day. It was too much. I withdrew my claim and I should have guessed that he would not let things be.

I knew I hadn't done anything illegal but proving it was

another thing. It was a stressful period. My baby brother, James, all grown up now of course, fell in love and married. As James was living abroad he sent me a ticket for the wedding, but I couldn't go; being on bail had its restrictions.

Eventually, the lawyer's bills exceeded our ability to pay them, and so just like that, our dream was put on the auction block and sold. I could hear the bidding from where I sat in the dining room and when it was all over I felt as though my heart would break. It was a big wide world out there and we were moving yet again.

Complete strangers would wait outside the court and give me hugs or stop me in the street and wish me all the best. And for their kindness I thank them. The papers were full of disbelief that an abuser could actually take out a private prosecution against his victim, and the law was powerless to do anything about it. No matter how unfair it seemed, I had to answer, rightfully so, to the charge.

I had new representation; my solicitor Mary-Jane Thomas, had taken my case *pro bono*. She was wonderful and exactly what I was looking for: a lawyer with teeth. In the end my father's witnesses were no competition for his own comments, on video, stating exactly what I had been saying all along. It was all over, yet again...

What am I saying? Of course, there were attempts at appeal. But then it finally came to an end. And touch wood, it has been very peaceful for the last two years.

We lost a dream, but you lose your dreams every time you wake up, so we simply looked for another dream, and we found it. A run-down (and I mean run-down) cottage. It was so dilapidated that we camped in it for the first three months, arriving in the middle of a harsh winter. To start with, there was no power, no water, and the only heating came from an ancient coal range that looked as though it shouldn't work, but somehow did. We spent a lot of time huddled over it, with the wind howling through the missing floor boards and holes in the walls. The dogs were not impressed (they'd never had it so rough)! Pukey, my darling old Boston terrier, is still with us. He is getting on now, and has a smattering of grey across his muzzle. His grand-daughter Pippi is a perfect copy of him, but in miniature. To give you an idea of how rough it was, we decided to renovate the bathroom first – washing in icy water in an old tin tub was becoming less than exciting. Finally it was finished – gleaming, pristine perfection down to the terracotta flooring and fluffy rug. In a simple way it inspired hope and courage that we really could renovate this house. Shortly afterwards I was horrified to discover that Pukey and Pippi had vanished. I hunted high and low, thinking the worst. Of course, I needn't have worried; they had sensibly moved into the bathroom, taken over the rug and refused to come out.

Over the last six months we have been transforming our new abode. A little bit like the transformation I have made to myself since the day I escaped from my father. It seems all so far away. I still have the occasional flashback though, and my last nightmare was only three weeks ago, but I can shrug them off now. Somehow, it's not so important anymore. What is important is the future and what I make of it.

I still wake every morning with an amazing feeling of elation and freedom, and these days my only stress factors are the normal ones, like 'Did I remember to pay the power bill?' (now that we have the power connected). 'Did we get enough milk for the weekend?' 'Is Pippi looking pale, perhaps her nose is too hot, too dry?'

It took me a while to get here though. Over the years I have moved from victim to survivor and beyond. Now I am more than a survivor. Now I am just an ordinary person, the girl next door. The one with laughter lines, a wicked sense of humour and more grey hair than is good for any woman's ego.

Bill and I have had a lot of fun and laughter renovating our cottage. We still have to plaster the hallway and one bedroom, and as I write this I notice flecks of white paint all over my hands. We have started the serious work of painting the exterior.

One day it will be a lovely house, with beautiful gardens filled with roses and dahlias; in the meantime, it's a lovely home, a home filled with sunshine, love and laughter – and the patter of tiny Boston terrier paws.